BURNOUT Paradise

PRIMA OFFICIAL GAME GUIDE

DAVID S. J. HODGSON

Prima Games
A Division of Random House, Inc.

3000 Lava Ridge Court, Ste. 100
Roseville, CA 95661
www.primagames.com

Product Manager: Todd Manning

Editors: Shaida Boroumand and John Browning

Design and Layout: José de Jesús Ramírez, Rick Wong, and Jamie Knight

Manufacturing: Stephanie Sanchez

David S. J. Hodgson

Originally hailing from Manchester in the United Kingdom, David left his role as a writer of numerous British video game magazines (including *Mean Machines*, *Computer & Video Games*, and the *Official Nintendo* and *Sega Saturn* magazines) and a bohemian lifestyle on a rusting, condemned dry-docked German fishing trawler to work on the part-fraternity, part-sanitarium known as *GameFan* magazine in 1996.

David helped to launch the fledgling GameFan Books and form Gamers' Republic in 1998, authoring many strategy guides for Millennium Publications, including *The Official Metal Gear Solid Mission Handbook*. After launching the wildly unsuccessful incite Video Gaming and Gamers.com, David began authoring guides for Prima Games in 2000. He has written over 60 strategy guides; including *The Legend of Zelda: Twilight Princess*, *Knights of the Old Republic*, *Crysis*, *Half-Life: Orange Box*, and even *Panzer Dragoon Orta*. He lives in the Pacific Northwest with his wife, Melanie, and an eight-foot statue of Great Cthulhu.

The author would like to thank: My loving wife Melanie; Bryn, Rachel and Samuel; Mum, Dad, Ian and Rowena; Laibach, Ladytron, and The Knife; Ron and Fez. Massive thanks to Todd Manning, Shaida Boroumand, John Browning, and José de Jesús Ramírez at Prima for their help and support during the creation of this guide.

This guide wouldn't have been possible without the massive amounts of help and support of Alex Ward, Paul Glancey, Charnjit Bansi, and all at Criterion Studios. In addition, thanks to Steve Watt, Matt Benson, and Dave Sage at Electronic Arts for their invaluable time and help on this project.

Special final thanks to the letter "Z" for Zillah, who drank too much gin.

ISBN: 978-0-7615-5580-3

Library of Congress Catalog Card Number: 2007920560

Printed in the United States of America

08 09 10 11 LL 10 9 8 7 6 5 4 3 2 1

CONTENTS

................SCHOOL...........................2
YOUR JOURNEY TO ELITE STATUS STARTS HERE!...........2
TRAINING PART 1: BASIC CAR TYPES AND MANEUVERS. 2
TRAINING PART 2: GOING ONLINE.............................6

02:
THE JUNKYARD...10
THE COMPLETE CAR COLLECTION........................10
STOCKTAKING IN YOUR GARAGE..........................18

03:
EVENT ADVICE..20
ROAD RAGE EVENTS......................................42
MARKED MAN EVENTS....................................47
BURNING ROUTE EVENTS.................................55
STUNT RUN EVENTS......................................63
ROAD RULES: TIME AND SHOWTIME EVENTS.............72

04:
TOUR OF PARADISE......................................76
WELCOME TO PARADISE CITY!...........................78
NEIGHBORHOOD 1: PALM BAY HEIGHTS...................79
NEIGHBORHOOD 2: DOWNTOWN PARADISE................92
NEIGHBORHOOD 3: HARBOR TOWN.......................109
NEIGHBORHOOD 4: WHITE MOUNTAIN....................125
NEIGHBORHOOD 5: SILVER LAKE.........................142

05:
APPENDICES...156
APPENDIX I: FREEBURN CHALLENGES....................156
APPENDIX II: PS3 PARADISE AWARDS...................168
APPENDIX III: XBOX 360 ACHIEVEMENTS................172
APPENDIX IV:
GOLD ELITE AND PLATINUM ELITE MEMBERS.............176

01: Advanced Training: Driving School

YOUR JOURNEY TO ELITE STATUS STARTS HERE!

Welcome to *Prima's Official Burnout Paradise Strategy Guide*. Here's a quick description of each chapter, so you know how to use this book:

POSTER: BU NOUT PARADISE

The biggest help to any driver is knowing where all 8 compass finishing places, 11 parking structures, 11 auto repair shops, 14 gas stations, 5 paint shops, 5 junkyards, and 120 billboards are. And that's not to mention every hidden area and shortcut! Fortunately, this map (and all maps in this guide) provide this information!

CHAPTER 1: DRIVING SCHOOL

Excellent work! You're reading this section now, which improves on the information learned in the Instruction Manual, and gives you a great overview of the different car types, the actions and maneuvers you can attempt, the drivethrus and other areas of the city you should pay attention to, and the basics of online gameplay.

CHAPTER 2: THE JUNKYARD

As the game progresses, you're given additional vehicles to drive, and this chapter reveals all of the available cars, along with their statistics, including how many "lives" a car has before it becomes a complete wreck in certain game modes. Then there's a progression chart for you to check how far you are from Elite status!

CHAPTER 3: EVENT ADVICE

The majority of your progression is spent completing seven different types of events: Races, Road Rages, Marked Man Events, Burning Routes, Stunt Runs, Time Road Rules, and Showtime Road Rules. In this chapter, you're given all the information you need to win every one of these 248 events!

CHAPTER 4: TOUR OF PARADISE

Half the game is about finding out the coolest and most interesting alleys and shortcuts, and figuring out where all the landmarks are so you can use your in-game map as little as possible, and concentrate on the road ahead. Thankfully, half this guide has segmented each of the five neighborhoods into districts, and revealed the major landmarks, thoroughfares, 35 drivethrus, 11 parking structures, and the three types of 570 discoveries (50 super jumps, 120 billboards, and 400 smashes) you can find!

CHAPTER 5: APPENDICES

Finally, there's descriptions of all the 350 online Freeburn Challenges you can complete, advice on receiving all 60 Paradise Awards (for PlayStation 3) or 50 Achievements (Xbox 360), and finally, the ultimate revelation: how to become a true ultimate **Criterion Elite** racer and finish 100 percent of the game!

> **NOTE**
>
> Now read the Instruction Manual and familiarize yourself with the game before reading the rest of this section!

TRAINING PART 1: BASIC CAR TYPES AND MANEUVERS

STARTING YOUR JOURNEY: DRIVETHRUS

Auto Repair: After you obtain your first vehicle from the junkyard, the first order of business is to find an auto repair shop. This is what one looks like. The guide maps shows where all 11 are. This is the first of the four types of drivethru. Drive through each auto repair shop to repair your car, and do this immediately, every time you win a new car.

> **NOTE**
>
> Once you repair your car for the first time, it needs further repair only if you knock into scenery or other vehicles but aren't wrecked. Once you wreck, your car is repaired when you reenter the city after the wreck cutscene.

Gas Station: The second type is a gas station. There are 14 to find. Drive through each so it appears on your in-game map. This refuels your boost meter, which is vital during certain events, or if you want to quicken your pace.

Junkyard: There are five junkyards. Drive through each, and you can choose a new car from the vehicles you have acquired, and then choose your car's color if you visited a paint shop. Check the Junkyard section for specific details on obtaining all the in-game cars.

Paint Shop: Lastly, you can change the color of your vehicle by driving through a paint shop. Do this the first time you obtain a new vehicle, because this unlocks an additional choice for this car, in the junkyard, from this point onward. You can choose any color you like for most cars!

NOTE

Most cars allow you to choose one of a number of color finishes:

Original: If you've been choosing paint finishes, and you want to revert to the original, press the Reset Settings button.

Finish 1, 2, 3: Metallic, Pearlescent, or Gloss

Gold: This feature is currently hidden!

Platinum: This color is also hidden!
Note that some finishes, cannot be changed if you drive through a paint shop.

STARTING YOUR JOURNEY: BOOST TYPES

Introduction: As the Instruction Manual states, there are three vehicle classes: Speed (yellow boost bar), Aggression (red boost bar), and Stunt Class (green boost bar). It is important to learn the strengths and minuses of each.

Speed-Class Vehicles: Use these vehicles when racing, or obtaining the quickest time possible (for Races, Burning Routes, and Time Road Rule Events). Perform dangerous actions (see below) to increase the boost bar. This bar

can **only** be used when it is completely full. However, this is the only class of vehicle you can "boost chain" with.

Boost Chaining (AKA Burnouts): Perform actions to increase your boost. When you're instructed that a boost is ready, start and continue the boost until the bar empties without stopping the boost, and the bar half-fills again. Use dangerous actions while you're boosting to top up the bar, and boost again. Combo these for a series of Burnout Chains. This is useful when racing. Attempt Burnout Chains on long, mountainous roads to the west.
Author High Score: 10 Chains

Aggression-Class Vehicles: This is the best class to use during Road Rage and Marked Man Events, as your boost refills quickly with hostile driving, and these vehicles are likely to be the toughest. However, when you're wrecked, your boost bar drops. Unlike the Speed-class vehicles, you can boost at any time.

NOTE

The different types of takedown you can try during Road Rages is shown in the Event Advice section.

Stunt-Class Vehicles: Arguably the most useful of all the classes, these receive quicker boost bar refills if you barrel roll, jump, drift, spin, get big air, or perform other such actions. You can use all other types of dangerous driving to refill the boost, and use the boost at any time. This means these vehicles are useful in almost every event, including races! Also use Stunt-class cars for any exploration.

OPTIMIZING YOUR JOURNEY: GENERAL ADVICE

Introduction: Next to learning the lay of the land, the most important thing to master is knowing how to increase your boost, and when to use it. Before we run through all the different ways to earn boost, here are a few general tactics:

1. Stay in the middle of the road. That way, you can edge in to attempt oncoming actions, but keep a look-out for oncoming traffic.

2. Perfect your racing line. View the map and learn to cut corners, driving as close to barriers as possible, so you are always driving the shortest distance between two points (such as subsequent bends in a road, as shown).

3. Camera change: Although the "chase" cam (picture 1) is preferred in almost every event, the "hood" cam (picture 2) is beneficial if you're heading down a hill. That way your vision isn't blocked by the back end of a car (important if another vehicle is incoming).

4. Looking back: Use this during events to see who's behind you, and if anyone is about to slam you. Quickly flick the rear view on, then flip back to regular view, so you don't crash!

5. Reversing: Remember your vehicle can reverse. Not only is this incredibly useful during Stunt Runs (see the Event Advice section for more information), but you can e-brake and spin the vehicle around 180 degrees. Use this technique to back out of awkward positions.

6. E-brake "tapping": Instead of letting go of your boost button to e-brake, try keeping your right thumb on the boost, then tap the e-brake and steer when you want to corner. You'll continue at a faster speed!

7. Know your vehicle: Each vehicle has its own inertia, weight, strength, and flexibility. Some ponderous vehicles are terrible at cornering, but remove rivals easily. Some are fantastic at barrel rolls, but pathetic when scraping against rivals. If you're finding a particular maneuver or event difficult, check your vehicle's statistics, and change vehicle classes.

OPTIMIZING YOUR JOURNEY: INCREASING YOUR BOOST BY ACTIONS

Introduction: Here are all the ways to increase your boost bar during your journey. Use any or all of them as much as possible, when the situation allows it! You know you're succeeding in one of these actions when a message appears in the screen's bottom left.

1. Get Airtime: Achieve this by launching off a ramp and flying through the air before landing safely. The longer the drop, the more airtime you get.

2. Flat Spinning: Drive up a ramp, or to an area where you know you're going to get airtime, and combine this with an e-brake, just as the car is about to leave the ramp. Rotate through the air and land (usually facing the way you came, unless the airtime is longer).

3. Landing a Barrel Roll: Locate the ramps throughout the city that have a second, steeper section to them. Accelerate strongly, so the two left or two right tires hit this ramp squarely. If you're at an angle, you usually crash. You rotate through the air, and must land on your tires. Longer jumps (especially in out-of-the-way areas), and different cars allow for multiple barrel rolls—the key to gigantic stunt scores!

4. Escaping a Crash: During a race or other event with rivals, many pile-ups are going on around you. Instead of becoming a victim of one, if you can drive under, through, or around a crash without being struck, expect a boost reward.

5. Drifting: Approach a long curved bend (like the ones on South Mountain Drive) and tap the brake (not the e-brake) while continuing to accelerate. The drift begins. Hold the drift by flicking the steering to maintain the turn. If you're boosting at the same time, you're boost drifting. If you e-brake instead, this isn't counted as a drift. The length of the drift, not the angle of the turn, is counted here.

6. Grinding a Rival or Another Player: This is done during events (notably Road Rages). Simply swerve into a rival or player and crush them against a wall as you both continue to move forward. This is grinding.

7. Using the E-Brake: Simply apply the e-brake, ideally at top speed, and your car spins around. Keep the spin going for more "distance" (the greater angle you turn, the more boost). E-brakes are vital for heading around sharp corners without slowing too much, or for avoiding obstacles. Remember e-brakes can be "dabbed," and used to power park, too.

8. Near Misses (Traffic or Rivals/Players): This is an easy action, and one to always use initially to gain boost; simply drive into oncoming (or same-way) traffic, and avoid hitting them!

9. Nudging or Trading Paint (with a Rival/Player): Not quite grinding; this is less vicious. Simply knock your rival back and forth a few times without either of you crashing into a wreck.

10. Oncoming: The other easy way to increase your boost is to simply drive on the "wrong" side of the road, into oncoming traffic, but miss them (combine this with near misses). The longer the distance, the more boost.

11. Shunting a Rival/Player from Behind: During Road Rage or Race Events, simply ram a rival from behind. They'll be angry, but you'll be boosting!

12. Shunting a Rival/Player from the Side: This is the same deal as Action #11, except this is more of a sideswipe, steering left or right into the side of a foe rather than ramming from the rear.

13. Smashing a Burnout Billboard: Locate any of the 120 billboards—whether you've crashed through them or not—head through them, and land safely.

14. Landing a Super Jump: Locate any of the 50 super jumps, whether you've completed them or not, and land safely.

15. Tailgating a Rival or Player: Match the speed of a foe, and follow their "slipstream" without nudging or overtaking them, and you're awarded with boost power.

16. Performing a Takedown: Simply ram a foe off the road in one of the many entertaining ways detailed in the Road Rage section of Event Advice.

17. Traffic Checking: Hit traffic and survive the collision. Almost similar to the near miss, except you glance into them as you pass, sometimes causing them to crash. Some Aggression-type vehicles are better at this; you can strike vehicles head-on and at greater speeds in a

Takedown 4x4, compared to a low-strength Speed-class car, for example.

CONTINUING YOUR JOURNEY: EXPLORATION

Now that you should have figured out the types of cars to use for specific events, and how to increase your boost, you can fully explore Paradise City. The overall plan is to strive for better licenses, until you reach Elite and Criterion Elite, status! Complete the following tasks:

Power Parking: This fun little mini-game also allows you to perfect tight e-braking. Approach a gap between two parked cars, and e-brake 180 degrees into the gap. Your car should spin around without touching the cars, and stop with the inside wheels just inches away from the curb. To perfect a 100 percent score, make sure you position your vehicle as shown (pictures 1, 2, 3), and have the vehicle parked parallel to the other cars. Remember you receive boost from the e-brake, too!

Events (120 Total): This occurs throughout the entire time you are obtaining licenses. Choose from Races, Road Rages, Marked Man Events, Burning Routes, and Stunt Runs. Basically, you drive to the nearest intersection and begin an event. Additional licenses are awarded, the more events you complete. Consult the Event Advice section for further information.

Road Rules (128 Total): Turn on Road Rules by hitting ⬥, and the signposts of upcoming roads turn from green to red. You have Time Road Rules (64 events), where you must beat each of the city's roads by driving from either end to the other, and Showtime Road Rules (64 events), where you must execute a crashing roll, and strike other vehicles and scenery for a massive score. Consult the Event Advice section for further information.

> **NOTE**
>
> Beat a Time Road Rule *or* a Show-time Road Rule on a particular road, and the road sign turns from red to silver. Beat a Time Road Rule *and* a Showtime Road Rule, and that road sign turns from silver to gold.

Shutdowns (29 total): Listen for announcements that a new rival has entered the city, and cruise around until you spot them. Then use a car (ideally Aggression class) and take them down to add that car to your collection.

> **NOTE**
>
> Remember! Double your car collection by completing the Burning Route Event for each vehicle you own, and claim a better version of the existing vehicle as a prize.

Car Collecting (76 total): You can obtain vehicles in various ways. They are awarded at licenses upgrades, after shutdowns, when you finish Burning Route Events, and after completing discoveries. Check out the Junkyard section for all the details.

Discoveries (570 total): The other main "collectible" aspect of this game are the three types of discoveries scattered throughout the city. Refer to the Tour of Paradise section to find them all!

Super Jumps (50): Look for ramps with three (or more) flashing cones to ram through. These lead to a slow-motion, epic jump. Land one to complete the super jump. There are 10 super jumps per neighborhood.

Billboards (120): Look for the specific red Burnout billboards, scattered across town (there are 20–30 per neighborhood). Crash through them and land without wrecking to add a billboard to your collection. Note that broken billboards are still counted during Stunt Events, so don't delay in crashing through them all!

Smashes (400): There are 50–90 wire fences per neighborhood with yellow warning signs on them. These are usually at the beginning or end of a shortcut and need to be crashed through. Note that you must destroy at least one of the fence's gates for the smash to count!

> **NOTE**
>
> Completing these tasks adds to your "percentage complete" total. Consult the Appendices to learn how to achieve 100 percent!

Additional Exploration: The largest part of your game plan should be exploration. Here are just a few of the options (check the guide map for all the information you need):

  1. Find all the shortcuts (and drive through multiple ones in the same direction).

  2. Locate all the "hidden" areas not on your in-game map (such as the Lone Peaks Quarry).

  3. Find all "non-road" areas, like the train tracks.

  4. Look for all the ramps (blue arrows on the guide map).

  5. Look for all the drops (black arrows on the guide map).

  6. Figure out where all eight compass finishing places are.

TRAINING PART 2: GOING ONLINE

Unlocking events and vehicles is only half the fun. Check out some incredible online antics, too! Get online, and hook up with your friends. The most important games you can choose from are the following:

TODAY'S BEST

First of all, you can simply lark about throughout the city, attempting various actions (tactics for them are shown earlier in this chapter). Here's what you can attempt:

AIRTIME

Simply hang in the air for the longest possible time. Try falling off Uphill Drive, or into the Lone Peaks Quarry.

BARREL ROLLS

Hit any ramp with a narrow, higher section. Try the ramp on South Mountain Drive, or at the top of the quarry.

BURNOUTS

Maximize your boost in a Speed-class car, and continuously Burnout to the max! The mountain roads, where only a few cars are seen, is the best place for this.

DRIFTS

Approach a long curved corner at speed (optionally while boosting), and tap the brake. South Mountain Drive is a great place to try this!

FLAT SPINS

Boost toward any ramp, and e-brake and turn at the last second. Try this from the quarry, too; massive flat spins are possible!

JUMP DISTANCES

Accelerate strongly, toward a ramp, and sail through the air for the longest possible time. As usual, the quarry is exceptional for this maneuver!

NEAR MISSES

Drive close to, but without hitting, any of the innocent, cross-town traffic. The populated areas are best for this.

ONCOMING

Drive on the wrong side of the road, dodging incoming vehicles (including your friends) if necessary. This is a great way to keep your boost up.

POWER PARKING

Find a gap between two cars, drive at speed parallel to them, then e-brake 180 degrees, and hope for a high percentage score!

SUMMARY

This gives you a running total of how many events you've got the best score at, compared to your friends.

FREEBURN CHALLENGES: RECORDED

Refer to the Appendices for the list of all 350 Freeburn Challenges. There are 50 per number of players (so, 50 for two players, 50 for three players, all the way up to 50 for eight players). Choose any one you like if you're hosting. For location-specific challenges, a red dot appears on your in-game map.

FREEBURN CHALLENGES: YO GJ, PUMP THIS PARTY!

As you play online with your friends continuously, you'll learn you don't have to simply play by the rules; think about creating your own types of gameplay. Be inventive, because Freeburn Challenges work on many levels. As the host, you should know the different properties that this mode has to offer. Consider yourself a Game Jockey (GJ), with a role to select and mix appropriate actions and events!

> **NOTE**
>
> Your mission as host is to maximize the energy and fun for the players within your game!

Here are just a few of the almost limitless types of "freeform" gameplay you should think about employing. Chat to your friends over headsets and let them know what your plans are:

1. Attempt the challenges: These are usually in order, and finishing them all gives you a great sense of achievement!

2. Adventures: Figure out an awesome path (using this guide's map for shortcut and off-road information); and get all your friends to follow you—convoy style—over ramps, under bridges, off-road into the stock car track. What stock car track? Exactly!

3. Convergence: Choose a destination (either one that's easy to find, like the Wildcats Baseball Stadium, or a difficult place to get to, like Silver Lake Island), and all meet up. Last one to reach the place loses!

4. Learning the basics: Make sure everyone warms up before starting any difficult challenges. For example, can everyone land a barrel roll every time? If not, show them how it's done! Now try multiple barrel rolls!

5. Invent your own challenges: Try jumping over all the other players, or achieving 10 (or any other number of) near misses on a specific road.

6. Other competitions: Pick a target (for example, locating 10 super jumps), and the first person to reach that target wins.

MAKE YOUR OWN CHALLENGES: EXAMPLES

INTERSTATE BATON RACE

1. Position two players at each interstate toll booth. Start a one-on-one race (in Instant Freeburn mode, not in Race mode), and have the first two rivals drive to the next toll booth. When one hits their friend, the "baton" is passed, and they drive to the next toll booth, and so on until an entire interstate loop is made. The fourth teammate who drives back to the first toll booth to hit his first teammate wins the game for the team!

STOCK CAR SLAMMING

2. Head to the stock car track. The last one to crash is the survivor, and winner!

BARN ROOF SUMO

3. Locate the top of a barn or warehouse roof, such as the one at guide map coordinates H4 (the junction of Nelson Way and Lewis Pass) as part of a Freeburn Challenge. When the challenge is over, knock each other off; last man standing wins!

RED ROVER

4. Known in the UK as *British Bulldogs*, this tag-like game has the first player driving from and to a preset destination, chosen by everyone, such as from the Lone Stallion Ranch to the Wind Farms, or across Silver Lake Island. The other players are positioned along the route, and the first player must reach the destination without being "tagged." "Tagged" can mean touched or wrecked, your choice, GJ!

PARKING PAPARAZZI

5. Start power parking near one another, and put additional pressure on the last player to finish this move by following him around, to watch his technique and put him off. However, the "paparazzi" players can't move or damage the parked cars!

HANGING ON

6. Drive to the airfield in Silver Lake, ideally to complete the Freeburn Challenge that requires you to barrel roll through the fuselage sections at this point. While the slackers finish up this event, the ones who have finished this challenge drive to the ramped top of any of the barn hangars, and try to stay there while rivals try to knock them off!

INSTANT COMPASS RACE

7. Forget the "proper" racing mode. Simply wait for the right moment, and shout to everyone to get to a specific compass finishing place. These ad hoc races are great fun, especially as you jostle for position!

HIDDEN HIDEAWAYS

8. Because you've bought this guide, you already have a massive advantage over your friends. Study the guide map and find every shortcut and hidden area. Become the coolest host around and guide other players to these crazy places!

TIP

We've only scratched the surface regarding the cool games you can invent with your friends! Don't forget to visit the following websites and forums (and listen to the Crash FM Podcasts) for the latest information on this topic, and a whole lot more:
www.burnout.ea.com
www.criteriongames.com
www.burnoutaholics.com

RACES

The other main online activity is an online race. Hosts can create races with up to 15 waypoints, plus a start and finish location. You can also select the type of car and laps, and previously created races are saved so you can replay them later if you want!

TIP

Use this guide's Tour of Paradise and Event Advice sections to fully learn each square inch of this city. That way, all your online races should result in victory, especially when you figure out all the shortcuts!

ROAD RULES: TIME AND SHOWTIME

The final online aspect to perfect is to aim for the highest possible Time and Showtime scores. Time Events have you racing from one end of a specific road to the other, and recording the time. Showtime has you demolishing as many vehicles as possible in a continuous roll. Consult the Event Advice section for all the information.

02: The Junkyard

THE COMPLETE CAR COLLECTION

This chapter details all the vehicles that you can unlock and collect during your License challenges. As a general rule, the later the vehicle is in the following list, the more powerful it is. The list includes an artist's rendition of each vehicle, the manufacturer's insignia, the name of the vehicle, the Boost type, and the stats. Obviously, the higher the statistic, the better. Note that the number of Lives statistic informs you how many times you can wreck the vehicle during a Road Rage or Marked Man Event. Then comes information on how the car is unlocked, and a description.

01

Hunter: Cavalry
Boost Type: Stunt

SPEED:	●●○○○○○○○○
BOOST:	●●○○○○○○○○
STRENGTH:	●●●○○○○○○○
LIVES:	●●●○○

How Unlocked: Awarded with your Learner License.
Description: Not bad for a beginner's car, right? Well we're not gonna make you roll into Paradise in some junk compact your mom gave you. A good all-rounder to get you started.

02

Hunter: Oval Champ 69, Boost Type: Aggression

SPEED:	●●○○○○○○○○
BOOST:	●○○○○○○○○○
STRENGTH:	●●●●●○○○○○
LIVES:	●●●●○

How Unlocked: Complete the previous vehicle's Burning Route Event.
Description: Hunter dominated the stock car racing circuits of the 1960s. The Oval Champ 69 builds on the successful Hunter Cavalry platform, adding greater strength and more responsive handling.

03

Hunter: Mesquite
Boost Type: Aggression

SPEED:	●●●○○○○○○○
BOOST:	●●○○○○○○○○
STRENGTH:	●●●●●●○○○○
LIVES:	●●●●○

How Unlocked: Complete two Events to upgrade your license. This car is awarded with your Class D License.
Description: Tough enough to take the knocks of rural life. Quick enough to blow the doors off of every preppie in the state.

04

Hunter: Mesquite Custom, Boost Type: Aggression

SPEED:	●●○○○○○○○○
BOOST:	●●●○○○○○○○
STRENGTH:	●●●●●●○○○○
LIVES:	●●●●○

How Unlocked: Complete the previous vehicle's Burning Route Event.
Description: This slick custom version might not be as valuable to snooty collectors, but to a street racer like you, that extra boost power will sure come in handy.

05

Nakamura: SI-7, Boost Type: Speed

SPEED:	○○○○○○○○○○
BOOST:	○○○○○○○○○○
STRENGTH:	○○○○○○○○○○
LIVES:	○○○○○

How Unlocked: Complete three Events*.
Description: Front wheel drive means no surprises in the drift, but no doughnuts either! It won't cause you many heart-stopping moments, but its slavish obedience will get you out of sticky situations.

06

Nakamura: Racing SI-7, Boost Type: Speed

SPEED:	○○○○○○○○○○
BOOST:	○○○○○○○○○○
STRENGTH:	○○○○○○○○○○
LIVES:	○○○○○

How Unlocked: Complete the previous vehicle's Burning Route Event.
Description: The Nakamura Racing Group know what to do when it comes to cars. They have race-tuned the engine for greater speed, but they've backed off the boost for increased reliability.

07

Hunter: Vegas
Boost Type: Stunt

SPEED:	●●●●○○○○○○
BOOST:	●●●○○○○○○○
STRENGTH:	●●●○○○○○○○
LIVES:	●●●○○

How Unlocked: Complete five Events*.
Description: Relaxed street cool is the order of the day here. The Hunter Vegas packs a wicked boost, but is just far too laid back for the aggro of tackling corners.

08

Hunter: Vegas Carnivale, Boost Type: Stunt

SPEED:	●●●●○○○○○○
BOOST:	●●●○○○○○○○
STRENGTH:	●●●○○○○○○○
LIVES:	●●●○○

How Unlocked: Complete the previous vehicle's Burning Route Event.
Description: How could you possibly improve on the perfect classic coupe? With an even sweeter paint job and by cranking up the boost! How else?

09

Krieger: Pioneer
Boost Type: Aggression

SPEED:	●●●●○○○○○○
BOOST:	●●●○○○○○○○
STRENGTH:	●●●●●●●●●○
LIVES:	●●●●●

How Unlocked: Complete seven Events*.
Description: Like an automotive sumo wrestler, the Krieger Pioneer may look like three tons of blubber, but it's surprisingly agile. Smash insignificant rivals into the wall as you scream past to glory!

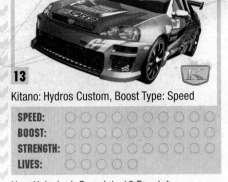

10

Krieger: Pioneer Super Gator
Boost Type: Aggression

SPEED:	●●●○○○○○○○○○
BOOST:	●●●●○○○○○○○○
STRENGTH:	●●●●●●●●●●●○
LIVES:	●●●●

How Unlocked: Complete the previous vehicle's Burning Route Event.
Description: The mighty Pioneer was no slouch, but the Super Gator packs even more boost power to help hunt down your prey.

11

Nakamura: Ikusa GT, Boost Type: Stunt

SPEED:	●●●●○○○○○○
BOOST:	●●●○○○○○○○
STRENGTH:	●●●○○○○○○○
LIVES:	●●●○○

How Unlocked: Complete nine Events to upgrade your license. This car is awarded with your Class C License.
Description: A Japanese take on the American muscle car, and one that has graduated to the level of a motoring legend—providing exceptional power at a bargain price. A solid all-round performer.

12

Nakamura: Ikusa Samurai, Boost Type: Stunt

SPEED:	●●●●○○○○○○
BOOST:	●●●○○○○○○○
STRENGTH:	●●●○○○○○○○
LIVES:	●●●○○

How Unlocked: Complete the previous vehicle's Burning Route Event.
Description: If you thought the Ikusa GT couldn't get any cooler, you were wrong! Custom Samurai artwork and extra boost power help you carve up the opposition.

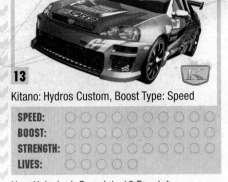

13

Kitano: Hydros Custom, Boost Type: Speed

SPEED:	○○○○○○○○○○
BOOST:	○○○○○○○○○○
STRENGTH:	○○○○○○○○○○
LIVES:	○○○○○

How Unlocked: Complete 10 Events*.
Description: The Kitano Hydros Custom is basically a front-wheel-drive shopping cart with a monster nitrous system. Don't expect to get too much out of it until you unleash the boost.

14

Kitano: Hydros Techno, Boost Type: Speed

SPEED:	○○○○○○○○○○
BOOST:	○○○○○○○○○○
STRENGTH:	○○○○○○○○○○
LIVES:	○○○○○

How Unlocked: Complete the previous vehicle's Burning Route Event.
Description: Check out the super cool Hydros Techno edition. The Techno's engine is tuned to provide extra speed without you needing to light up the boost.

15

Hunter: Reliable Custom, Boost Type: Aggression

SPEED:	●●●●●●○○○○
BOOST:	●●●●○○○○○○
STRENGTH:	●●●●●●●●○○○
LIVES:	●●●●○

How Unlocked: Complete 13 Events*.
Description: Looks like an antique, but above-average strength and a gentle drift make quite a handy package. An unconventional little all-rounder.

16

Hunter: Reliable Special, Boost Type: Aggression

SPEED:
BOOST:
STRENGTH:
LIVES:

How Unlocked: Complete the previous vehicle's Burning Route Event.
Description: Eye of the tiger! The wild Hunter Reliable Special packs extra boost power to bring more thrill to your fight!

17

Watson: R-Turbo Roadster
Boost Type: Stunt

SPEED:
BOOST:
STRENGTH:
LIVES:

How Unlocked: Complete 16 Events*.
Description: Light, agile, and with phenomenal grip, the Watson R-Turbo Roadster is the choice for drivers out to run rings around bigger vehicles. Don't expect to win many fights with it though.

18

Watson: Burnout Roadster
Boost Type: Stunt

SPEED:
BOOST:
STRENGTH:
LIVES:

How Unlocked: Complete the previous vehicle's Burning Route Event.
Description: Burnout branding and Burnout pace, with more boost power. You won't miss the loss of speed when you stop boosting because you won't stop boosting. Will you?

19

Rossolini: LM Classic
Boost Type: Speed

SPEED:
BOOST:
STRENGTH:
LIVES:

How Unlocked: Complete 19 Events*.
Description: There's nothing particularly complicated going on under the sleek chassis of the Rossolini LM Classic. Just lots of really simple stuff doing exactly the right thing.

20

Rossolini: LM Classic
Boost Type: Speed

SPEED:
BOOST:
STRENGTH:
LIVES:

How Unlocked: Complete the previous vehicle's Burning Route Event.
Description: This full on track-tuned version is honed for power on the straights, with even more boost power. Keep your boost chains going to get the most from her.

21

Hunter: Manhattan
Boost Type: Stunt

SPEED:
BOOST:
STRENGTH:
LIVES:

How Unlocked: Complete 22 Events*.
Description: It handles like a barge, but when you're sailing through the air doing a double barrel roll you won't go unnoticed! Showing off is the order of the day here.

22

Hunter: Manhattan Custom, Boost Type: Stunt

SPEED:
BOOST:
STRENGTH:
LIVES:

How Unlocked: Complete the previous vehicle's Burning Route Event.
Description: With the magnificent Manhattan Custom it's all about what's under the hood. The Custom packs an upgraded engine, giving you a much improved cruising speed.

23

Carson: Fastback
Boost Type: Speed

SPEED:
BOOST:
STRENGTH:
LIVES:

How Unlocked: Complete 24 Events to upgrade your license. This car is awarded with your Class B License.
Description: More than just a car, the Carson Fastback is a celebration of freedom. Freedom of expression. Freedom of spirit. Freedom of cornering—really, really sideways!

24

Carson: Fastback Special, Boost Type: Speed

SPEED:
BOOST:
STRENGTH:
LIVES:

How Unlocked: Complete the previous vehicle's Burning Route Event.
Description: The limited edition Fastback Special is the highest specification model that Carson produced. The Track Package extras bring increased boost power for those brave enough to keep it locked in.

25

Carson: Grand Marais
Boost Type: Aggression

SPEED:	●●●●●●○○○○
BOOST:	●●●●●○○○○○
STRENGTH:	●●●●●●●○○○
LIVES:	●●●●○

How Unlocked: Complete 26 Events*.
Description: Loved by Hollywood glitterati and mafia bosses alike, the Carson Grand Marais is the ultimate getaway car. It takes a while to get rolling, but it really takes some stopping!

26

Carson: Grand Sicilian
Boost Type: Aggression

SPEED:	●●●●●●○○○○
BOOST:	●●●●●●○○○○
STRENGTH:	●●●●●●●○○○
LIVES:	●●●●○

How Unlocked: Complete the previous vehicle's Burning Route Event.
Description: Don't worry, the bullets missed all the important bits. This Sicilian modster packs extra boost power to get you across the border.

27

Montgomery: Hyperion
Boost Type: Stunt

SPEED:	●●●●●○○○○○
BOOST:	●●●○○○○○○○
STRENGTH:	●●●●○○○○○○
LIVES:	●●●●○

How Unlocked: Complete 30 Events*.
Description: The Montgomery Hyperion has a few surprises up its sleeve. The problem isn't that it doesn't do what you tell it to, more that it does it all a bit too eagerly!

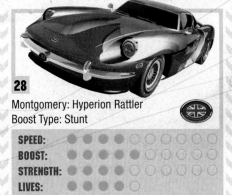

28

Montgomery: Hyperion Rattler
Boost Type: Stunt

SPEED:	●●●●●●○○○○
BOOST:	●●●●●○○○○○
STRENGTH:	●●●●○○○○○○
LIVES:	●●●●○

How Unlocked: Complete the previous vehicle's Burning Route Event.
Description: The Hyperion Rattler is hot. Hot car. Hot spray-job. They've even managed to squeeze more power out of the boost system.

29

Krieger: 616 Sport, Boost Type: Speed

SPEED:	○○○○○○○○○○
BOOST:	○○○○○○○○○○
STRENGTH:	○○○○○○○○○○
LIVES:	○○○○○

How Unlocked: Complete 34 Events*.
Description: High tech doesn't even begin to describe it. Computer-controlled supercar power. Computer-controlled all wheel drive. Computer-controlled traction aid. This car's probably smarter than you are!

30

Krieger: 616 Arachno Sport, Boost Type: Speed

SPEED:	○○○○○○○○○○
BOOST:	○○○○○○○○○○
STRENGTH:	○○○○○○○○○○
LIVES:	○○○○○

How Unlocked: Complete the previous vehicle's Burning Route Event.
Description: This sublime custom 616 packs a smoother, more powerful engine. It's not all about the boost in this ride. You'll leave people standing without it!

31

Hunter: Spur
Boost Type: Aggression

SPEED:	●●●●●●○○○○
BOOST:	●●●●●●○○○○
STRENGTH:	●●●●●●●●○○
LIVES:	●●●●○

How Unlocked: Complete 38 Events*.
Description: A pure street brawler. It can be stubborn around corners, so don't be afraid to use the handbrake or, alternatively, the side of a rival's car to help make a turn.

32

Hunter: Hotspur
Boost Type: Aggression

SPEED:	●●●●●●●●○○
BOOST:	●●●●●●○○○○
STRENGTH:	●●●●●●●○○○
LIVES:	●●●●○

How Unlocked: Complete the previous vehicle's Burning Route Event.
Description: This is the Hotspur, with a smokin' hot paint job and a super-tuned motor for increased cruising speed. It still won't go around corners, but now the paint you scrape off is much more expensive!

33

Montgomery: GT 2400
Boost Type: Speed

SPEED:	○○○○○○○○○○
BOOST:	○○○○○○○○○○
STRENGTH:	○○○○○○○○○○
LIVES:	○○○○○

How Unlocked: Complete 42 Events*.
Description: An out-and-out track car. Light, powerful, and so much grip that it takes a lot of persuading to make it go sideways. Watch out for some understeer when cornering at speed.

34

Montgomery: Sabotage GT 2400
Boost Type: Speed

SPEED:	○○○○	○○○○	○○	
BOOST:	○○○○	○○○○	○○	
STRENGTH:	○○○○	○○○○	○○	
LIVES:	○○○○	○		

How Unlocked: Complete the previous vehicle's Burning Route Event.
Description: The awesome Sabotage Racing GT 2400 squeezes every last drop out of the car's boost system. The speed drops off a bit more when you stop boosting, but why would you do that?

35

Jansen: P12
Boost Type: Stunt

SPEED:	●●●●	●○○○
BOOST:	●●●●	●○○○
STRENGTH:	●●●	○○○○
LIVES:	●●●	○○

How Unlocked: Complete 46 Events*.
Description: Known by its fans as The Pocket Rocket, the Jansen P12 is grippy and maneuverable. If you want to get the back end out, thump the throttle down.

36

Jansen: P12 Track Package
Boost Type: Stunt

SPEED:	●●●●	●○○○
BOOST:	●●●●	●○○○
STRENGTH:	●●●	○○○○
LIVES:	●●●	○○

How Unlocked: Complete the previous vehicle's Burning Route Event.
Description: This spectacular Jansen P12 track package gives even more top end boost than the street version. Just make sure you keep pulling enough stunts to keep it burning!

37

Carson: Inferno Van
Boost Type: Aggression

SPEED:	●●●●●●●	○○○
BOOST:	●●●●●	●○○○○
STRENGTH:	●●●●●●	●●●●
LIVES:	●●●●●	

How Unlocked: Complete 51 Events*.
Description: Handles like a tank. Hits like a tank. Basically, it is a tank. It just looks like a van.

38

Carson: Inferno BRT Van
Boost Type: Aggression

SPEED:	●●●●●	●○○○○
BOOST:	●●●●	●○○○○
STRENGTH:	●●●●●	●●●●●
LIVES:	●●●●●	

How Unlocked: Complete the previous vehicle's Burning Route Event.
Description: The fearsome Inferno Van just got harder to outrun! The Burnout Race Team only knows one way to tune an armor-plated racing van. Give it more boost!

39

Rossolini: Tempesta
Boost Type: Speed

SPEED:	○○○○	○○○○
BOOST:	○○○○	○○○○
STRENGTH:	○○○○	○○○○
LIVES:	○○○○	○○

How Unlocked: Complete 50 Events to upgrade your license. This car is awarded with your Class A License.
Description: The Rossolini Tempesta looks good and you want one. So don't focus on the blistering power or the punchy, responsive drift. Winning isn't everything. Looking good while you're winning is essential.

40

Rossolini: Tempesta GT
Boost Type: Speed

SPEED:	○○○○	○○○○
BOOST:	○○○○	○○○○
STRENGTH:	○○○○	○○○○
LIVES:	○○○○	○○

How Unlocked: Complete the previous vehicle's Burning Route Event.
Description: The Rossolini Tempesta GT is a real prize. Lighter and faster across the board, this full GT racing conversion offers more of pretty much everything. If you can handle it.

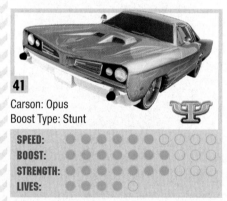

41

Carson: Opus
Boost Type: Stunt

SPEED:	●●●●	●●○○○
BOOST:	●●●●	●●○○○
STRENGTH:	●●●●	●○○○
LIVES:	●●●	●○○

How Unlocked: Complete 56 Events*.
Description: The Carson Opus is the ultimate in pimpin' street cool! It's not the nimblest stunt car around, but that extra weight comes in handy when things get rough.

42

Carson: Opus XS
Boost Type: Stunt

SPEED:	●●●●	●●○○○
BOOST:	●●●●	●●○○○
STRENGTH:	●●●●	●○○○
LIVES:	●●●	●○○

How Unlocked: Complete the previous vehicle's Burning Route Event.
Description: The Opus XS brings a lot more to the party, with a cool graffiti spray job and a tuned engine for a higher cruising speed. So get cruisin'!

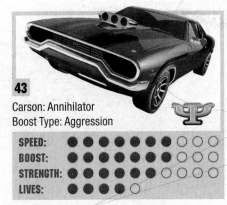

43

Carson: Annihilator
Boost Type: Aggression

SPEED:	● ● ● ● ● ● ● ○ ○ ○
BOOST:	● ● ● ● ● ● ○ ○ ○ ○
STRENGTH:	● ● ● ● ● ○ ○ ○ ○ ○
LIVES:	● ● ● ● ○

How Unlocked: Complete 61 Events*.
Description: Affordable big block muscle, home customized into a supercar stomping street machine. It may not be refined; but it's brash, it's effective, and it's a lot of fun.

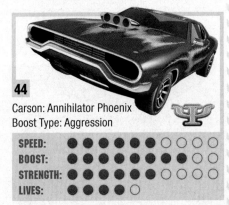

44

Carson: Annihilator Phoenix
Boost Type: Aggression

SPEED:	● ● ● ● ● ● ● ○ ○ ○
BOOST:	● ● ● ● ● ● ● ○ ○ ○
STRENGTH:	● ● ● ● ● ● ○ ○ ○ ○
LIVES:	● ● ● ● ○

How Unlocked: Complete the previous vehicle's Burning Route Event.
Description: This is the awesome Annihilator Phoenix. Use it to rise from the ashes, and burn your opposition with an amped-up boost system.

45

Jansen: X12 Supercar, Boost Type: Speed

SPEED:	○ ○ ○ ○ ○ ○ ○ ○ ○ ○
BOOST:	○ ○ ○ ○ ○ ○ ○ ○ ○ ○
STRENGTH:	○ ○ ○ ○ ○ ○ ○ ○ ○ ○
LIVES:	○ ○ ○ ○ ○

How Unlocked: Complete 66 Events*.
Description: It's fast. It's a bit mental. And it doesn't like you very much. But if you've got the skills to tame it, there aren't many cars faster.

46

Jansen: XS12
Boost Type: Speed

SPEED:	○ ○ ○ ○ ○ ○ ○ ○ ○ ○
BOOST:	○ ○ ○ ○ ○ ○ ○ ○ ○ ○
STRENGTH:	○ ○ ○ ○ ○ ○ ○ ○ ○ ○
LIVES:	○ ○ ○ ○ ○

How Unlocked: Complete the previous vehicle's Burning Route Event.
Description: If the X12 was mental, this baby's completely loco! The Jansen XS12 is the street-legal track package. Somehow the Jansen guys have squeezed even more boost out of it. Hang on!

47

Kitano: Touge Sport, Boost Type: Stunt

SPEED:	● ● ● ● ● ● ● ○ ○ ○
BOOST:	● ● ● ● ● ● ● ○ ○ ○
STRENGTH:	● ● ● ● ● ● ○ ○ ○ ○
LIVES:	● ● ● ● ○

How Unlocked: Complete 71 Events*.
Description: A delicately balanced drifting machine, the Touge's GT pedigree also gives it a straight line speed that's not to be laughed at.

48

Kitano: Touge Criterion, Boost Type: Stunt

SPEED:	● ● ● ● ● ● ● ● ○ ○
BOOST:	● ● ● ● ● ● ● ● ○ ○
STRENGTH:	● ● ● ● ● ● ● ○ ○ ○
LIVES:	● ● ● ● ○

How Unlocked: Complete the previous vehicle's Burning Route Event.
Description: This hot street machine has been race-tuned by the Criterion team to give you even more boost. Everybody loves more boost!

49

Hunter: Takedown 4x4
Boost Type: Aggression

SPEED:	● ● ● ● ● ● ● ○ ○ ○
BOOST:	● ● ● ● ● ○ ○ ○ ○ ○
STRENGTH:	● ● ● ● ● ● ● ● ● ○
LIVES:	● ● ● ● ●

How Unlocked: Complete 77 Events*.
Description: This is the ideal choice for bullies. In the Hunter Takedown 4x4, it's always *your* right of way.

50

Hunter: Takedown Dirt Racer
Boost Type: Aggression

SPEED:	● ● ● ● ● ● ● ○ ○ ○
BOOST:	● ● ● ● ● ● ● ○ ○ ○
STRENGTH:	● ● ● ● ● ● ● ● ● ○
LIVES:	● ● ● ● ●

How Unlocked: Complete the previous vehicle's Burning Route Event.
Description: Check out the monstrous Dirt Racer edition of the Hunter Takedown. It's packing extra boost power to help you plow through your rivals.

51

Carson: 500 GT
Boost Type: Speed

SPEED:	○ ○ ○ ○ ○ ○ ○ ○ ○ ○
BOOST:	○ ○ ○ ○ ○ ○ ○ ○ ○ ○
STRENGTH:	○ ○ ○ ○ ○ ○ ○ ○ ○ ○
LIVES:	○ ○ ○ ○ ○

How Unlocked: Complete 83 Events*.
Description: A true-blood racer's car. Low-tech, tricky to master, but devilishly quick if you're good enough. Are you good enough?

52

Carson: Racing 500 GT
Boost Type: Speed

SPEED:	○○○○○○○○○○○○
BOOST:	○○○○○○○○○○○○
STRENGTH:	○○○○○○○○○○○○
LIVES:	○○○○○

How Unlocked: Complete the previous vehicle's Burning Route Event.
Description: If you thought the 500 GT was fast, then you ain't seen nothing yet. The Carson Racing 500 GT is the full GT racing package with even more blistering boost power!

53

Hunter: Racing Oval, Boost Type: Aggression

SPEED:	●●●●●●●●●○
BOOST:	●●●●●●●●○○
STRENGTH:	●●●●●○○○○○
LIVES:	●●●●○

How Unlocked: Complete 89 Events*.
Description: Straight from the racing ovals, this is a hot, race-tuned stock car. It's nimble and stable in a straight line, but its racing pedigree makes drifting a bit uncomfortable.

54

Hunter: Racing BRT Oval Champ, Boost Type: Aggression

SPEED:	●●●●●●●●○○
BOOST:	●●●●●●●○○○
STRENGTH:	●●●●●○○○○○
LIVES:	●●●●○

How Unlocked: Complete the previous vehicle's Burning Route Event.
Description: The Burnout Race Team brings its own special brand of performance enhancement to the Hunter Oval Champ. And you know what that means. More boost!

55

Carson: GT Concept
Boost Type: Stunt

SPEED:	●●●●●●●●●●
BOOST:	●●●●●●●●●●
STRENGTH:	●●●●●●●●●●
LIVES:	●●●●○

How Unlocked: Complete 90 Events to upgrade your license. This car is awarded with your Burnout License.
Description: The new generation of American muscle cars is here, and they've finally put the *muscle* back in. What's more, it might even make it round the occasional corner.

56

Carson: GT Flame
Boost Type: Stunt

SPEED:	●●●●●●●●○○
BOOST:	●●●●●●●●●○
STRENGTH:	●●●●●○○○○○
LIVES:	●●●●○

How Unlocked: Complete the previous vehicle's Burning Route Event.
Description: The stunning Carson GT Flame brings a lot more than a cool spray job. Its ramped up boost power makes it one of the fastest cars in Paradise.

57

Hunter: Citizen
Boost Type: Aggression

SPEED:	●●●●●●●●○○
BOOST:	●●●●●●●●○○
STRENGTH:	●●●●●●●●●○
LIVES:	●●●●

How Unlocked: Complete 98 Events*.
Description: Paradise City's idea of law enforcement. It's more like a battle cruiser than a police cruiser. It takes an age to turn, but you'd need a torpedo to stop it!

58

Hunter: Civilian
Boost Type: Aggression

SPEED:	●●●●●●●●●○○○
BOOST:	●●●●●●●●●○○○
STRENGTH:	●●●●●●●○○○
LIVES:	●●●●

How Unlocked: Complete the previous vehicle's Burning Route Event.
Description: This is the Hunter Citizen on its day off, with less armor plating and more boost. If the Citizen is too much of a tank for you, this could be exactly what you're looking for.

59

Watson: 25 V16 Revenge
Boost Type: Speed

SPEED:	○○○○○○○○○○○○
BOOST:	○○○○○○○○○○○○
STRENGTH:	○○○○○○○○○○○○
LIVES:	○○○○○

How Unlocked: Complete 107 Events*.
Description: This car has an awful lot of torque. Too much for it to handle. It's driven it mad. Drunk with power. It's practically foaming at the grill!

60

Watson: Revenge Racer
Boost Type: Speed

SPEED:	○○○○○○○○○○○○
BOOST:	○○○○○○○○○○○○
STRENGTH:	○○○○○○○○○○○○
LIVES:	○○○○○

How Unlocked: Complete the previous vehicle's Burning Route Event.
Description: The mind-blowing Watson Revenge Racer packs even more boost power than the stock version. Revenge is a dish best served at 200 miles an hour.

61
Montgomery: Hawker
Boost Type: Stunt

SPEED:
BOOST:
STRENGTH:
LIVES:

How Unlocked: Complete 116 Events*.
Description: The Montgomery Hawker is, to put it simply, crazy. As well as being a competitive racer, this is the ultimate stunt car. Find a split ramp and land some barrel rolls!

62
Montgomery: Hawker Solo
Boost Type: Stunt

SPEED:
BOOST:
STRENGTH:
LIVES:

How Unlocked: Complete the previous vehicle's Burning Route Event.
Description: The Montgomery Hawker Solo boasts the coolest spray job in Paradise. It's a shame all that extra boost power means no one will get the chance to see it as you fly by.

63
Krieger: Uberschall 8
Boost Type: Speed

SPEED:
BOOST:
STRENGTH:
LIVES:

How Unlocked: Complete 128 Events*.
Description: If you can keep it under control, this is a seriously rapid piece of equipment. In drifts, use the throttle to get the back end moving, then hold on tight.

64
Krieger: Uberschall Clear-View
Boost Type: Speed

SPEED:
BOOST:
STRENGTH:
LIVES:

How Unlocked: Complete the previous vehicle's Burning Route Event.
Description: With the spectacular Uberschall Clear-View you can see exactly where all that power is coming from. And there's plenty of it, with boost speed pumped to the max.

65
Carson: Thunder Custom
Boost Type: Aggression

SPEED:
BOOST:
STRENGTH:
LIVES:

How Unlocked: Complete 140 Events*.
Description: Great on the straightaways and not too bad in a fight. When this monster hits the streets, the only safe place is behind the wheel.

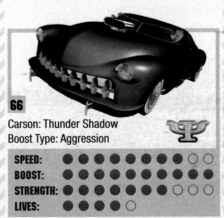

66
Carson: Thunder Shadow
Boost Type: Aggression

SPEED:
BOOST:
STRENGTH:
LIVES:

How Unlocked: Complete the previous vehicle's Burning Route Event.
Description: As black as night and twice as frightening. The boost power on this baby is just phenomenal. As the saying goes, they can't outrun your Shadow.

67
Carson: Hot Rod Coupe
Boost Type: Stunt

SPEED:
BOOST:
STRENGTH:
LIVES:

How Unlocked: Complete 154 Events*.
Description: For burning up straight roads, the Hot Rod Coupe is second to none. Watch out for the boost wheelie at low speed.

68
Carson: Tribal Special
Boost Type: Stunt

SPEED:
BOOST:
STRENGTH:
LIVES:

How Unlocked: Complete the previous vehicle's Burning Route Event.
Description: The Tribal Special is the cruising man's Hot Rod. Slightly less boost power, but more cruising speed means if you shut it off, the whole pack won't go strolling past.

69
Krieger: Racing WTR '07
Boost Type: Speed

SPEED:
BOOST:
STRENGTH:
LIVES:

How Unlocked: Complete 168 Events*.
Description: Have you ever wondered what top-flight motor sport would be like on Planet Burnout? The Krieger Racing WTR is the ultimate Burnout racecar.

70

Krieger: PCPD Special
Boost Type: Speed

SPEED:	
BOOST:	
STRENGTH:	
LIVES:	

How Unlocked: Complete the previous vehicle's Burning Route Event.
Description: This is the ultimate in law enforcement. Nobody outruns the PCPD special pursuit vehicle! This baby's got all the boost power you could ever need.

71

Carbon Ikusa GT
Boost Type: Aggression

SPEED:	●●●●●●●●○○
BOOST:	●●●●●●●○○○
STRENGTH:	●●●●●○○○○○
LIVES:	●●●●○

How Unlocked: Beat all the Time Road Rule times.
Description: Awarded for beating all the Time Road Rules, this limited edition aerospace Ikusa GT comes with Aggression Boost as standard and a stronger carbon fiber body shell.

72

Carbon Hydros Custom
Boost Type: Stunt

SPEED:	
BOOST:	
STRENGTH:	
LIVES:	

How Unlocked: Beat all the Showtime Road Rule scores.
Description: Awarded for beating all of the Showtime Road Rules, this unique Hydros Custom comes with Stunt Boost and a rear wheel drive conversion for more extreme stunt performance.

73

Carbon GT Concept
Boost Type: Speed

SPEED:	
BOOST:	
STRENGTH:	
LIVES:	

How Unlocked: Smash all 400 fences.
Description: Awarded for finding all the smashes in Paradise City, this exclusive GT Concept boasts a chrome trimmed carbon fiber chassis and a Speed Boost conversion. Perfect for cruising.

74

Carbon Hawker
Boost Type: Speed

SPEED:	
BOOST:	
STRENGTH:	
LIVES:	

How Unlocked: Destroy 120 billboards.
Description: Awarded for hitting all the billboards in Paradise City, this custom built Montgomery comes with a gorgeous carbon fiber and chrome finish and a Burnout chaining Speed Boost conversion.

75

Carbon X12
Boost Type: Stunt

SPEED:	
BOOST:	
STRENGTH:	
LIVES:	

How Unlocked: Complete all 50 super jumps.
Description: Awarded for landing all the jumps in Paradise City, this astonishing X12 is stronger, lighter, and faster thanks to a space-age carbon fiber construction. A Stunt Boost conversion completes the package.

76

Carbon Krieger Uberschall 8
Boost Type: Stunt

SPEED:	●●●●●●●●○○
BOOST:	●●●●●●○○○○
STRENGTH:	●●●●○○○○○○
LIVES:	●●●●○

How Unlocked: Complete two sets of online Freeburn Challenges**
Description: Awarded for completing two full sets of Freeburn Challenges, this special Uberschall 8 has been converted to run on Stunt Boost. Whiplash also comes as standard. A neck-brace is advised.

(* Once unlocked, a rival will start driving this car around Paradise City. Shut him down to acquire this car.)

(** A set of Freeburn Challenges means a complete selection with a specific number of players; so for example, all the two-player Freeburn Challenges comprise a set.)

STOCKTAKING IN YOUR GARAGE

The following information summarizes the number and type of vehicles in your collection:

THE DIFFERENT METHODS OF UNLOCKING VEHICLES

HOW UNLOCKED?	NUMBER OF CARS UNLOCKED IN THIS MANNER
Complete a number of Events	35
Complete a Burning Route	35
Complete all Road Rule Events	2
Complete all Discoveries	3
Complete some Freeburn Online Challenges	1
Grand Total	76

TOTAL VEHICLE TYPES AVAILABLE

STUNT TYPE	AGGRESSION TYPE	SPEED TYPE	GRAND TOTAL
26	24	26	76

LEGEND
- SPEED
- AGGRESSION
- STUNT

DRIVER'S LICENSE PROGRESSION CHART

LICENSE GRADE	CAR NAME (& NUMBER IN CHAPTER)	WINS TO UNLOCK	REQUIREMENT TO REACH NEXT LICENSE CLASS
BURNOUT ELITE LICENSE		183–210*	MAIN GAME PROGRESSION IS COMPLETE 100%
	Krieger Racing WTR (69)	168	
	Carson Hot Rod Coupe (67)	154	
	Carson Thunder Custom (65)	140	
	Krieger Uberschall 8 (63)	128	
	Montgomery Hawker (61)	116	
	Watson 25 V16 Revenge (59)	107	
	Hunter Citizen (57)	98	
BURNOUT LICENSE	Carson GT Concept (55)	**90**	Number of events for game completion **85 events + Remaining Burning Routes**
CORE GAME COMPLETION + CREDITS	Hunter Racing Oval Champ (53)	89	
	Carson 500 GT (51)	83	
	Hunter Takedown 4x4 (49)	77	
	Kitano Touge Sport (47)	71	
	Jansen X12 Supercar (45)	66	
	Carson Annihilator (43)	61	
	Carson Opus (41)	56	
	Carson Inferno Van (37)	51	
CLASS A LICENSE	Rossolini Tempesta (39)	**50**	Next License upgrade in **40 events**
	Jansen P12 (35)	46	
	Montgomery GT 2400 (33)	42	
	Hunter Spur (31)	38	
	Krieger 616 Sport (29)	34	
	Montgomery Hyperion (27)	30	
	C&B Grand Marais (25)	26	
CLASS B LICENSE	Carson Fastback (23)	**24**	Next License upgrade in **26 events**
	Hunter Manhattan (21)	22	
	Rossolini LM Classic (19)	19	
	Watson R-Turbo Roadster (17)	16	
	Hunter Reliable Custom (15)	13	
	Kitano Hydros Custom (13)	10	
CLASS C LICENSE	Nakamura Ikusa GT (11)	**9**	Next License upgrade in **15 events**
	Krieger Pioneer (9)	7	
	Hunter Vegas (7)	5	
	Nakamura SI-7 (5)	3	
CLASS D LICENSE	Hunter Mesquite (3)	**2**	Next License upgrade in **7 events**
(START GAME) LEARNER LICENSE	Hunter Cavalry (1)		Next License upgrade in **2 events**

*The exact figure depends on the number of Burning Routes completed during your progression from Learner up to the Burnout License, as these event wins are not reset at license upgrades.

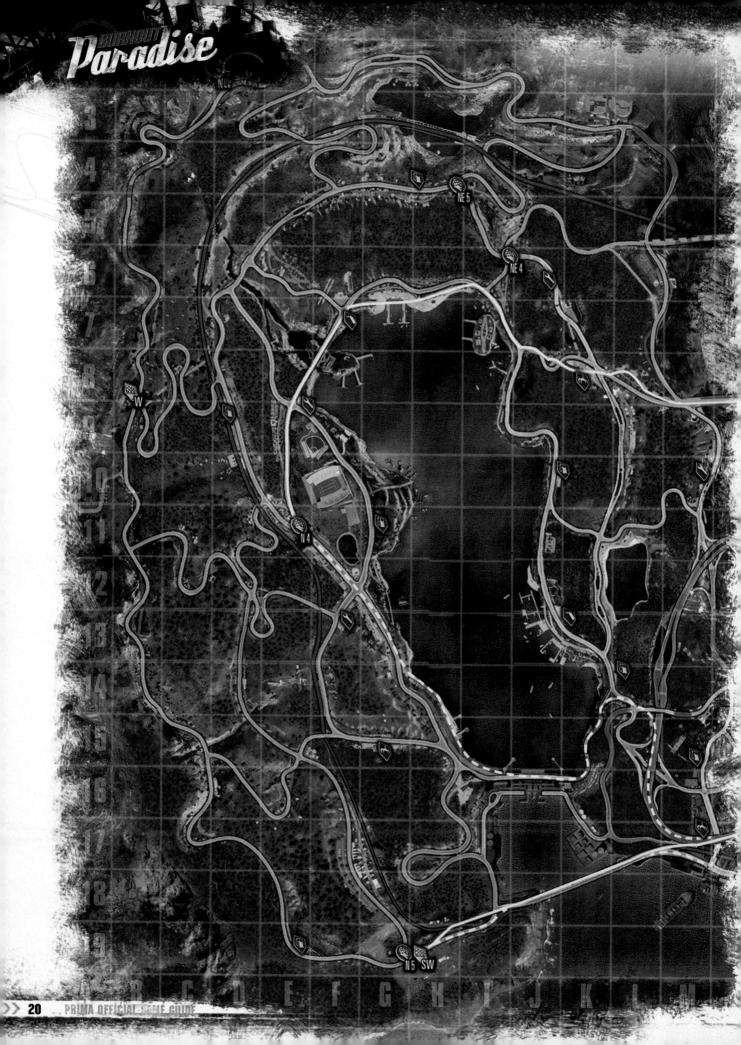

**NORTH AND NORTHEAST
RACE ROUTES**

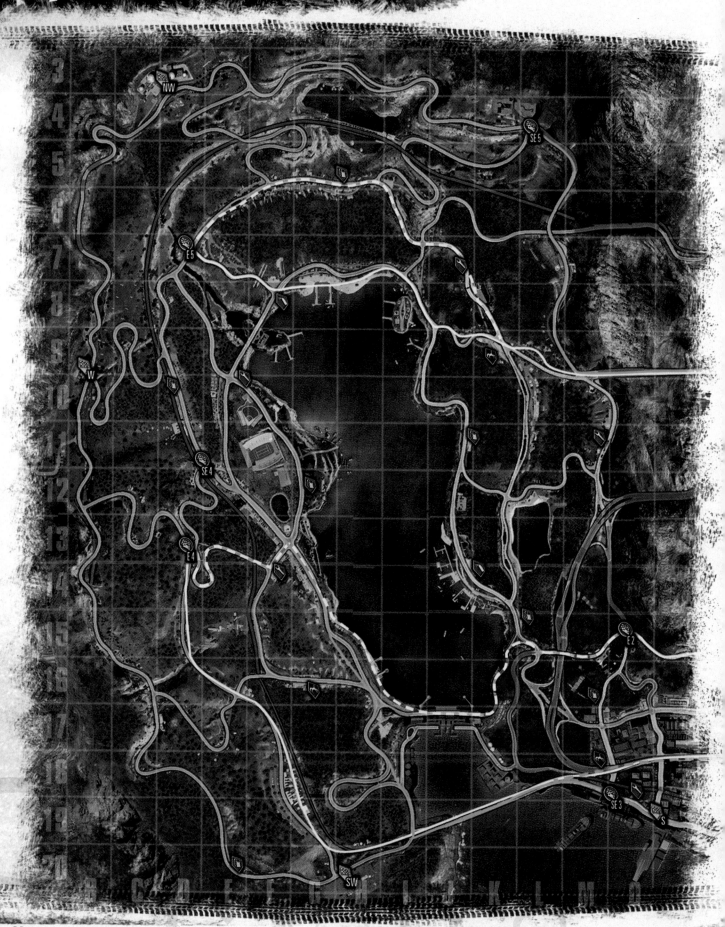

**EAST AND SOUTHEAST
RACE ROUTES**

SOUTH AND SOUTHWEST
RACE ROUTES

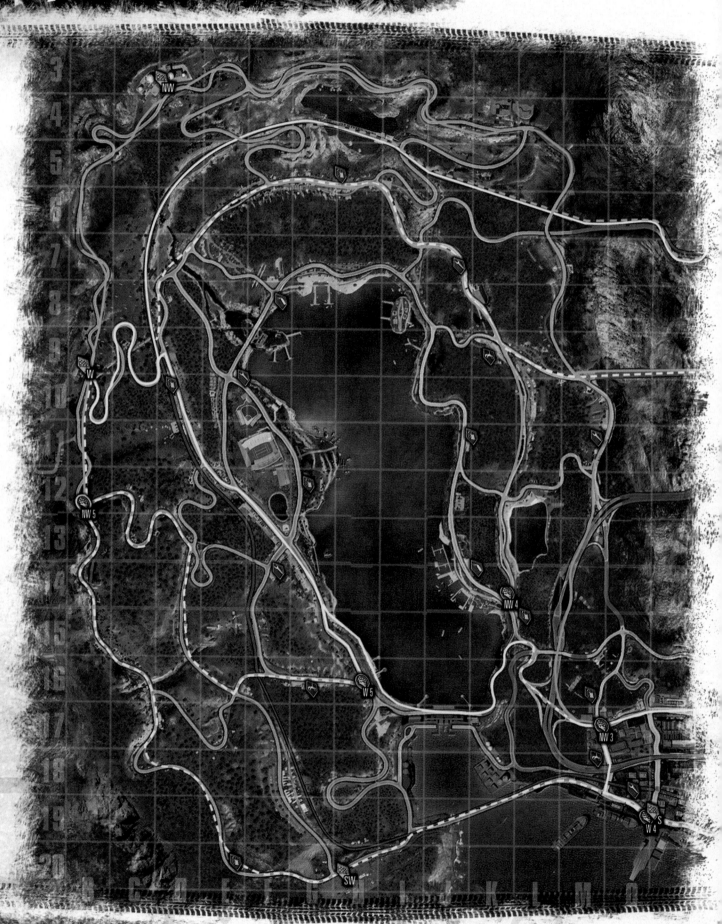

WEST AND NORTHWEST RACE ROUTES

OVERVIEW

There are two different types of Race Events in *Burnout Paradise*: duels and regular races. Duels involve you and a rival. Other races involve up to eight total drivers. The objective is simple: reach the finishing place first! If you don't come in first, you get nothing, so strategies for beating all the other cars will be essential.

However, the route you take is completely up to you! Therefore, it becomes important for you to pore over this strategy guide map (showing all the shortcuts) in great detail, so you can learn the quickest routes possible. With this in mind, this portion of the book splits the races into different sections.

Each section showcases all the races ending at a particular compass direction, starting with north, and ending with northwest. From there, two excellent and cunning routes are plotted out for you, along with screenshots showing points of interest along the way.

MAP LEGEND

- 🏁 STARTING POINT
- 🏁 DUEL STARTING POINT
- 🏁 DRIVE THRUS
- ▬ ROUTE 1
- ■ ■ ROUTE 2
- 🏁 FINISHING PLACES

RECOMMENDED VEHICLES

AMATEUR

RACING SI-7

HYDROS TECHNO

LM TRACK PACKAGE

Or use any Stunt or Aggression vehicle, if boosting is a problem for you.

PROFESSIONALS

TEMPESTA GT

XS12

RACING 500 GT

REVENGE RACER

SEMI-PROFICIENT

FASTBACK SPECIAL

616 ARACHNO SPORT

SABOTAGE GT 2400

Or use any Stunt or Aggression vehicle, if boosting is a problem for you.

ELITE STATUS

CARBON GT CONCEPT

CARBON HAWKER

UBERSCHALL CLEAR-VIEW

PCPD SPECIAL

ADDITIONAL PRE-RACE ADVICE

The better you know your way around the streets of Paradise City, the bigger the advantage you'll have over your rivals.

It's essential to choose the right car before you race. To reach the finish line before anyone else, your best bet in a race is a Speed car. You can win races in any class of car, but speed is ultimately your goal.

Your car's indicators blink when you approach a turn that is advantageous to your route.

If you're in a Stunt or Speed car, look out for all the jumps along the way to get some boost. If you're in an Aggression car, which is generally stronger than the other two classes of car, take down your rivals up to first place and earn extra boost chunks.

If you're having problems being pushed around, move from a Speed to a stronger Stunt class vehicle.

Look at the plotted-out race routes throughout this chapter, and drive them, memorizing the turns prior to a race!

Many races go past gas stations. Keep an eye out for them on the Crashnav when planning your route to gain a boost refill.

Check out this guide's map poster to see where all the ramp opportunities are. The blue arrows show where to get quick boost refills.

Speed cars work supremely well in the White Mountain and Silver Lake neighborhoods. Boost chain through the drift corners to keep your speed maxed out.

When you really learn the city, you can plan and take your own route to the finish line rather than following the indicator signs. There may be a straighter or faster way there, especially if the race goes near the interstate.

At that point in the game, you may find the compass more useful than the flashing street signs.

When you become a Grand Master at *Burnout Paradise*, you'll ignore all the compass and map information completely, and use in-game landmarks to find your way around!

NOTE

The following routes represent some of the fastest ways to reach each of the eight compass direction finishing places. However, you may want to consider other shortcuts if you're finding these routes difficult. You might even figure out a quicker way!

NOTE

The race numbers in this guide are arbitrary; they are purely to reference the guide's maps and waypoints. You can complete any race in any order you like.

PART 1: NORTH (THE MAPLEMOUNT COUNTRY CLUB)

1. RAT RACE

Start Point: 2nd and Webster

ROUTE 1

Make a left turn onto 2nd as you begin. Accelerate northwest, head into the park, and enter the arched southeast corner entrance of it, on 2nd and Glancey.

Cut across the park diagonally, and drive onto 3rd and Root. Continue to speed west, to the major intersection of Paradise Square.

Drift right onto Franke Avenue, and begin to increase your speed heading northwest. Cross the bridge, and continue up Franke. Cross Young, and drive into the left-hand shortcut. Continue along it and merge onto 7th.

Continue west on 7th Street, choosing either a gap between the buildings or the stepped area at the corner of Lambert Parkway to skid right.

Head north on Lambert Parkway, accelerating strongly as it changes into Newton Drive, and cross the finishing line at the Maplemount Country Club.

ROUTE 2

Instead of turning left onto 2nd, accelerate north for two blocks to Andersen, and swing left. Accelerate quickly, heading west (and slightly south), avoiding the El Train ramp, and blast through the mall, joining route 1 at the intersection of Paradise and Franke. Now finish the race as described previously).

2. RIVERSIDE RUN

Start Point: Andersen and Glancey

ROUTE 1

Turn left immediately, and continue heading west (and slightly south), avoiding the El Train ramp, and blast through the mall, joining the race #1 route at Paradise and Franke. Now finish the race as described previously.

ROUTE 2

Stay on Glancey and accelerate north, passing the intersections with 4th and Young, and ignoring the left turn at 7th (by the Twin Bridges). One option is to skid left here and travel along the sunken highway all the way to Lambert Parkway.

Cross 7th street: Glancey ends and 9th Street begins. Follow the path of the river (on your left) around to the west, and accelerate all along 9th Street. Skid sharply right at the end of 9th, onto Lambert Parkway. Now finish the race by heading to the country club.

☐ 🏁 3. HEADS UP
Start Point: Gabriel and Manners

ROUTE 1

Continue north along Gabriel, and merge onto Lambert Parkway while still heading north. Before you reach the intersection, optionally enter the building site to the right, and use the ramped exit onto Lambert.

Simply drive through the traffic, ideally staying in the middle of Lambert Parkway, all the way north, passing all the major intersections to your right. Eventually, you reach the Ocean View archway and can continue through to the finish.

ROUTE 2

Instead of heading north directly, turn right and continue along Manners. Gain more speed as you head through the fishing market warehouses and over the ramps, before merging back onto Manners.

Take the small shortcut onto Evans and accelerate north. Although this route is longer, there's less traffic to worry about and Evans is a straight shot all the way to Franke. Head left, into the Franke Avenue shortcut, and onward to the finish.

☐ 🏁 4. DRIVING OFF
Start Point: West Lake and Nelson

ROUTE 1

Accelerate north on West Lake, ignoring the shortcut on your left, and power through the intersection with Chubb Lane. Continue heading northeast.

Drive onward, over the two steel bridges, optionally using the super jump on your right. At the paint shop, swerve right, and enter the marina shortcut; it's quicker than continuing onto East Lake.

Drive onto the marina, back up, and merge back onto East Lake. Ignore the junction with West Crawford, and instead merge left at the intersection with Ross Drive.

Optionally gain some boost by using the banked shortcuts and gaps, landing and boosting through the junkyard, crossing Nelson, and optionally using the snaking shortcuts to reach the junction with Lawrence.

Enter Lawrence Road Tunnel, and accelerate strongly, optionally dropping into the left lane at the gap, toward the eastern end.

Emerge from the tunnel, and immediately make a very sharp left turn onto Newton Drive. Follow this north to the finishing place. If you overshoot Newton, skid left onto Lambert instead.

ROUTE 2

Swing around and journey southeast down West Lake Drive. At the parking lot, merge onto the shortcut road by the side of Silver Lake.

Accelerate down the hill, using the ramps on the building to gain boost, and merge onto Geldard Drive at the top of the dam. You can optionally drop down onto Casey Pass here, but a safer option is to stay on Geldard.

Follow the winding tunnels to the intersection with East Lake Drive, and head east, but slow down so you make the shortcut curve through the billboard, and onto I-88. Turn right so you don't

land in the middle of the interstate wall and crash. Accelerate strongly as you speed south down the interstate, as it curves around to the east. Continue on this easterly path, keeping to the far left.

As you approach over Parr Avenue, brake sharply, spin 180 degrees, and drop off the gap from the interstate to Parr. Then speed up as you head toward the finish on Lambert Parkway.

> **NOTE**
>
> You can continue along the interstate before dropping off near Manners Ave. Look for these opportunities, as there are many, and some don't involve braking.

☐ 🏁 5. HIGH NOON CLUB
Start Point: South Mountain and Lucas

ROUTE 1

Upper: Head northeast from the starting point, and head left, onto the shortcut that leads to the train tracks. Accelerate across the bridge, staying on the tracks.

Accelerate strongly and line yourself up for the ramp at the northeastern end of the train tracks, leap over, and land on the interstate itself. Drop off onto Parr and continue up Lambert Parkway to the finish.

ROUTE 2

Lower: Jet off the starting line, ignoring the shortcuts, and aim for the suspension bridge entrance. Accelerate through the bridge, using the super jumps if you wish.

Head along South Bay Expressway, but slow as you reach Hall Avenue, and swing left, heading north. At the next turn (Manners), make a right, and follow Manners east. Use the shortcut off Manners to cut across to Evans. Proceed to Franke and continue on to the finish as described in race #1.

PART 2: NORTHEAST (THE COAST GUARD HEADQUARTERS)

1. ROLLERCOASTER

Start Point: Young and Hubbard

ROUTE 1

Start by heading north along Hubbard, ignoring the shortcuts, and accelerating past the right turn onto 2nd. Pass the interstate bridge to your left, and at the long looping corner, use the shortcut to your right.

Merge back onto Hubbard at the top of the turn, then make a sharp left onto Lambert Parkway and accelerate north.

Pass by 9th Street, then look for a line of white barriers on your right. Skid through them, before you reach East Crawford, and drive onto the train yard. Head through the warehouse and onto the northern end of Hamilton, then merge onto East Crawford.

Follow East Crawford Drive along the beachfront area, weaving in and out of traffic and avoiding the central road islands. Use any of the ramps if boosting is an issue. The gas station at Nakamura should have solved that problem, though.

Boost east, passing all the luxury hotels to your right, and aim straight for the Coast Guard HQ finishing place, just past Patterson.

ROUTE 2

Follow Hubbard north, but cut through the shortcut to your right, just before 2nd. Merge onto 2nd,

and follow it all the way through to the bridge. Speed through Downtown, avoiding the traffic, and look for signs for Root Avenue up ahead.

Merge into the park entrance on your left. Speed through the park, and stay heading northeast, into the construction yard. Keep right so you enter the narrow lower shortcut that brings you out onto Webster heading north; don't take the super jump because your direction after landing isn't ideal.

Enter the tunnel on Webster, accelerating north out of it, pass the parking structure, steer right slightly at the junction with 7th, under the interstate bridge, and continue north to the finish.

2. AVANT GUARD

Start Point: Young and 1st

ROUTE 1

Turn and head east on 1st Street, and look for either of the construction shortcuts on your left, before you hit Evans. Follow this underground shortcut north, on a parallel route to Evans. Merge back onto Evans at the intersection with 5th Street.

Immediately steer right slightly onto the grassy shortcut that cuts across Franke, emerging onto Young at the auto repair shop. Cut across into the underground parking lot at the corner of Young and Paradise, then drive north on Paradise to the sunken 7th Street highway. Skid right, onto any of the three parallel roads of 7th Street. Follow one of them east to the Twin Bridges, and join Webster at 4th. Then head to victory!

ROUTE 2

Instead of heading east, continue north on Young. Make sure you bear right at the junkyard and intersection with Hamilton, and continue to speed up as you enter the Twin Bridges district.

Continue toward the auto repair shop (on your right), skid into the underground parking lot, and follow the route to the finish.

3. COAST TO COAST

Start Point: Warren and Manners

ROUTE 1

This is very straightforward. Accelerate north on Warren toward the four-way intersection, then keep straight onto Hamilton. Drive northeast, either to the start of Race 2 (Young and 1st), or through the warehouse shortcut to your right, and through the construction shortcut that leads to Lambert Parkway. Either way, continue to your goal using either of Race 2's routes.

ROUTE 2

Ignore the route to the north, and turn right, continuing northeast along Manners, crossing the river bridge, and heading through the shortcut at King Avenue and Harber.

Skid onto Fry and head north, using the shortcut under the police headquarters to cut the corner of Fry and 2nd. Follow 2nd east, to the park and the Root intersection. Proceed on the shortcut, following the route to the finish.

4. SAVE FERRIS

Start Point: West Crawford and Nelson

ROUTE 1

Begin heading north on West Crawford, and follow the road as it winds through the countryside. Just before the Crawford Tunnel, skid right, and head into the shortcut to the right. Accelerate through the muddy tunnel, emerging on North Rouse Drive heading south. Keep your speed up now that you're on the tarmac!

Use the shortcuts on North Rouse if you wish, but slide left as you reach the entrance to the Lawrence Road Tunnel. Accelerate all the way through to the other side, and make your second turn left, sharply skidding onto Lambert. Follow that north to the finish.

ROUTE 2

Ignore West Crawford, and instead head southeast along Nelson Way, optionally using the shortcut at the ranger station. At the junction with Ross Drive, skid left, optionally using the snaking paths that run parallel. You end up at the junction with North Rouse and Lawrence Road Tunnel. Enter the tunnel and follow the route northeast to East Crawford and the finish.

5. GOING COASTAL

Start Point: Nelson and Lewis

ROUTE 1

This starting point is only one junction away from Race #4, so simply journey southeast along Nelson to the junction with West Crawford, and follow either of the routes of the previous race.

ROUTE 2

Try this variation: follow the path to take the Crawford Tunnel, emerging on the winding path that eventually leads toward East Crawford. Pass Newton as you enter Palm Bay Heights, and stay on Crawford all the way to the finishing place.

PART 3: EAST (THE WATERFRONT PLAZA)

1. PLAIN SAILING

Start Point: East Crawford and Moore

ROUTE 1

Follow East Crawford, dodging the traffic and road islands, and head toward the northeastern finishing place at the Coast Guard HQ.

Accelerate through the warehouse shortcut from Crawford, bringing you out onto Angus Wharf. Accelerate south on Angus.

Keep your speed up as you race south on Angus Wharf, all the way to the finishing place.

ROUTE 2

Start by heading east on Crawford, but look for the shortcut on your right, just before you reach Patterson. This leads to a ramped area that allows you access onto the interstate.

Speed up on the interstate. You can fly off at

the billboard if you wish, but a quicker path is to pass by the toll booths on the right, exiting onto Webster via the shortcut.

Emerge from the covered area heading south on Webster, and look for the red stripes of the construction yard at the corner of Webster and Andersen. Skid left sharply, and cruise to the finish.

2. WATERWAY TO GO

Start Point: Hubbard and South Rouse

ROUTE 1

Head east along Hubbard, optionally heading through the tunnel for a shorter excursion to the junction with Harber.

Ignore this turn and instead continue north to the shortcut just before 2nd Street. Cut across the corner of 2nd, and continue traveling east on this road.

Pass the junction with Lambert Parkway and boost forward, heading directly for the bridge that leads into Downtown.

Once over the bridge, avoid the traffic and continue along 2nd until you reach the intersection with Root Avenue. Cut across the park, then head through the construction building, choosing either the ground or super jump exit, quickly dropping onto Andersen, heading east to the finish.

ROUTE 2

Accelerate along Hubbard using the same path

as Route 1, but swing right at the junction with Harber. Follow it as it winds south then meets up with the junction of Young and Lambert.

You can choose Route 1 or 2 of Race #3 from here, or head northeast along Lambert, to the junction with 2nd Street, and boost east, following this race's Route 1.

3. PLEASURE CRUISE

Start Point: Harber and Lambert

ROUTE 1

Journey north to the triangular intersection with 1st Street, and boost east, maximizing your speed for the jump over the broken bridge, into Downtown.

Land on 1st Street in the River City District near Downtown, and boost along 1st. Although you can head up the ramp to the El Train, then drop off and head to the Wildcats Baseball Stadium, it is slightly quicker to cut the corner at 1st and Root.

Use another shortcut through construction to steer onto 2nd, but ignore the park and continue east, all the way to Angus Wharf. Skid left, and use the Rayfield Grand Hotel shortcut to the goal.

ROUTE 2

Instead of heading along Lambert, follow Harber east and then turn northeast on Hamilton, using the warehouse shortcut to reach 1st Street. Then complete the race using Route 1.

4. EASTERN PROMISE

Start Point: Lucas and Schembri

ROUTE 1

Swing around and ensure you're traveling south on Lucas, using the shortcut on the left, through the timber building to reach the intersection with Hans.

Continue south through the trailer park, and skid left onto the shortcut leading to the train tracks. Boost across the suspension bridge above the expressway.

At the eastern end of the bridge, locate the ramp on the train tracks, and use it to land on the interstate. Head east at top speed along this intersection section.

Stay on your preferred side of the interstate, either heading into traffic for extra boost, or remaining on the other side for a safer path.

Continue all the way to the toll booth in Downtown Paradise.

Pass through the toll booth, and head into the tunnel under Webster (you can take the shortcut leading to the Wildcats Baseball Stadium before the tunnel, if you wish). Head north on I-88, then locate the ramp in the middle of the road that lands you on Webster above. Skid right off the shortcut, and proceed to the goal.

ROUTE 2

For the alternate route, weave down Schembri (or take the Super Jump), merge onto Chubb, and take West Lake southeastwards, across the parking lot to the shortcut: the lakeside road that leads to Geldard, above the dam.

Cross the dam, then wind through the tunnels to the junction with Manners, East Lake, and Hubbard. Continue east, along Hubbard, crossing the bridge over the Interstate, through another small tunnel and out to the junction

with South Rouse. The remainder of the race should be selected from either path on Race #2 (detailed previously).

5. PLAZA ENDURANCE

Start Point: Cannon and Nelson

ROUTE 1

Begin this cross-city race heading southeast along Cannon Pass, cutting through the parking lot at the junction with West/East Lake, and then drive onto the marina shortcut.

Skid back onto East Lake Drive, and continue heading southeast until you reach the junction with Ross. Turn left slightly, onto Ross.

Cross Nelson and stay on Ross, optionally using the snaking shortcut for additional boost. Then cross into Lawrence Road Tunnel and increase your speed.

Head directly east as you zoom out of the tunnel, onto 7th Street, and look for the shortcut on your right, just before you spot the El Train tracks. Skid right, and drive onto Franke Avenue.

Once on Franke, it's a straight shot across the bridge and into Downtown. At Paradise City Square, skid left and head into the base of the shopping mall, then out onto Andersen. Optionally take the El Train ramp, land back on Andersen, and accelerate straight to the finish.

ROUTE 2

Instead of heading down Cannon Pass, journey northeast along Nelson Way, optionally using the storage barn shortcuts to the south along the way.

Continue along Nelson until you reach the junction with Lewis Pass, and ignore it. Stay on Nelson as it bends southeast.

At the next junction with West Crawford Drive, jet across to the east, then follow the road southeast, all the way to the junction with Ross, and continue to the tunnel. Follow Route 1 to the finish.

PART 4: SOUTHEAST (THE WILDCATS BASEBALL STADIUM)

☐ ◉ 1. STEALING 1ST

Start Point: Webster and 7th

ROUTE 1

Immediately continue along Webster, weaving south, passing the parking structure, entering the small tunnel, and heading out the other side.

Continue heading south on Webster, watching for cross-traffic and using the middle ramps if extra boost is needed.

Continue on Webster heading directly south. The road passes under another small tunnel, and once on the other side, you should be able to spot the finish.

It is important to learn that the finishing place is outside the baseball stadium, on the intersection of Angus Wharf, Webster Avenue, and 1st Street.

ROUTE 2

This takes a little more skill. Head onto the parking lot to the left of Webster, and locate the ramp pointing toward the interstate. Leap onto the toll booth, and land without crashing.

Drive into the interstate tunnel underneath Webster, and increase your speed. At any time before you reach the southern corner, move to the middle and line yourself up with a ramp. Jump out, onto Webster, and follow the remainder of Route 1 to your goal.

☐ ◉ 2. CURVEBALL

Start Point: Lambert and East Crawford

ROUTE 1

Accelerate south down Lambert before making a sharp left turn at 7th Street, heading down the southern of the two split lanes.

Skid right, head into the shortcut that leads to Franke Avenue, and then follow Franke southeast, toward the bridge leading to Downtown.

Once in Downtown, pass through the middle of Paradise Square, continue on Franke to its end, and merge onto 2nd Street heading east.

Pass the park and make a sharp right turn onto Webster. You're a block north of your goal

ROUTE 2

Instead of turning left onto 7th, make a sharp, controlled left turn a block from your starting point, onto 9th Street, and follow it east, locating this shortcut on the corner of 9th and Nakamura. This allows a straight shot onto the interstate on-ramp. Once on the interstate, accelerate wildly, and follow the road south, through the toll booths to 2nd Street. Proceed on the same route as described in race #16 (route 2) to the finish.

☐ ◉ 3. RACE FOR THE PLATE

Start Point: South Bay Expressway and South Rouse

ROUTE 1

Travel east along the expressway, optionally using any of the parallel shortcuts to increase your boost.

Keep this up until you reach the junction with Manners; keep to the right and use the shortcut by the ocean. Keep this up as you reach the fish market warehouses on your left and right. Stay right, and merge onto Harber.

Keep up your speed as you head along Harber, and be sure to head into the covered Exhibit Hall thoroughfare, leading to the left curve. Avoid heading into the baseball stadium itself; stay on the road to reach the finish.

ROUTE 2

Alternately, follow Route 1 until you reach the junction with Gabriel. Skid left and travel north up this road. A block farther north is the interstate on-ramp.

Turn right, head onto the interstate route, and keep going along it at high speed, making sure you have a good, straight racing line as you pass through the toll booths.

As the road drops down into the tunnel, look for a shortcut on the right side, and take it, leading onto the Exhibit Hall main road. Follow it as it curves around to the finish line.

☐ 🏁 4. CALL OF THE WILD

Start Point: Nelson and Lucas

ROUTE 1

Ignore Lucas and instead head southeast on Nelson and onto West Lake, optionally using any of the parallel shortcuts. Power across the junction with Chubb.

Keep on your southeast trajectory, staying on West Lake all the way to the junction with South Mountain Drive.

Accelerate down South Mountain Drive, and line yourself up with the ramp that allows you to fly off the cliff, landing on the road below. Skid left at the junction with the expressway, and cross the suspension bridge.

Cross the bridge, and continue to work your way along the South Bay Expressway, all the way to the junction with South Rouse, after which you can choose either of the routes from the previous Race.

ROUTE 2

Begin as you did in route 1, but once on the bridge, use a middle ramp to land on the train tracks, and stay on them instead of dropping down.

Continue along this train track above the road bridge until you reach this ramp, and land on the interstate, accelerating and heading east until you reach the victory line.

☐ 🏁 5. BASEBALL BATTLE

Start Point: North Rouse and Lewis

ROUTE 1

Begin with a strong acceleration southeast, through the tunnel, and down North Rouse heading along this mountain road.

Head farther down North Rouse, past the heliport, and winding down to the junction with Lawrence Tunnel. Enter the tunnel heading east at speed, and exit out onto 7th Street. Now follow the rest of Race #2 Route 1 to the finish.

PART 5: SOUTH (THE NAVAL YARD)

☐ 🏁 1. DEEP SOUTH

Start Point: East Crawford and Hudson

ROUTE 1

Head south on Hudson, then make a cunning off-road decision and steer onto the railroad tracks, and boost southeast.

Skid south and launch over 7th Street using one of the concrete ramps, land in the train yard, then exit via Smash #12, landing after the short drop onto Glancey.

If you land perfectly, you'll have an excellent racing line at the junction of Glancey and 4th Street, into the shortcut that cuts diagonally, leading you into Andersen.

Jet across Anderson, up the concrete short-cut, and off the drop, driving from north to south through the park.

Continue due south, into the shortcut in the middle of the park block of 2nd Street, which curves west slightly and allows you access onto Harber Street on the opposite side of the road from the auto repair shop.

Boost west along Harber until you reach the fish market warehouse shortcuts, and power through them, merging onto the expressway soon afterward.

Keep your speed up as you head along the South Bay Expressway, all the way to the naval yard, which is just before Hall Avenue.

ROUTE 2

This is slightly less direct, but offers wider thoroughfares. Start by driving east, then southeast onto the shortcut leading through the billboard, and onto the interstate.

Increase your speed as you tear along the interstate, boosting past the toll booths, and into the tunnel under Webster. Continue at speed, and choose a central ramp, or roadway either side, to merge up and into Webster.

Once on Webster, tear under the southeast finishing place by the Wildcats Baseball Stadium, skid right, and power along Harber before following the remainder of Route 1 to your goal.

☐ 🏁 2. THE DUEL

Start Point: Hamilton and 7th

ROUTE 1

Head directly south down Hamilton, past the parking structure after zipping between 3rd Street's crossroads.

After Hamilton merges, continue almost directly south, passing the junkyard and gas station, and keep pointing south as you cross 1st Street.

Continue south all the way to the intersection where Hamilton ends and Harber continues in a southwest direction. Almost instantly, make an easy left onto Shepherd, taking you across Manners and all the way to the expressway, and the final race to the finish!

ROUTE 2

There's a slight variation to this route; begin by heading south as in Route 1, but at the intersection with Harber, head south onto Warren Avenue.

A block later, you're on Manners, and the junction where the expressway begins. Boost south onto the expressway, opting to use the shortcut warehouse ramps at the fish market if you wish, and continue on to the finish.

☐ 🏁 3. MAN O' WAR

Start Point: 3rd and Angus

ROUTE 1

Begin with a boost south, along Angus Wharf, and curve your racing line around to the junction with Webster, heading under the southeast finishing place. Then continue on the road as it turns into Harber. Then follow Race #1 Route 1 from that point to the victory line.

ROUTE 2

Turn right, and jet off west along 3rd for two blocks, lining yourself up with the park entrance. Blast through the concrete arch, across the park, and onto 2nd Street.

Remain on 2nd Street through the rest of Downtown, heading west across the bridge, and a block after Evans, make a sharp left, onto Hamilton. You can now choose either of Race #2's routes.

☐ 🏁 4. TORPEDO RUN

Start Point: North Mountain and Hans

ROUTE 1

The reason for this race name becomes apparent when you reach the suspension bridge. To get there, head south as North Mountain becomes South Mountain. Use this shortcut if you wish. Power down this mountain road, passing the gas station and Lone Stallion Ranch, and make a massive acceleration across the suspension bridge, from the west to eastern end. From here, it is two short blocks to the finish.

ROUTE 2

A longer, but no less entertaining route can lead you away from the rival drivers. Head east along Hans, following the road and the shortcut, to this junction with Lucas. Optionally, head south down Lucas, and join Route 1.

Or, build up speed heading from Hans, past the junkyard, to South Mountain Drive and south, past the quarry entrance, and then off the cliffside jump. A block later, take a sharp left, onto the suspension bridge. Then follow Route 1 for the rest of the race.

☐ 🏁 5. HARD FORT

Start Point: North Rouse and Read

ROUTE 1

The first part of this race is concerned with exiting the northwestern region; head east, using North Rouse's shortcut, and cut the corner. Keep going to the tunnel entrance.

The next route is long, but simple. Stay on North Rouse and ride it all the way past the intersection with Ross and Lawrence, head across the interstate, drive into the tunnel, and emerge as the road changes to South Rouse, in Harbor Town. Travel south a block, then turn left on Hall, and follow that across Lambert Parkway, for a straight shot down to the victory line. Don't forget to skid left across the finish!

ROUTE 2

Follow the path of Route 1 all the way to the junction with I-88. Instead of cutting across and continuing on Rouse, enter the interstate, driving to the left side, and heading to the first off-ramp. This leads to Lambert Parkway, and a turn back onto South Rouse. Follow that to a right turn onto the expressway, and the naval yard.

PART 6: SOUTHWEST (THE LONE STALLION RANCH)

☐ 🏁 1. HORSE POWER

Start Point: 8th and Hudson

ROUTE 1

Turn to face west, and drive a couple of blocks to Moore. Head right, and then drive up and onto I-88. Accelerate strongly along the interstate, all the way to the toll booths, curving round to the south, across the bridge. Keep right as you enter the interstate tunnel.

Emerge from the tunnel, keeping to the right, and head through another set of toll booths. Make a right on the off-ramp road, which winds back and around onto the end of Lambert Parkway. At the junction, turn left onto Manners. Speed through the tunnel, then turn right at the exit, into the tunnel.

Emerge from the tunnel onto Casey Pass, drive over the super jump at the base of the dam, skid around the corner, and drive up and onto South Mountain Drive, heading south. Follow the bend to the right, and the finish is up ahead, just before the junction with Lucas.

ROUTE 2

Instead of heading east, move southeast down Glancey and follow the edge of the river, turning onto 4th Street heading west. This becomes King Avenue. Continue to boost south before merging onto Harber.

A second later, merge onto the beginning of South Bay Expressway, using the fish market warehouses as a shortcut. Follow the expressway west, all the way to the suspension bridge, where this joins Route 1 near the finish.

2. FINAL FURLONG

Start Point: Hamilton and 3rd

ROUTE 1

A straightforward run south is all that's needed here. Boost through the junction with 1st Street, following Hamilton as it changes into Harber Street, and at the next left, skid onto Shepherd Street, heading south. Cross Manners to reach the expressway. The rest of the route is west along the expressway to the suspension bridge, then along South Mountain Drive to the finish.

ROUTE 2

Follow under the El Train to the junction with 1st, then make a right and merge onto Lambert Parkway, heading southwest. At the grassy corner with Parr, drive onto Parr until you reach Manners, and skid right. Head west one block, then turn sharply left, moving south on Hall. Then drive to the expressway bridge, and then the Ranch.

3. SPAGHETTI WESTERN

Start Point: Harber and Glancey

ROUTE 1

Begin by looking for the steps at the starting junction that allow you to head up and onto the interstate, then boost toward the toll booths at high speed, and follow the interstate as it winds southwest, then west again.

After you see the parking structure on your right, continue to boost, but look for the flashing warning barriers on the right edge, and drop down. Land on Manners and continue west, then swerve left at Hall, and continue to the goal.

ROUTE 2

This is a simple affair. Boost west along Harber Street, passing the auto repair shop and staying under the interstate bridge, before you merge onto Race #1's Route 2 at King Avenue. Follow that path along the South Bay Expressway to the goal.

4. FULL GALLOP

Start Point: Nelson and Chubb

ROUTE 1

Take Nelson south, all the way down past the gas station, through the junction with Lucas, and make the turn at Chubb. Boost south past Tindle's Mine to Hans, and screech right, then almost immediately left so you skid onto Lucas. Accelerate south all the way to the end of Lucas, and skid left, through the finishing place.

ROUTE 2

This starts with the same boost south along Nelson, but instead of turning at the intersection with Chubb, continue on Nelson, passing the parking lot, until you hit South Mountain Drive, then accelerate down South Mountain, and over the ramp that cuts out the final loop. Land and drive to the finish.

5. DEMOLITION DERBY

Start Point: East Lake and Ross

ROUTE 1

Head south down East Lake, following the coast of the lake itself, optionally heading into the tunnel, and following the road to the junction with Nelson. From here, head to Geldard and speed onto the dam.

As soon as you round the corner onto the top of the dam, find the opening on your left, and drop off the side of the dam to the metal platform halfway down. Drive west, off the edge of the platform, land on Casey Pass, and follow it south to South Mountain Drive, then onward to victory!

ROUTE 2

This route is exactly the same as Route 1, until you reach the dam. Instead of the potentially dangerous drop down to Casey Pass, head to the shortcut area that merges onto South Mountain Drive, then take the clifftop ramp drop down, and proceed to the goal.

PART 7: WEST (THE WIND FARM)

□ ◎ 1. RACE TO THE SUMMIT
Start Point: Franke and Young

ROUTE 1

Take a trip south down Young, using the parking lot shortcut by the gas station to merge onto 2nd Street. Then skid onto Lambert Parkway, follow that past the triangular intersection, and stay on Lambert as it winds west.

Follow Lambert all the way to the junction with Manners and Geldard, and cross Manners, looping around into the Geldard Tunnel that leads to the top of the dam. Speed across it, into the shortcut by the water's edge. Boost out onto West Lake, and accelerate through Sunset Valley village, all the way to the junction with Nelson.

Follow Nelson northwest to the junction with Uphill Drive, and make a sharp left onto this road. There's a trio of nasty switchbacks as you rise up; take the shortcut as you reach the

middle one if you need to. Continue all the way to the junction with North Mountain, and the finish line.

ROUTE 2

Ignore Young and instead look for the road to the right of Franke Avenue. Head down Evans, along the southbound covered roadway, until you reach the expressway. Use the regular shortcuts if you wish, traveling all the way along the expressway and over the bridge.

Travel west, passing Lone Stallion Ranch, and then drive up South Mountain Drive along the twists and turns, finding the shortcuts that you need. Pass Schembri, and enter the shortcut through the concrete pipe just north of here, dashing out at the junction with Uphill Drive and through the finish line.

□ ◎ 2. GO WEST!
Start Point: Newton and East Crawford

ROUTE 1

Make a turn right, moving onto West Crawford, and enter the hills, making sure you maneuver into the tunnel.

The rest of the middle of your journey is along these train tracks. Ride them across the rickety bridge, across the northern suspension bridge, through the tunnel, and between the two dirt ramps and sheds leading to billboards. Pass

through the yellow steel bridge, and power south toward the bridge where Uphill Drive starts. Take the shortcut on the right, join Uphill just right of the bridge over the train tracks, and wind up Uphill Drive to finish.

ROUTE 2

Make a quick acceleration south, but skid right at the tunnel entrance, onto Lawrence Road. Speed through the tunnel, exiting at the junction with North Rouse. Speed across onto Ross, and follow that to the junction with Nelson. Here, make a right, and head northeast, past the ranger station.

Stay on Nelson as you head past West Crawford, and wind through the mountains, passing the storage depots, zipping past Frankie's Campground on your left, and winding up the vista hill to the junction with Uphill Drive. Finish using this switchback-heavy road.

□ ◎ 3. SPIN CITY
Start Point: 1st and Glancey

ROUTE 1

Jet forward heading west along 1st Street; this is an excellent run, especially if you head up the ramp onto the El Train, and jump the broken bridge from this height. Continue to blast forward, toward the triangular junction where you can easily merge onto Lambert. Follow Race #1's Route 1 the rest of the way.

ROUTE 2

Start by heading along 1st Street west as you would in Route 1, but turn left through the shortcut across Fry, then through the forecourt shortcut near the sundial to reach Harber and King. Cross the bridge, and merge onto Race #1's Route 2, following that to the goal.

4. CATCH MY DRIFT

Start Point: South Bay Expressway and Hall

ROUTE 1

Make sure you learn Race #1's Route 1 before you try this one. Launch your vehicle heading west on the South Bay Expressway, but skid right onto South Rouse, traveling up two blocks to Lambert Parkway, and follow Race #1 Route 1 the rest of the way.

ROUTE 2

This starting point occurs midway through Route 2 of Race #1. Therefore, you should also attempt to continue west along the expressway, following the middle and latter part of this earlier route, to the goal.

5. POWER SURGE

Start Point: Hans and West Lake

ROUTE 1

Steer northwest along West Lake as it heads into Sunset Valley village, and continue to your goal by following the latter portions of Race #1 Route 1.

ROUTE 2

This is a good alternate route, if you can properly skid through the sharp curves and corners. Head west along Hans, and then skid right at the junction with Lucas. Follow Lucas, ideally using the timber building shortcut. At the junction with Schembri Pass, make a left and go up the pass all the way to South Mountain Road. The goal is north of you.

PART 8: NORTHWEST (CRYSTAL SUMMIT OBSERVATORY)

1. TUNNEL VISION

Start Point: Glancey and 7th

ROUTE 1

The first half of this road trip is almost entirely straight. Head straight along 7th, down into the sunken highway before emerging and continuing west through the junction with Lambert, into Lawrence Road Tunnel. At the western end, swerve right, and begin to climb North Rouse.

The road north is winding, but keep on North Rouse for the most direct path. Pass over the tunnel, through the tunnel to the weather station area, and continue, heading west, across the entirety of hillside pass (this part of North Rouse road). Use the shortcuts, especially in the middle of the road as the main paths split slightly.

Race across the junction of North Mountain Drive and Read Lane, and almost immediately skid left into the shortcut, bearing right as the shortcut path branches left and right. This leads to a drop and the straightest shot to the finish line!

ROUTE 2

Route 2 is a little more convoluted, but still worth a shot. Head west on the sunken highway, as in Route 1, but make a sharp right onto Newton, then skid left onto West Crawford.

Follow the winding path to the tunnel entrance, and make sure you head into the train tunnel.

Emerge at full speed from the tunnel, and cross the rickety bridge, boosting west and crossing the suspension bridge, but slow down for an accurate escape onto the narrow dirt exit path just before the tunnel. This allows access onto Read Lane. Drive up, along the switchback to the junction with North Mountain Drive, and complete the race using the shortcut.

2. FAR, FAR AWAY

Start Point: 2nd and Root

ROUTE 1

This is one of the longest races, so prepare yourself! Begin on Root, but head up Franke Avenue, crossing the bridge, and taking the shortcut that allows you access onto 7th Street. Here, you can choose to continue on Race #1's Route 1 or 2.

ROUTE 2

Begin on Root as before, heading up Franke, but turn left just after crossing the bridge, driving into the covered section of 5th Street. Accelerate up and out, then make a right turn onto Hamilton. Skid left onto 7th Street. Here, you can choose to continue on Race #1's Route 1 or 2.

3. REACH FOR THE STARS

Start Point: South Rouse and Lambert

ROUTE 1

The first route is straightforward. Boost onto the interstate on-ramp and roar north, through the toll booths and crossing the broken overpass sections and onto North Rouse itself. Follow this road to the junction with Ross, and from here, continue using the plans detailed in Route 1 of Race #1.

ROUTE 2

This is a completely new route compared to the previous plans. Begin by heading west along

Lambert, but head under the interstate bridge, and wind up at the start of East Lake Drive, and the junction where Race #4 begins.

From here, head right onto Nelson Way and boost north, heading up past the airfield (on your left), passing the junction with Ross and the junction with West Crawford. Continue along Nelson through the mountains near the storage depots.

Make the turn at Read Lane's southern end, and power up this winding road, joining Race #1 Route 2 as it merges onto Read Lane. Then continue up to the top of Read, and use the shortcut to reach the finishing place.

4. LAKESIDE GETAWAY

Start Point: Nelson and East Lake

ROUTE 1

The first route to take from this starting place is the last 80 percent of Race #2's Route 2. Start at the junction with Rack Way and follow Nelson Way north.

ROUTE 2

Route 2 begins similarly, with you driving north on Nelson, but when you reach Rack Way, make a right, and wind past the water treatment facility, all the way to North Rouse. Join this, and head north, completing the race using the course from Race #1, Route 1.

5. MANO A MANO

Start Point: North Mountain and Schembri

ROUTE 1

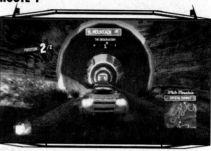

This exciting duel race is simply a task to see who can head north along South Mountain Drive, then North Mountain Drive the fastest. Begin by heading into the shortcut, moving through the concrete pipe, and out at the Wind Farm .

Continue to boost north, leaping the gap where the billboard is, and then optionally taking the shortcut to avoid the small tunnel and S bends.

Continue along North Mountain Drive, and into the two small tunnels that lead to Dead Man's Curve. Use the super jump shortcut to easily sail past your foe! For a finale, head up the shortcut and drop off the concrete area next to the finish line. A vertical Takedown (almost impossible to time) is an impressive (but purely optional) way to win!

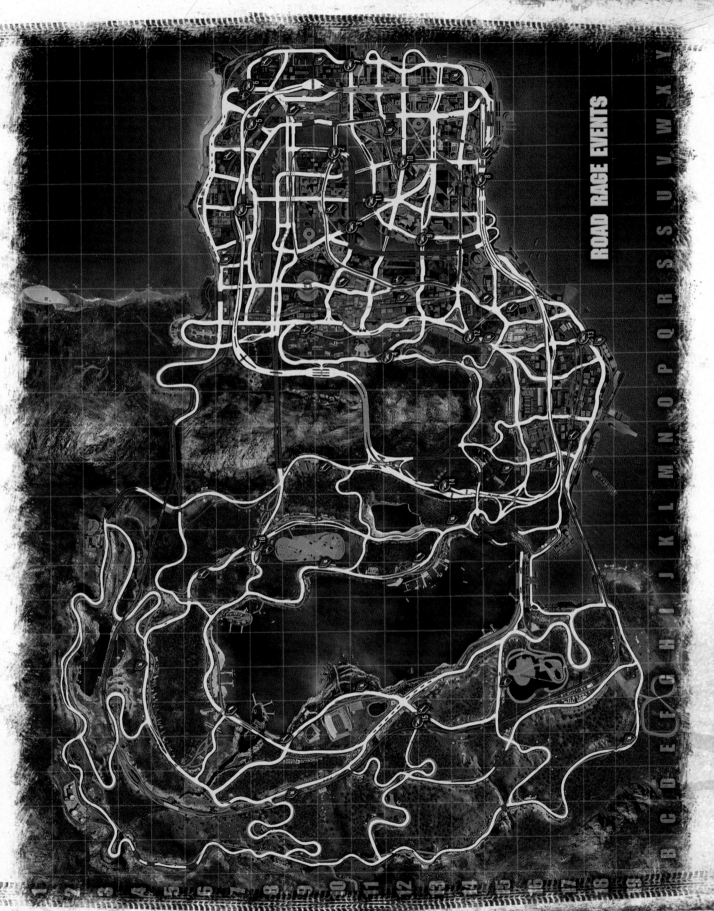

ROAD RAGE EVENTS

ROAD RAGE EVENTS
OVERVIEW

Welcome to Road Rage! This type of event has you swiping, crashing, and finally taking down a series of rivals before a time limit runs out or your vehicle becomes completely wrecked. This chapter details the possibilities and tactics to ensure that you finish these events with the maximum number of Takedowns and the minimum number of crashes. Use the cunning tactics herein to ensure a decisive victory, and earn a Takedown score you can boast to your friends about!

PART 1: BEFORE YOU RACE

1. When cruising the mean streets of Paradise City for a Road Rage Event, make sure that your vehicle is up to the task. Choose an Aggression-class vehicle; it increases its boost when you execute a Takedown, which is the main task in this event! Choosing other classes makes your Road Rages more difficult.

2. Before the race begins, double-check your vehicle's statistics in the Junkyard section of this book. You want a car with high strength and lives. Strength is important, as the stronger the car, the easier it is to crash into other cars and take them down. You can also view adversaries during a race, compare their strength to yours, and learn which vehicles are going to be easier to slam into than others.

3. Study the map of Paradise City, and pay attention to the 11 auto repair shops, and (to a lesser extent) the 14 gas stations dotted throughout the city. Although you can drive anywhere during a Road Rage, heading to auto repair shops becomes important to continue your Road Rage Event.

4. The number of Takedowns you must complete varies throughout your game. The same event requires more Takedowns the farther into the game you are. Also, the type of rival cars you have varies depending upon your vehicle, so you won't be completely outclassed. The number of takedowns starts at three, and maxes out at 25 (when you're approaching Elite status).

PART 2: TAKEDOWN TACTICS

1. Once you begin a Road Rage Event, you have a group of five or six rivals, all jostling you. They swarm around you but you don't need to follow them (although it helps your timer if you do follow, then slam into them). You have three to five minutes (depending on your License grade) to complete as many Takedowns as you want. For every Takedown you manage, five seconds is added to your timer.

2. Executing a Takedown is straightforward: simply knock into a car and cause it to crash into a wall or other vehicle. Remember! The stronger your vehicle, the easier these maneuvers are to execute! Try one of these initial methods:

A. You can do this by tapping your front corner into their back corner and causing them to fishtail.

B. You can ram them squarely in the trunk.

C. You can sideswipe them.

D. You can crash into their front corners with your front corners.

3. You can attempt a number of different takedowns during the course of a Road Rage. All give you one additional point, so none are necessarily "better," although some take more skill to pull off:

A. The Takedown: Simply strike an opponent so they crash.

B. Vertical Takedown: Land on top of a rival. Accomplish this using a drop or a nearby ramp. Most of the time, this is due to luck, but if you study the guide map for ramps and drops, you'll know where to try this!

C. T-bone Takedown: Ram the side of a rival's car with your hood.

D. Grinding Takedown: Force a rival into a wall, and grind them against it as the sparks fly, until they crash.

E. Traffic checking Takedown: Strike a traffic vehicle not associated with this event, so it's shunted into the path of your rival, causing him to hit the innocent vehicle!

F. Head-on Takedown: Ram them hood-to-hood. For best results, your vehicle should ideally be stronger or moving faster. Spin around during a Road Rage and approach a car behind you to try this.

G. Car Takedown: Force a rival into a traffic car not associated with this event, causing your rival to crash.

H. Bus Takedown: Force a rival into a bus, causing your rival to crash. Stationary buses (shown on the Road Rules Event section) are easier.

I. Van Takedown: Force a rival into a traffic van, causing your rival to crash.

> ## NOTE
> All of these Takedowns are available online as well! Although there are no online Road Rage Events, you can create rivalries by executing any Takedown you want during Freeburn Challenges or races, or if you're simply messing about!

PART 3: ADVANCED TACTICS

When you've got the hang of this event and want to increase your score, heed the following advice:

1. Once you begin a Road Rage, be sure you know where your nearest auto repair shop is. The Road Rage continues until either the timer counts down to zero, or you are struck and wrecked once all your lives are gone. If you achieve your target before the timer runs out, you can end your run early by finding a safe shortcut to stop in.

2. With this in mind, begin your Road Rage and focus on Takedowns. Keep a mental note of how many times you are wrecked, compared to your vehicle's lives. Once you're down to two lives, or one (when you're given a "Damage Critical" warning), attempt the next plan.

> ## NOTE
> Although your vehicle shows signs of damage, you can also tell how many lives you've lost as the colors on-screen begin to turn from a bright, full-color spectrum, to a duller, more monotone hue.

3. Locate an auto repair shop and drive through it. This essentially "heals" you back up to your maximum lives! Theoretically, if your car has five lives, and you can locate all 11 auto repair shops, you can withstand 55 wrecks during the course of a single Road Rage Event! Remember that you can only visit an auto repair shop once, so do so when you're almost completely wrecked, not after one crash!

> ## NOTE
> Drive in a looping (and long) circle that passes an auto repair shop every two minutes or so, so you can drive in if you need to. Then move to another area and circle the auto repair shop, and continue with this plan.

4. Changing direction is important too; rivals appear depending on where you are, so you don't need to chase them all. However, slowing and stopping, or changing direction, leaves you open to attack, so keep your speed up, and e-brake to head down a different path. You should only be concerned with auto repair shop locations, although long, uninterrupted stretches (like Mountain Drive) mean less cross-traffic.
5. You are encouraged to "go for it!" by attacking rivals viciously. If you're heading for an impact, thanks to a tiresome foe, fight back so he crashes first before you're taken down. You're automatically saved during the Takedown cinema!
6. Cross-traffic is nasty, and parked cars, buses, and other innocent vehicles can cause you to crash (as well as barriers and corners

you misjudge). Negate some of these problems by choosing a vehicle with an incredibly high strength, such as the Takedown Dirt Racer. You can actually survive low and mid-speed head-on collisions with other vehicles, pushing them out of the way instead of becoming wrecked yourself! Obviously, this is a tremendous help in this game mode!

7. One of the biggest problems when you're becoming truly adept at this mode, is knowing when a rival has crashed. When you're jostling with a foe, you can ram and smash him. However, if that foe is taken out ahead of you by another rival, his vehicle becomes an obstacle you must avoid, or you'll hit it and become wrecked! Always attempt evasive steering if this occurs.

8. When Elite drivers try this mode, it becomes less about the Takedowns and more about keeping the Takedowns going so you don't run out of time. For this reason, keep your speed up, and your Takedowns continuous instead of heading off down other roads or looking for auto repair shops; do that only when you really have no other choice.

NOTE

At the highest levels of skill, there's no reason to visit a gas station, because you gain boost on every Takedown. Also, there isn't any reason to boost continuously. Dab the boost to catch up and when you're ramming. It's easier to maneuver if you aren't boosting and accelerating at once.

When your score goes over 100 (as shown), you should think of yourself as a true Elite at this event type. Obviously, with skill (and a little luck) you can keep this event going almost infinitely.

OVERVIEW

AMATEUR

OVAL CHAMP 69

MESQUITE CUSTOM

PIONEER SUPER GATOR

IKUSA SAMURAI

PROFESSIONALS

ANNIHILATOR PHOENIX

TAKEDOWN DIRT RACER

CITIZEN

SEMI-PROFICIENT

RELIABLE SPECIAL

GRAND SICILIAN

HOTSPUR

INFERNO BRT VAN

ELITE STATUS

CARBON IKUSA GT

THUNDER SHADOW

CIVILIAN

IMPORTANT PRE-ROAD RAGE ADVICE

Keep an eye on your target score and pace yourself. The game will continue after you reach the target. Don't worry about the Road Rage ending if you reach your target score; you can carry on as long as you like!

Spend some time exploring Paradise City to find all the auto repair shops and use your map to remind you where the nearest one is.

Use auto repairs wisely. They close after you've used them once, so don't waste the opportunity.

Don't forget that once you've hit your target score, you can stop your car to end the Road Rage and still win. You may have to pull off the road, otherwise the other cars will keep charging at you.

If you're at Damage Critical and you're heading to the nearest auto repair, duck into the shortcuts. The other cars won't follow you in there. This includes shortcuts, alleys, the El Train track, train track, dirt roads, building corner cuts, etc. If you spot a shortcut with a smash gate, use it!

Take a look at the car statistics in the Junkyard section of this guide and use the car that best suits your driving style. High strength cars have more "lives" and can recover from more Takedowns. Pick cars like the Krieger Racing WTR at your own risk. It will go much faster but you've only got two lives till you're out!

This guide's Junkyard section has an additional statistic—Lives—which isn't found in your in-game Junkyard information. This is vital to your Road Rage completion, and it tells you how many times you can be wrecked! Check this statistic out, and choose vehicles (ideally from the Aggression class) with lives of 4 or 5.

NOTE

The Road Rage Events numbers in this guide are arbitrary. They are purely to reference the associated map, and you can complete any Road Rage in any order you like, depending on the area of the map you've unlocked.

ROAD RAGES

☐ 🚗 1. ONCOMING ONSLAUGHT
Start Point: I-88 and Moore
Direction: West

☐ 🚗 2. CROSS-TOWN CARNAGE
Start Point: Young and Riverside
Direction: West

☐ 🚗 3. FRANKE EXCHANGE
Start Point: Franke and 5th
Direction: Northwest

☐ 🚗 4. SUBURBAN SCRAP
Start Point: Hubbard and 2nd
Direction: North

☐ 🚗 5. MOTOR CITY MAYHEM
Start Point: Patterson and I-88
Direction: Southwest

☐ 🚗 6. LIGHTHOUSE ROCK
Start Point: East Crawford and Angus
Direction: North

☐ 🚗 7. ANGUS WHARFARE
Start Point: 4th and Angus
Direction: South

☐ 🚗 8. TAKING ITS TOLL
Start Point: I-88
Direction: West

☐ 🚗 9. CENTRAL SQUARE-OFF
Start Point: King and 2nd
Direction: East

☐ 🚗 10. RUSH HOUR
Start Point: 3rd and Root
Direction: North

☐ 🚗 11. RIVER CITY RAMPAGE
Start Point: 4th and Paradise
Direction: West

☐ 🚗 12. WRECKING YARD
Start Point: Lambert and 1st
Direction: Southwest

☐ 🚗 13. BLOCKADE RUN
Start Point: South Bay Expressway and Gabriel
Direction: Southwest

☐ 🚗 14. FREEWAY FRENZY
Start Point: I-88
Direction: North

☐ 🚗 15. SUNSET SHOWDOWN
Start Point: Schembri and Chubb
Direction: Northeast

☐ 🚗 16. HALF NELSON
Start Point: Ross and Nelson
Direction: Northwest

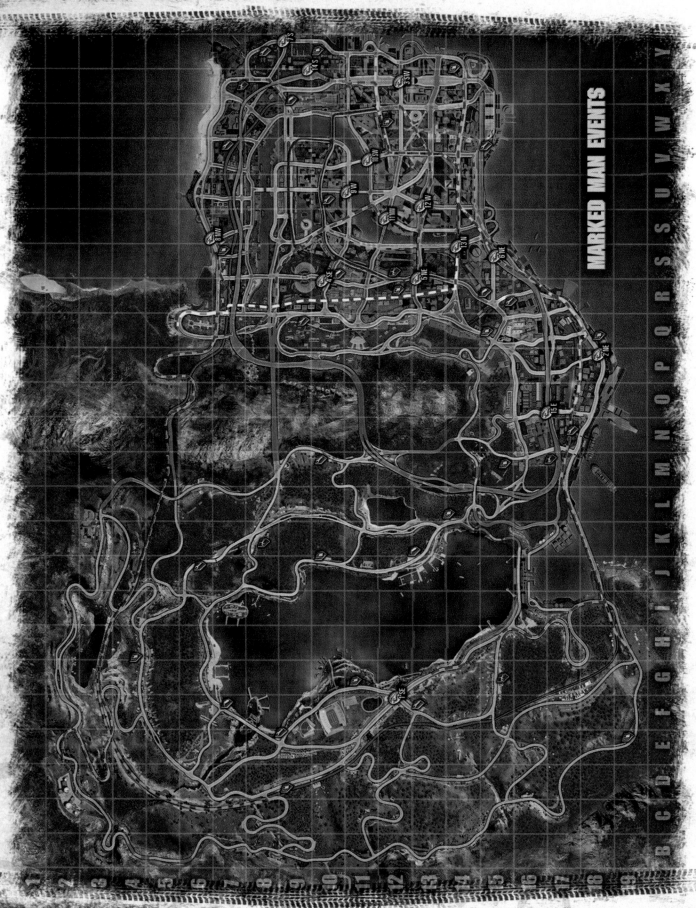

MARKED MAN EVENTS

MARKED MAN EVENTS
OVERVIEW

What begins as a regular race soon turns nasty as you realize that a number of black saloon cars, which are almost always stronger than you, are doggedly attempting to swipe, smash, and crash you into an obstacle or other vehicles, and wreck your car! You can choose a steed that is faster than these foes, or one that can compete, strength-wise. However, the best plan is to plot a path full of shortcuts from the start to your goal. Fortunately, the guide map shows every possible shortcut there is! And, we've found some great routes to try for each of these events.

MAP LEGEND

 DRIVE THRUS

 ROUTES

 FINISHING PLACES

RECOMMENDED VEHICLES

Choose your vehicle based on your style of play:

If you enjoy outrunning foes and can easily boost, find a Speed-class car.

If you're finding this event tricky, and you're being wrecked constantly, choose a Stunt or Aggressive car with a high strength.

These black, unmarked cars are Hunter Citizens. Look at the Junkyard section of this book at this vehicle's statistics, and choose a vehicle that has better strength than it, or comparable stats.

ADDITIONAL PRE-RACE ADVICE

The black cars are special versions of the Hunter Citizen. They're heavy cars, so they can deliver quite a shunt if you're in one of the low-strength cars.

The black cars usually stay on the main road. When competing in a Marked Man, try to find the shortcuts and off-road areas and stick to them. This includes shortcuts, alleys, the El Train track, train tracks, dirt roads, building shortcuts, and anything else shown on the guide map.

As with Road Rage, choose the car for your driving style. You can out-run the black cars if you have a really fast car, but it might be safer to pick a car with high strength, as that lets you survive more Takedowns.

Auto repair shops are your best friend in this mode. Find them all, learn the locations, and use them wisely. The following routes don't feature auto repair shops, so detour to the nearest one if you need to.

If you're trying to out-pace your opponents, you need to keep your boost topped up. Learn the locations of the gas stations along the route to the finish line to help you with this plan.

Look at the Junkyard section and choose a vehicle with the largest number of lives; this helps out immensely during this event.

> **NOTE**
>
> The following routes represent the fastest way to reach each of the eight compass direction finishing places using the most off-road areas and shortcuts (as the black Hunter Citizens don't follow you into these areas). However, you may consider other shortcuts, or simply use the main roads. You might even figure out a quicker way, too!

> **NOTE**
>
> The Marked Man Events numbers in this guide are arbitrary. They are purely to reference the guides maps and waypoints, and you can complete any race in any order you like.

PART 1: NORTH (THE MAPLE-MOUNT COUNTRY CLUB)

☐ 🏁 1. CLUB SANDWICH
Start Point: Evans and 1st

Turn and travel west for a block, looking for the smash on your right. Drive off the road, into the long train tracks.

Accelerate north, unimpeded by foes. Head through the train yard area with the billboard and ramps, and straight through the tunnel under 7th Street.

Keep heading up this train track until you reach the small yard just south of Crawford. Skid left, then immediately right onto the top end of Lambert Parkway. You're a block from the finish, on Newton!

PART 2: NORTHEAST (THE COAST GUARD HEADQUARTERS)

☐ 🏁 2. EMERGENCY 911
Start Point: 2nd and Hamilton

Boost east, directly along 2nd, and keep the enemies at bay as you pass the branching 2nd, which soon merges again. Look for Root Avenue coming up, and steer left, diagonally heading into the park.

Accelerate through the park without any problem, jet across the intersection, and head into the construction shortcut, keeping right to head down the slope and out onto Webster.

Accelerate north for one block, then steer left slightly, entering the right side of the train station, into the tunnel.

Head through the train yard at your leisure, and journey up the concrete ramp, onto 7th Street, but don't accelerate too quickly and miss the right turn! Try the super jump for the correct direction.

Then simply gas your car up to the finishing place, just north of the junkyard.

☐ 🐉 3. MAYDAY, MAYDAY

Start Point: Harber and Manners

Begin by heading east on Harber, across the bridge, then cut in by the sundial shortcut on the corner of King Avenue, and shoot across to Fry.

Skid onto 1st Street and immediately ramp up onto the El Train track. You're safe up here, as long as you stay on it!

Drive along the El Train track, turning the corner and avoiding the two drops as you head north above Root Avenue. Slow as you reach the corner above Andersen; there's no barrier to stop you falling.

Stay on the El Train tracks above Andersen, heading northeast, and drop off at the next corner, slowing so you don't overshoot the shortcut between the tenement buildings. Merge at the corner of 4th and Webster, and follow the route described previously to your goal.

☐ 🐉 4. RESCUE ME

Start Point: South Bay Expressway and Parr

This is a cunning course. Begin by locating the fence to the right and drive in, to the right of the gas station, and continue along this oceanside shortcut and optionally leap this super jump near the pier.

Boost back onto the expressway, then steer right, onto the shortcut leading to the interior fish stalls shortcut under the interstate. Emerge on the Harber and Manners intersection. Now follow Marked Man #3's course to the Coast Guard HQ.

PART 3: EAST (WATERFRONT PLAZA)

☐ 🐉 5. HOSTILE WATERS

Start Point: Hall and Manners

Accelerate south on Hall, passing the parking structure, and skid up the concrete ramp on the left, connecting the railroad bridge. Skid left, and accelerate along the train tracks heading east.

Keep speeding east until you spot the shortcut on your right that brings you out at the junction of South Bay Expressway and Gabriel Avenue. Head northeast, onto the shortcut. Then follow the previously described route.

Accelerate all the way to the El Train track area on Andersen, and drop off the eastern edge. Instead of heading into the tenement shortcut, continue driving east, all the way to the finish.

PART 4: SOUTHEAST (WILDCATS BASEBALL STADIUM)

☐ 🐉 6. STRIKE OUT

Start Point: Hamilton and 5th

Boost west for a moment on 5th, then drop down onto the railroad tracks so you aren't followed. Accelerate south three blocks, staying on the sunken tracks.

Head up the concrete slope and onto 1st Street, which is a straight shot to your goal. Skid east and accelerate quickly toward Evans, launching yourself across the broken bridge.

Land on 1st, and immediately accelerate toward the ramp leading through the billboard and onto the El Train tracks. Then drop off the end, back onto 1st, and keep your speed up as you head straight for the finish line.

☐ 🐉 7. RUN HOME

Start Point: West Lake and Chubb

This is the most difficult of the Marked Man Events, so choose your vehicle wisely. Boost off the starting line, immediately turning right so you enter the shortcut behind the stores that runs parallel to West Lake. Exit, and then keep right, using the dirt path shortcut to the intersection with Hans.

Boost across this intersection, and prepare for jostling for a moment as you career down South Mountain Drive, but make sure you aim for this ramp, cutting the S-bend to the west out completely.

Drift onto the South Bay Expressway, heading across the suspension bridge, and use any of the concrete ramps in the middle to land on the train tracks above. Without enemies, you can easily follow the tracks east, all the way to the exit shortcut onto the intersection of the expressway and Gabriel.

Accelerate northeast along the expressway, steering right, into the shortcut, and then drive over the fish market warehouse ramps and out onto Harber, crossing the bridge.

Cut across the sundial shortcut from King to Fry Avenues, and merge onto 1st Street, then accelerate up the El Train ramp and through the billboard. Finish with a straight shot to the goal.

PART 5: SOUTH (NAVAL YARD)

8. SAFE HARBOR

Start Point: Watt and Angus

Begin with a dangerous southern acceleration along Angus, driving through the gas station and skidding through the small shortcut onto 4th Street. A block later, locate the shortcut between the two tenement buildings.

Drive southwest, between the tenement blocks, and emerge heading south on Glancey. A block later, skid right, and head into the park, moving southwest.

Instead of completing this diagonal route, drop off the ledge where the billboard is so you're heading south, and drive over 2nd, and into the shortcut that crosses two blocks, bringing you out under the suspension bridge near the auto repair shop.

Head down Harber for a moment, and optionally drive up the steps on the right, and into the covered mall, then through the parking lot on the corner of Fry, and out onto Harber again.

Skid left, into the shortcut across the ramps of the fishing market warehouses, and merge onto the expressway. After a couple of blocks, look for the shortcut onto the train tracks at the junction with Gabriel.

These tracks offer security as you boost west. When you reach Hall, skid off the tracks, boost south along Hall, and speed through the finish.

9. PRESS GANGED

Start Point: I-88

This route is almost exactly the same as for Marked Man #8. However, first get off I-88 by driving right of the toll booth, through the shortcut and onto Webster. Emerge from the tunnel and look at the shortcut between the tenement blocks. Then follow Marked Man #8's route to the goal.

PART 6: SOUTHWEST (LONE STALLION RANCH)

10. STAMPEDE

Start Point: 3rd and Webster

Memorize most of the route you used for Marked Man Events #8 and 9; this uses most of them! Start by traveling west on 3rd, and then head into the park at Waypoint H3. Continue using Marked Man #8's route toward Hall. Instead of heading south at Hall, continue on the train tracks, all the way across the suspension bridge. Stay on the train tracks and head left at the fenced shortcut, straight through the Lone Stallion goal.

11. STEEPLECHASED

Start Point: 4th and Root

This path is mainly the Marked Man #10 route. Head south on Root, and skid left into the park entrance. Journey on this paved path, then skid right, under the bridge so you're heading south. The rest of the journey is the same as Marked Man #10.

PART 7: WEST (THE WIND FARM)

12. RUN LIKE THE WIND

Start Point: Paradise and 5th

Begin by heading west on 5th until you reach Franke, then turn right and follow Franke northwest, shrugging off enemy attacks. Skid into the shortcut on the left. Emerge onto 7th, then quickly dart left into another small shortcut.

Merge onto 7th, and at the large intersection with Lambert, skid right and launch across the pond using the super jump. Land and continue along the grassy verge of Newton, until you turn left onto Crawford. Head for the hills!

Accelerate toward the tunnel on Crawford, and enter the train tunnel slightly north of the road. This gives you miles of freedom! Now accelerate along the tracks heading west, across the rickety bridge.

Cross the north suspension bridge, passing the shortcut that leads to Read Lane, and continue along the railroad, crossing the yellow bridge.

Steer to the right at the end of this massive off-road area, up the narrow track and onto Uphill Drive, then power up it, skidding into the smaller loop shortcut along the way to the Wind Farm finishing place.

13. POWER STRUGGLE

Start Point: 2nd and Fry

Head west along 2nd and cross the bridge, skidding right and then accelerating north along the left side of Evans. When you reach the fence, take the shortcut—an enclosed tunnel that merges you back onto Evans as the covered portion of the road ends. Head across the shortcut to Franke. Then use Marked Man #12's route to the Wind Farm.

14. SEEING STARS

Start Point: East Crawford and Sullivan

Travel west on Crawford for a couple of blocks, then cut in on Hamilton for a second, driving into an open warehouse, and through a small train yard. Exit, weave back onto Crawford, and then follow Marked Man #12's route onto the train tracks.

Continue following this route across the suspension bridge, but slow down as you near Read Lane. Use the shortcut here to cross onto Read, and then follow it as it winds to the junction with North Rouse and North Mountain. Turn left, and immediately head into the shortcut that leads to the drop onto the finishing place.

15. RUN TO THE HILLS

Start Point: King and 3rd

This route is almost identical to Marked Man #12's; however, you start heading northeast on King Avenue. Then skid left, across the bridge on Franke Avenue and onto 5th. Follow Marked Man #12's route until you meet up with Marked Man #14's route to the observatory.

NORTH AND NORTHEAST BURNING ROUTES

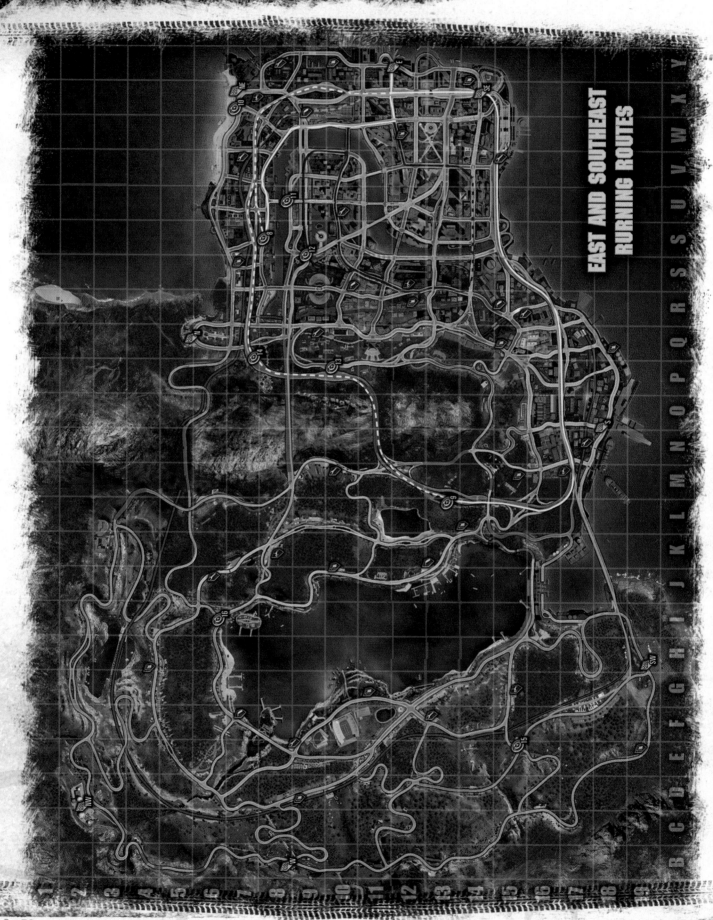

EAST AND SOUTHEAST
RUNNING ROUTES

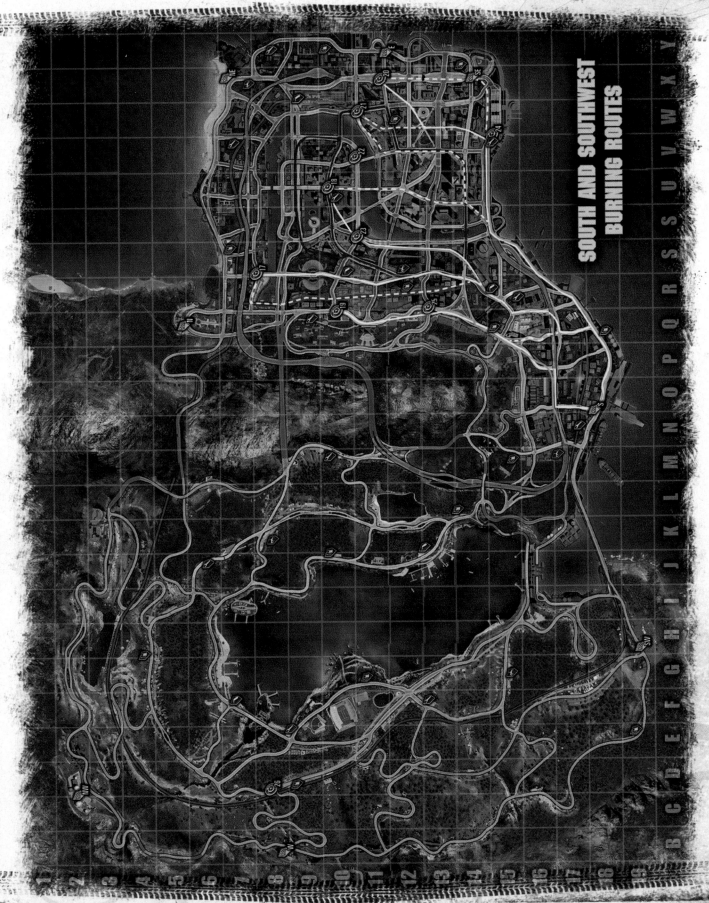

SOUTH AND SOUTHWEST
BURNING ROUTES

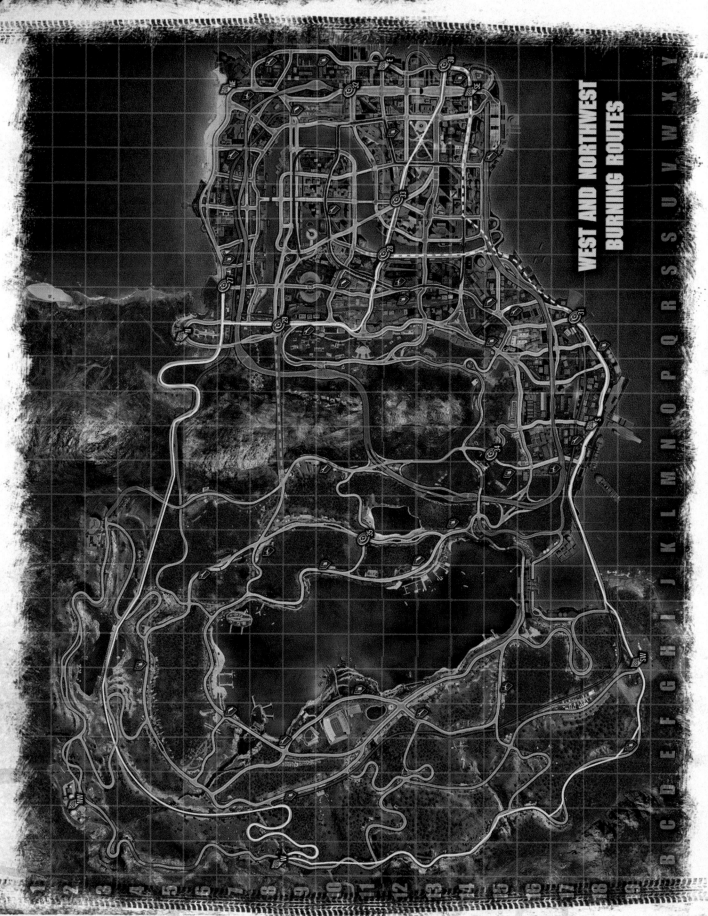

WEST AND NORTHWEST
BURNING ROUTES

BURNING ROUTE EVENTS

OVERVIEW

Burning Routes are the next largest event type after Races for you to attempt during your quest for Elite License status. For this event, first obtain the specific vehicle needed (listed in your in-game map, and also as the title of each route description, to come), and begin the race. There's only you, the goal, and cross-town traffic to navigate to reach the finishing place.

Simply beat the time, and you win the "special" version of the car you used. Check the Junkyard section of this guide to see what car you get. Finally, if you're after another challenge, try to beat the times the guide author set! There's only a feeling of smug satisfaction if you do, though!

TIP

How to read this chapter: check the in-game map, and find the finish for the Burning Route event you want to complete. Then look for the compass direction from the tactics listed below.

MAP LEGEND

 DRIVE THRUS

 ROUTES

 FINISHING PLACES

PRE-RACE ADVICE

Burning Route times are set pretty aggressively, especially for the later cars. You may need to race them a couple of times first and learn the route before you go for the win.

If your Burning Route is in the city, don't forget to use all the alleys, shortcuts, and the El Train track!

Watch for the traffic. The traffic in Paradise City is dynamic but it does have some patterns. Maybe some traffic lights are always red when you get there, perhaps there's always a truck passing nearby. Learn these little quirks and your Burning Routes will become easier. This only comes with practicing the routes shown below.

NOTE

The following routes represent the two fastest ways for each Burning Route, from the start to the compass direction finishing place. However, you might want to figure out another way.

NOTE

The Burning Route Events numbers in this guide are arbitrary. They are purely to reference the guide's maps and waypoints, and you can complete any event as soon as you receive the appropriate vehicle in your junkyard.

PART 1: NORTH (THE MAPLEMOUNT COUNTRY CLUB)

1. HYPERION

Start Point: 3rd and Glancey
Target Time: 1:15
Author Best Time: 0:49.78
Turn left in your Hyperion, and gun it along 3rd to Paradise Square. Turn right onto Franke, and accelerate northwest.

Look for the shortcut on the left. Skid in and use the next, smaller shortcut to merge onto 7th Street. Make a careful, but quick right at the junction with Lambert. Floor it as you head north, all the way to the goal.

2. IKUSA GT

Start Point: 2nd and Glancey
Target Time: 1:15
Author Best Time: 0:51.85

Follow the same route as for Burning Route #1, except at the start, turn northwest, and drive into the park, merging onto 3rd at Root. Then follow Route #1 the rest of the way.

3. OPUS

Start Point: 1st and Webster
Target Time: 1:20
Author Best Time: 0:52.47

The previous route in Burning Route #2 is all you need to finish quickly; head up Webster for a block, and skid left onto 2nd Street. When you reach the park, head across it, then follow Burning Route #1 to the country club.

4. R-TURBO ROADSTER

Start Point: King and Harber
Target Time: 1:15
Author Best Time: 0:50.87

ROUTE 1

Journey north along King Avenue, boosting four blocks to the junction with Franke, then skid left, heading northeast across the bridge. Then follow Burning Route #1 to the finish.

ROUTE 2

An alternate route is to head west over the bridge, and immediately drive north on Evans for a block. Skid left onto 1st and drive west to the triangular junction with Lambert Parkway.

Accelerate north on Lambert, winding up the road and taking any available shortcuts you wish, and continue north to the goal.

PART 2: NORTHEAST (THE COAST GUARD HEADQUARTERS)

☐ ◎ 5. INFERNO VAN

Start Point: 1st and Fry
Target Time: 1:20
Author Best Time: 0:41.07

ROUTE 1

Begin with a journey north on Fry for two blocks, until you reach Paradise Square. Then locate the mall to the northeast and accelerate through it.

Boost out onto Andersen, and keep your speed up as you avoid the El Train ramp, pass the gas station, and then turn left slightly, at the junction with Glancey, into the shortcut.

Head through the tenements and out the other side, then journey north on Webster. Steer right slightly as you continue on Webster, under the interstate, past the junkyard on your left, and to the goal.

ROUTE 2

Accelerate east, avoiding the El Train ramp, but cutting in on the corner of 1st and Root. Head north for a second, then skid right, into the park, and drive northeast across it.

Exit the park, head straight into the construction building, keeping right so you head down to the ground exit, and skid north onto Webster. Drive north to the goal from here.

☐ ◎ 6. X12 TURBO

Start Point: Manners and Parr
Target Time: 1:25
Author Best Time: 1:02.92

ROUTE 1

Start with a dash northeast up Parr to the junction with Lambert, and merge onto that road until you reach the triangular junction, and head east on 1st. Accelerate so you leap the broken bridge. A block later, you're at 1st and Fry; choose either of Burning Route #5's routes to complete this journey.

ROUTE 2

Continue east on Manners, merge onto Harber, and accelerate toward the Wildcats Baseball Stadium. Head through the Exhibit Hall covered area, skid around the curve to Webster, and accelerate north, until this route merges with Burning Route #6's.

☐ ◎ 7. HOT ROD COUPE

Start Point: West Lake and Cannon
Target Time: 1:50
Author Best Time: 1:19.50

ROUTE 1

Accelerate southeast, and make the first left turn off West Lake, onto Ross. Follow Ross across Nelson, and then enter the Lawrence Road Tunnel. Emerge on 7th Street.

Continue east on 7th, entering the sunken highway area, and boost through the Twin Bridges, steering left slightly as you merge onto Webster, heading north under the interstate bridge, and through the finish line.

ROUTE 2

Begin by heading east, then turn northeast and enter West Crawford. Follow this winding road through the tunnel, appearing out the other side, and drive down into Palm Bay Heights from the hills.

Continue boosting east along East Crawford, avoiding the road islands and traffic, and continuing all the way to the goal. Follow Crawford for almost the entire journey.

PART 3: EAST (THE WATERFRONT PLAZA)

☐ ◎ 8. SI-7 TURBO

Start Point: Sullivan and 9th
Target Time: 1:00
Author Best Time: 0:41.63

ROUTE 1

Accelerate east along 9th, following it south as it becomes Glancey, before making a sharp left onto Andersen. The goal is two blocks away from here.

ROUTE 2

Turn left slightly, and drive through the courtyard shortcut, then up the on-ramp to I-88. Follow this interstate east and then south, through the toll booths.

Keep right at the toll booths so you can use the shortcut onto Webster. Follow Webster south to the turn with Andersen, and skid left. You're a block away from the finish.

☐ ◎ 9. OVAL CHAMP 07

Start Point: I-88
Target Time: 1:30
Author Best Time: 1:19.05

Accelerate southbound on the interstate, using the flow of traffic to gain incredible speed as you race east, above Manners, and continue all the way across town. Continue on the interstate as it descends into a tunnel.

Once in the tunnel, look for a central ramp, or one of the side off-ramps that lead up to Webster. Once you're on the ground level, race to Andersen, and make a sharp right, heading to the goal a block east.

PART 4: SOUTHEAST (THE WILDCATS BASEBALL STADIUM)

☐ ◉ 10. CAVALRY

Start Point: East Crawford and Patterson
Target Time: 1:10
Author Best Time: 0:38.39

ROUTE 1

Boost south on Webster, passing the junkyard, heading under the bridge, and continuing south, passing the parking structure to your left.

Accelerate along the raised area of Webster, crashing through billboards for boost, and avoid cross-traffic as you continue on Webster all the way to the goal.

ROUTE 2

For a little variety, head down Patterson to 9th, and drive south as it becomes Glancey. Continue south all the way to 2nd and make a left. Skid right onto Webster immediately afterward, and into the finish.

☐ ◉ 11. GRAND MARAIS

Start Point: Root and Paradise
Target Time: 1:05
Author Best Time: 0:34.56

ROUTE 1

Head east along Root until you reach the edge of the sunken highway. Drive down onto it, heading east on 7th across the Twin Bridges. Then skid right and follow Glancey south, using Burning Route #10 Route 2 to complete your run.

ROUTE 2

Boost straight south on Paradise, crossing the bridge and heading straight through Paradise Square, and onto Franke as it curves and points east. Merge onto 2nd, then follow this to Webster, skid right, and into the goal.

☐ ◉ 12. VEGAS

Start Point: 7th and Franke
Target Time: 0:50
Author Best Time: 0:35:80

There's really only one acceptable and fast route from this point. Boost southeast, down Franke Avenue, across the bridge, and through Paradise Square. Then use the latter half of Burning Route #11 Route 2 to the finish.

☐ ◉ 13. HYDROS CUSTOM

Start Point: Hubbard and I-88 Bridge Exit
Target Time: 1:05
Author Best Time: 0:49.42

ROUTE 1

Head south along Hubbard, and use the shortcut to drop down onto 2nd Street, following it to the junction with Lambert. Continue along 2nd, increasing your speed and eventually passing the park on your left. Skid right onto Webster, and drive a block south to the finish.

This excellent route is great fun: follow Route 1 to Lambert, but then head south and merge onto 1st at the triangular junction. Increase your speed and leap the broken bridge, landing on the other side. Drive up the El Train ramp, continue to boost, and fall off the end. It's a straight shot to victory from here!

☐ ◉ 14. WTR

Start Point: I-88 Toll Booth
Target Time: 1:00
Author Best Time: 0:55.13

This is the most difficult Burning Route because the vehicle is insane to drive! Accelerate east, ideally through traffic going the same direction unless you can handle dodging oncoming traffic for boost.

Speed east, follow the interstate south through the toll booths, and descend into the tunnel under Webster. Locate any of the middle ramps and leap out, onto the raised middle of Webster, and boost through the finishing place.

☐ ◉ 15. GT CONCEPT

Start Point: Lucas and Hans
Target Time: 1:50
Author Best Time: 1:24.96

ROUTE 1

Turn southeast, and drive down Lucas, optionally heading through the trailer park, and skid left onto the railroad tracks. Race across the suspension bridge.

At the eastern end of the bridge, line up a ramp and jump it, landing on the interstate. Now simply follow the interstate east, passing the toll booths and exiting via the shortcut on the right, just before the tunnel that leads to the final curve and the victory line (picture 2).

ROUTE 2

Take a trip east this time, boosting along the road to the junction with West Lake, and skid right, following South Mountain Drive to the clifftop ramp. Jump it and land safely. Skid left and drive across the suspension bridge. In the middle, use a concrete ramp and land on the train tracks, then follow Route 1 to the goal.

☐ ◉ 16. GT 2400
Start Point: East Lake and West Crawford
Target Time: 1:40
Author Best Time: 1:23.45

There's only one advantageous route to take here: southeast along East Lake until you reach Ross, then along Ross to the Lawrence Road Tunnel.

Head out of the tunnel, onto 7th Street, and then head down Franke Avenue. The rest of the route is the same as Burning Route #12.

PART 5: SOUTH (THE NAVAL YARD)

☐ ◉ 17. PIONEER
Start Point: Hamilton and 9th
Target Time: 1:25
Author Best Time: 1:01:45

ROUTE 1

Speed south, down Hamilton, passing the parking structure, and continuing all the way to the junction with Harber. Head down Harber for a second.

Immediately steer south onto Shepherd and follow this for a block. Then skid onto Manners, left onto Gabriel, and cut in the corner as you head onto the South Bay Expressway and toward the finish.

ROUTE 2

Instead of jetting off down Hamilton, head west on 9th for a moment, and then drop down and head south along the train tracks. Merge back onto Hamilton when the tracks end, then complete the remainder of Route 1.

☐ ◉ 18. TEMPESTA
Start Point: Paradise and Young
Target Time: 1:05
Author Best Time: 0:49.88

ROUTE 1

Jet off heading southwest on Young, passing the auto repair shop and using both grassy shortcuts to merge onto Evans. Head into the tunnel here.

Follow the tunnel to its exit, cross over 1st, and head through the left side of the warehouse shortcut until you merge with Hamilton. Now follow Burning Route #18 Route 1's racing course to the naval yard.

ROUTE 2

Another choice is to head directly south on Paradise, instead. When you reach Paradise Square, steer right slightly, joining Fry, and drive two blocks south until you reach the shortcut at the five-way interstection.

Head southwest, across the sundial shortcut, and across the bridge, before looking for the fish market warehouses near the entrance to the expressway. Use this shortcut, merge onto the South Bay Expressway, and continue down this road to your goal.

☐ ◉ 19. MESQUITE
Start Point: Lambert and 5th
Target Time: 1:20
Author Best Time: 0:47.18

ROUTE 1

Race south down Lambert Parkway. Keep your speed up, but aim for Parr as you reach the grassy triangular area.

Scoot down Parr to the junction with Manners, cut the corner while skidding right, and follow Manners for a block until you reach Hall. Skid left, and drive south on Hall to the finish, skidding left under the finish line itself.

ROUTE 2

For an alternate route, follow Lambert to the grassy triangular junction, but head directly south down Gabriel, all the way to the expressway, and turn right. The goal is two blocks west.

☐ ◎ 20. MANHATTAN

Start Point: Webster and Andersen
Target Time: 1:20
Author Best Time: 0:59.25

ROUTE 1

Instead of taking Webster, turn and head into the construction path moving southwest. Emerge by the park, and drive through the corner entrance, to the middle, swerving off the ledge, through the billboard.

Keep heading south across 2nd, and into the shortcut that cuts through two blocks and merges onto Harber Street. Now follow the remainder of Burning Route #18 Route 2 to the finish.

ROUTE 2

This variation enables you to boost south along Webster, heading around and merging onto Harber, then following that west. Use the remainder of Burning Route #18 Route 2 to complete this course.

☐ ◎ 21. 616 SPORT

Start Point: Glancey and 4th
Target Time: 1:15
Author Best Time: 0:59.66

ROUTE 1

Head down the shortcut through the open mall area, heading southwest. Then head south, crossing Andersen, dropping into the park, and driving south, straight across. Then use Burning Route #20 Route 1 to complete your run.

ROUTE 2

Or, head west along 4th for a block, cutting the corner as you reach Root Avenue, then boosting south.

Zoom past 2nd, make a right corner cut under the El Train, and drive west on 1st, until you reach the sundial shortcut. Then use Burning Route #18 Route 2 to the finishing place.

PART 6: SOUTHWEST (THE LONE STALLION RANCH)

☐ ◎ 22. UBERSCHALL 8

Start Point: 5th and Root
Target Time: 1:30
Author Best Time: 1:15.08

ROUTE 1

Wrestle this beast of a car west, to the junction of 5th and Evans, and then take the tunnel shortcut parallel to Evans south, exiting onto 1st Street. Drive to the west end of 1st, and continue along Lambert Parkway.

Two blocks later at the grassy triangle, drive down Parr to Manners, and skid right onto Manners heading west. Head all the way to South Rouse and turn left, so you arrive on South Bay Expressway. Drive west, across the suspension bridge, to the finish.

NOTE

You can also try Burning Route #23 Route 2 as a third possible course.

ROUTE 2

Alternately, drive south down Root, then steer right, under the El Train corner cut onto 1st Street. Follow 1st for a block, then use the sundial shortcut to Harber.

You should know this area by now! Cross the bridge, look for the shortcut on your left, and head through the fish market warehouses, merging onto the South Bay Expressway. Continue west, all the way over the bridge to the ranch.

☐ ◎ 23. CITIZEN

Start Point: Evans and 5th
Target Time: 1:35
Author Best Time: 1:19.56

ROUTE 1

As this starting point is only a block west of Burning Route #22, follow that exact path (Route 1) to the goal.

ROUTE 2

Instead of following previous routes, you can emerge from the tunnel shortcut on 1st, and immediately cross into the warehouse shortcut, driving out onto Hamilton. A second later, head south down Shepherd, and merge onto Manners. Then follow Burning Route #22 Route 1 the rest of the way.

☐ ◎ 24. FASTBACK

Start Point: Harber
Target Time: 1:30
Author Best Time: 1:14.10

This course joins Burning Route #22 Route 2 at Harber. Just accelerate west and aim for the fish market warehouses. Alternate routes take longer.

☐ ◎ 25. LM CLASSIC

Start Point: Lambert and 2nd
Target Time: 1:25
Author Best Time: 1:02.28
Follow the course provided for Burning Route #22 Route 1 to the ranch after traveling south.

☐ ◎ 26. RELIABLE CUSTOM

Start Point: Nelson and Uphill
Target Time: 1:35
Author Best Time: 0:58.13

ROUTE 1
Speed up as you fly south down Nelson Way, optionally heading through the shortcut to West Lake Drive, and using the alleys to negotiate Sunset Valley village.

Head out of the village, continuing southeast across the dirt shortcut to the junction with Hans and South Mountain Drive. Tear down South Mountain, jumping the clifftop ramp, and skidding right, toward the goal.

ROUTE 2

This follows a similar path until you reach the intersection of West Lake and Chubb, where you can drive southwest down Chubb instead. At the junction with Hans, make a sharp right, then left, onto Lucas. Then tear south down Lucas to the goal.

PART 7: WEST (THE WIND FARM)

☐ ◎ 27. TOUGE SPORT

Start Point: East Crawford and Hamilton
Target Time: 2:35
Author Best Time: 1:47.69

There's only one real route to take to get to the Wind Farms in double-quick time, and that's to head west along East Crawford, driving along the winding path after it turns into West Crawford, and entering the tunnel.

Increase your speed as you roar through the tunnel, across the rickety train bridge, and dash over the northern suspension bridge. Keep going over the yellow bridge.

Max your speed as you drop toward the bridge at the base of Uphill Drive. Take the narrow dirt shortcut to the right that merges onto Uphill, and ride the S-bends to the top, and the Wind Farm goal.

☐ ◎ 28. 500 GT

Start Point: Evans and 3rd
Target Time: 2:35
Author Best Time: 2:04.76

ROUTE 1
Boost west, skid onto Lambert Parkway, and drive north, through the junction with Lawrence and 7th Street. Now follow Burning Route #28 to the finish.

ROUTE 2
This is trickier, and usually a little longer, but you don't need to worry about crashing on the railroad. Head directly south on Evans, using the shortcut at the south end.

Merge onto the expressway, and use the warehouses to gain boost. Speed through this shortcut, onto the South Bay Expressway heading west. Keep going across the suspension bridge, and pass the Lone Stallion Ranch.

Now follow the winding South (then North) Mountain Drive all the way north to the goal. Use the shortcuts and gaps for boost power, and don't forget to use the concrete pipe shortcut at the construction yard that brings you out at the goal itself.

☐ ◎ 29. THUNDER CUSTOM

Start Point: Lambert and Lawrence
Target Time: 2:10
Author Best Time: 1:48.56

This Burning Route follows almost exactly the same path as #27. Head north along Lambert and start your run west along West Crawford, the train tracks, and finally up Uphill Drive.

☐ ◎ 30. HAWKER

Start Point: 2nd and Angus
Target Time: 2:45
Author Best Time: 2:22.45

ROUTE 1

This is the longest Burning Route of all! Head west along 2nd, and cut through the park, merging onto 3rd at Root. Follow 3rd all the way to the Lambert Parkway, where you can use Burning Route #28 Route 1.

ROUTE 2

Or, move south and west onto 1st, and accelerate hard, all the way to the sundial shortcut. Merge onto Harber, then cut through the fish market warehouses. The rest of the path follows Burning Route #28 Route 2.

☐ ◎ 31. P12

Start Point: South Bay Expressway and Shepherd
Target Time: 2:10
Author Best Time: 1:47.88

This route follows the last two thirds of Burning Route #28 Route 2 perfectly. Simply boost west along the expressway, and drive toward the long climb up South and North Mountain Drives.

PART 8: NORTHWEST (THE CRYSTAL SUMMIT OBSERVATORY)

☐ ◎ 32. ANNIHILATOR

Start Point: Webster and 4th
Target Time: 2:35
Author Best Time: 2:19.56

ROUTE 1

This is a long run, so plan it carefully. Head west a block onto Glancey, and turn right. Drive up to the Twin Bridges, steer left onto 7th, and cross the sunken highway.

From here, skid right at the junction with Lawrence and Newton, avoiding the pond. Continue left, on West Crawford, and drive along the winding road to the double-tunnel entrance. Choose the railroad tunnel.

Follow the train tracks over the rickety bridge and the suspension bridge. Slow down as you finish crossing the suspension bridge and take a shortcut on your left, leading to Read Lane.

Drive onto Read Lane, and follow it up to the junction with North Mountain and North Rouse. Skid left onto North Mountain and cut in at the shortcut, driving right at the shortcut fork so you can drop down onto the road at the goal.

ROUTE 2

Follow the path for Route 1, but instead of turning right onto Newton at the Lawrence Road Tunnel, head west, straight through the tunnel, and then speed across North Rouse and into Ross.

Drive west on Ross for a block, but make sure you turn right onto Nelson Way. Follow this road over the ranger station, cross the junction with West Crawford, then keep going to the right turn onto Read Lane. Ascend this lane to your goal.

☐ ◎ 33. 25 V16 REVENGE

Start Point: 3rd and Fry (Paradise Square)
Target Time: 2:05

Author Best Time: 1:49.99
Piggyback onto Burning Route #32's choice of paths (Route 1 or 2) after you drive northwest along Franke, all the way to 7th Street.

☐ ◎ 34. TAKEDOWN 4X4

Start Point: South Rouse and Hall
Target Time: 2:20

Author Best Time: 1:48.74
This is another route that joins the main thoroughfare paths already detailed in Burning Route #32. Head north into the tunnel, cross the broken interstate area, continuing north on Rouse until you reach the junction with Lawrence and Ross. Steer left on Ross because it's slightly quicker than taking North Rouse to the goal.

☐ ◎ 35. SPUR

Start Point: Nelson and Rack

Target Time: 2:05
Author Best Time: 1:47.55
This course quickly merges in with Route 2 of Burning Route #32. Head north on Nelson, passing the entrance to the airfield, then continue up Nelson toward the ranger station when you reach the junction with Ross.

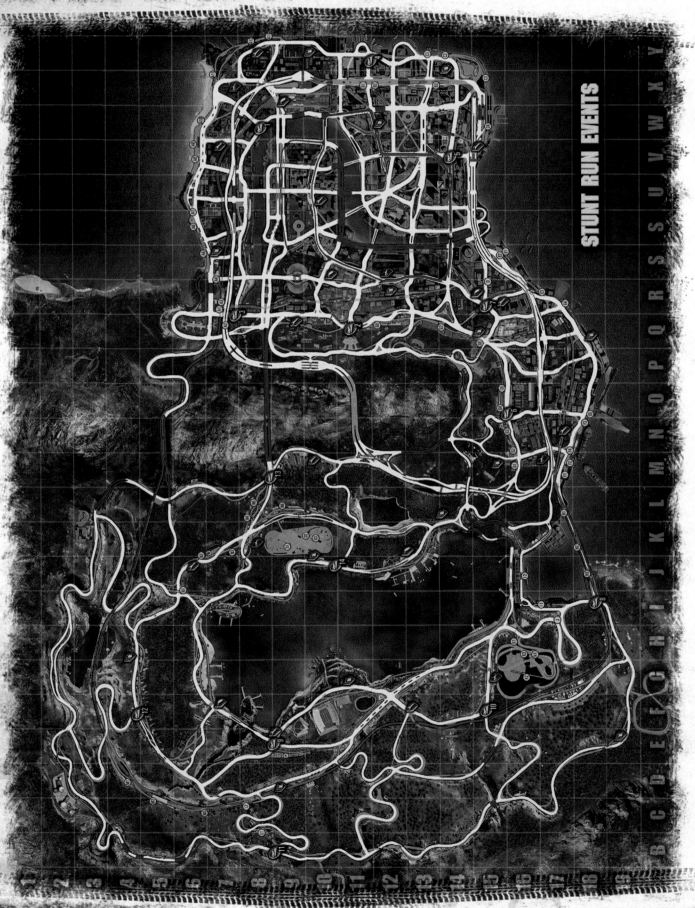

STUNT RUN EVENTS

STUNT RUN EVENTS

OVERVIEW

Although Stunt Events are relatively few, especially compared to Races and Burning Routes, they offer the most exhilaration as you attempt to gain incredible scores. The plan is simple: execute a series of stunts, and keep the stunts going to combo a massive score. Of course, you need to do all of this without crashing or letting the Stunt Timer fill to red! It's vital to learn the basics of Stunt Runs before trying any high scores in this event. Stunt Runs contain two elements: points and multipliers.

MAP LEGEND

 DRIVE THRUS

(A1) WAYPOINTS

STUNT RUN STARTS

PART 1: GAINING STUNT POINTS

Points are awarded when you attempt any of the following actions. Remember that actions appear on the screen's bottom-left during usual gameplay, too.

A. Getting Airtime: Speed off a ramp or drop, and the time spent in the air is added to your points total. Flat Spins also count towards your total.

Getting airtime off a short ramp: 700+ points

Getting airtime off a long drop: 2,500+ points

Reverse airtime: Double points

B. Successfully Landing a Barrel Roll: One of the most lucrative actions, and the most difficult unless you line it up correctly, is landing the right way up after a barrel roll. The points you receive make this worth it, however!

Landing a barrel roll off a short ramp: 6,500+ points

Landing a double barrel roll off a long ramp or drop: 14,000+ points

C. Boosting: The key to lengthening your Stunt Run is to boost, which also resets the Stunt Timer. You can boost to your car's maximum speed or tap the boost to reset the Stunt Timer.

Boosting to maximum speed: 400+ points

Tapping boost to reset the Stunt Timer: 5 points

D. Drifting and Boost Drifting: Only to be attempted when you have few or no obstacles to ruin your fun (such as on the slopes of South Mountain Drive), try drifting with and without a boost, for some easy points.

Boosting or drift boosting (per second): 500+ points (plus boost points)

E. Using the E-Brake: Heading forward, then swinging your vehicle around in an e-brake spin nets you some points, and resets the timer!

E-brake turn (per degree): 1+ point(s)

Example: 200-degree e-brake turn = 200+ points

F. Reversing: This excellent tactic not only scores a reasonable number of points, but this also resets the Stunt Timer and keeps it filled! This means you can reverse as long as you want. Combine this with an e-brake turn and a boost forward. Reversing is the key to a long Stunt Run.

Maxing out a reverse: 400+ points

Landing a reverse jump: Double points

> **NOTE**
>
> All other actions (such as near misses and oncoming) simply refuel your boost, which is also very important in this event.

PART 2: GAINING STUNT MULTIPLIERS

The second type of award during a Stunt Run is the multiplier: This adds a number (usually +1) to the multiplier of your points. For example, if you have 10,000 x1 points, then crash through a billboard and finish a Stunt Run, you receive +1 for the billboard, giving you 10,000 x2 points = 20,000 points.

As you'll find out, the key to massive point totals is to continuously receive multipliers! Here are the ways to get them:

A. Super jumps: Locate any of the 50 super jumps throughout the city, and land one successfully. The locations for all the super jumps are shown in the Tour of Paradise section.

Multiplier: +1

B. Billboards: Locate any of the 120 billboards throughout the city, and crash through one, landing successfully. The locations for all the billboards are shown in the Tour of Paradise section.

Multiplier: +1

C. Flat spins: Executing flat spins during a jump gives you a multiplier, too! Simply drive up a ramp at speed, and e-brake at the very last second.

Multiplier: +1

D. Big air: Whether you're heading over a super jump or not, if you can manage around a second of hang time from a jump, you receive a multiplier bonus! Look at the poster map for all the blue arrows and black arrows; these can give you big air if you're fast enough!

Multiplier: +1

E. Barrel Rolls: Dangerous and difficult to land if you don't approach them exactly (so you hit the upper part of the ramp with both your left or right tires), this also awards you with a +2 multiplier! Practice these until you can land your car each time.

Multiplier: +2

PART 3: STUNT RUN TACTICS

1. This event benefits the most from a thorough knowledge of Paradise City. With a bit of experience you'll learn the locations of the highest-scoring stunts near each start line (which are also shown below), and the highest-scoring routes between them. Plan your route!

2. Keep the combo going to gain the high scores you need later in the game. When the next air or billboard is down the road somewhere, use boost and drift to keep your combo going.

3. Stunt Runs are much easier in a Stunt car (as boost—the life blood of this event—is awarded for each action you perform). In a Speed car

you can only boost when the bar is full, which makes it harder to run a combo. An Aggression car is better, but with no-one to take down, you can't quickly fill up your bar.

4. Remember, unless you're in a Speed car, you can reset the combo timer by "pulsing" the boost as it's about to run out. Tap the boost button and reset the timer. There's no need to rush everywhere; take your time, and tap the boost. You'll have more time to react to a barrier, vehicle, or obstacle.

5. If you're running out of boost, try a stunt, and quickly! If you aren't near, or can't find a stunt, simply attempt near miss and oncoming actions to refill the meter. Or, swing your car around and reverse to refill your Stunt Timer. Also reverse if you get stuck facing a wall or land awkwardly. Reverse is a Stunt Run lifesaver!

6. Try pulling the e-brake just as you leave a ramp to add a spin to your jump. This adds one more to your multiplier, so you'll most likely get airtime and spin. Some cars spin better than others, and you need to hit the ramp with a lot of speed to get a full spin before you land.

7. Barrel rolls can be your best friend or worst enemy. Learn where the barrel roll jumps are and practice them before the event. Nail them in your Stunt Run to pick up a x2 multiplier, and stay in the air long enough to gain x3!

8. You can visit some hidden areas during your Stunt Run. These locations work extremely well—combo all of them for an extreme score (they are detailed in the next part of this section).

> The quarry
> The airfield
> The train track
> The drop down steps on Uphill Drive
> Southbay Expressway and the crane yard run
> Beachfront in Big Surf Beach

9. Until you become "hardcore" at this event, you won't usually reach the higher score targets during the time limit, so continue the combo after the time is over. Continue driving to build up multipliers and increase your score.

10. Don't forget that you can't use a particular stunt location twice in the same combo. If you get a jump off a split ramp, you can't go back and barrel roll off it. Therefore, try tactic #9 and gain the most multipliers you can. Check the Combos section for all the advice you need!

11. Remember that chaining combos together can lead to monstrous scores! As long as you don't crash, you can also enter parking structures and drive off the roofs. You don't necessarily need to be traveling quickly to add to your multiplier!

PART 4: COMBOS

Now that you've learned exactly how your score increases during this event, figure out how to obtain the most massive score possible! Best tactic? Combos!

1. In this example, we show you how it is possible to triple your score, approaching a ramp on the South Bay Expressway bridge:

A. A regular ramp. Land this for a +1 multiplier (big air).

B. A super jump ramp (with flashing cones). Land this for a +2 multiplier (big air and super jump).

C. Retaking the super jump ramp: Execute a flat spin as you launch, for a +3 multiplier (big air, super jump, flat spin).

2. In this example, check out the huge multiplier if you can combo:

A. A small ramp with a barrel roll opportunity: Drive over it too slowly and all you receive is a boost increase.

B. Drive over it quickly, and you receive a boost, and a +1 multiplier (big air).

C. Complete the barrel roll, however, and you get a +3 multiplier (big air, barrel roll). Now complete the same ramp heading in the opposite direction, and you've suddenly obtained +6 to your multiplier on a single ramp!

3. In this final example, check out another monster multiplier!

A. Locate this ramp (icon K1 on the Stunt Run map) at the top of the quarry. Drive off it, and complete a double barrel roll (two complete rotations!) for a massive +6 multiplier: barrel roll x2, big air, super jump. Can you land a triple barrel roll though? These ramps over long drops are scattered throughout the city.

RECOMMENDED VEHICLES

AMATEUR

CAVALRY

VEGAS CARNIVALE

IKUSA SAMURAI

BURNOUT ROADSTER

SEMI-PROFICIENT

MANHATTAN CUSTOM

HYPERION RATTLER

P12 TRACK PACKAGE

OPUS XS

PROFESSIONALS

TOUGE CRITERION

GT FLAME

CARBON HYDROS CUSTOM

ELITE STATUS

CARBON X12

HAWKER SOLO

TRIBAL SPECIAL*

(* The wheelie this vehicle does while initial boosting can make this a challenging choice!)

NOTE

The Stunt Run Events numbers in this guide are arbitrary. They are purely to reference the associated map, and you can complete any Stunt Run in any order you like, depending on the area of the map you've unlocked. Also note that the target score is based on the maximum needed; if you finish this event earlier during your licenses, the score will be lower.

STUNT RUN COMBO AREAS

The following areas of the city have a high density of ramps, billboards, super jumps, and drops that allow you to gain multipliers to your total quickly, as long as you're precise! Elite players attempt each of these, one after another, for truly mind-boggling scores!

NOTE

There are dozens of other areas, too. Basically, check the Tour of Paradise section, and investigate any area with a super jump or billboard.

AREA A

A1. Start in the train yard, and drive west up the super jump onto the interstate (+2).

A2. Spin around on the interstate, locate the ramp, and land in the oncoming lane (+2).

A3. Head off the side of the interstate through the billboard (+1).

A4. Jump the ramp after heading out of the train yard (+1).

A5. Drop down onto the beach pier, and drive over the ramp, landing on the roof (+2).

A6. Drive up the ramp near the semicircular vantage point. Optionally head west and crash through the billboard (+2).

A7. Head up the construction ramp and out the other side.

A8. Drop down to the beach area, and use this ramp heading west (+1).

A9. There are two small ramps with barrel roll opportunities here (+6).

A10. Exit onto East Crawford via the sloping ramp (+1).

A11. Enter this shortcut by the lighthouse.

A12. Hit the ramp and sail through the billboard (+2).

A13. Land, and do the same again (+2). There's no need for massive speed here; slow down so you have a good racing line for both ramps.

Now try this in the opposite direction!

Aim for: +22 multiplier for a single race west to east, and a few more going the opposite direction.

AREA B

B1. Travel south on Webster and drive onto the upper middle area. Use the short ramp, and crash through the billboard (with an optional flat spin) (+2 or +3).

B2. Attempt the same again at B2 (+2 or +3).

B3. There's a third opportunity here (or you can head under Webster on I-88, and take the super jump, landing near B3 and hitting the billboard, too!) (+2 or +3)

Aim for: +6 multiplier or more.

AREA C

C1. Head south down Angus Wharf, passing through the Rayfield Grand Hotel shortcut, and line up with the ramped scaffold.

C2. Enter the parking lot and drop through the billboard near the stadium (+2). There's a big air drop if you're heading north through this parking lot.

C3. Head around the perimeter of the stadium, then drive up the ramp, through the billboard, and onto the top of the Exhibit Hall (+2).

C4. Drop down near the auto repair shop (+1).

Aim for: +4 multiplier or more.

AREA D

D. Attempt this a simple small ramp with a barrel roll opportunity from both directions (+6).

Aim for: +6 multiplier.

AREA E

E1. Enter the fish market warehouses at top speed to gain the big air from the jumps here (+1). Flat spins are also available.

E2. Spin around, gain big air, and crash through a billboard (+2).

E3. Head through this shortcut. If you're approaching from the opposite side, you can launch into a billboard. Make sure you have the speed, and watch out when entering the interstate.

E4. Enter the super jump over the pier (+2).

E5. Exit onto South Bay Expressway.

Aim for: +5 multiplier or more.

AREA F

F1. Ideally attempt this after the suspension bridge stunts (H). Head east, through the right gap in the containers, gaining air through the billboard (+2).

F2. Accelerate and hit the super jump ramp (+2).

F3. Drive up the ramp and flat spin through the billboard (+3).

F4. Return to the western end, drive through the left gap in the containers, drop down, and launch into the billboard while flat spinning (+3).

Aim for: +9 multiplier or more.

AREA G

G1. Start by launching through the pipes and over the road (+2).

G2. Accelerate east, up the ramp and onto the roof (+1).

G3 and G4. Hit the next ramp, landing on the road near another ramp (G4) and launch up off that (+3).

G5. Accelerate across the roof and through the billboard (+2).

G6. Line up for the ramp over the roof.

G7. With enough speed, you can clear this drop through the billboard, heading the wrong (northeast) direction (+2).

G8. Launch at the billboard along the platform and ramp (+2).

Aim for: +8 multiplier or more.

AREA H

H1. Hit the super jump ramp while flat spinning (+3).

H2. Hit the next ramp and crash through both billboards (+4).

H3. Hit the other super jump ramp while flat spinning (+3).

Aim for: +8 multiplier or more.

AREA I

I1. Crash through the fence, drop down the construction yard, and head through the billboard (+3).

I2. Swerve and attack the super jump across the dam base with extreme speed. Avoid the parked cars on the southern part of the road (+3).

Aim for: +4 multiplier or more.

AREA J

J. Hit this barrel roll super jump ramp at full speed, and attempt a double barrel roll (+6).

AREA K

K1. Launch from this super jump barrel roll ramp (+6).

K2. Accelerate over the gap through the billboard, between the towers (+2). Then complete the barrel rolls from both ground ramps (+6), and the two jumps across the water (+2).

K3. Drop from the upper road, through the billboard while flat spinning (+3).

K4. Do the same, but from this vantage, and try to catch the billboard (+3).

Aim for: +20 multiplier or more.

AREA L

L1. Accelerate down the drops and off the super jump, landing on the road after executing a flat spin (+4).

L2. Attempt the same plan again, but this time through a billboard (+4).

Aim for: +8 multiplier or more.

AREA M

M1. Charge west along the train track, and boost into the billboard. Stop, and then do the same with the second, flat spinning if possible (2x +3).

M2. Launch off the ramp onto the bridge roof and through the billboard (+2). Then execute the super jump on the broken area next to the bridge (+2).

M3. Drop off the end of this ledge, flat spinning through this billboard (+3).

Aim for: +11 multiplier or more.

AREA N

N1. Accelerate up and over the rickety bridge at speed, through the billboard (+2).

N2. Boost off the drop, through the billboard just north of the ranger station (+2).

N3. Leap the gap over the pond, through the billboard (+2).

N4 and N5. Execute the jumps across the snaking roads, covering both gaps, one of which has a billboard (+3).

N6. Crash through the billboard at the sawmill (+2).

Aim for: +10 multiplier or more.

AREA O

O1. Enter the airfield, and immediately leap the curved ramped warehouse in both directions (2x +2).

O2. There are four barrel roll ramps, which can theoretically be completed in either direction, for a massive multiplier (if you get big air)! (4x +3).

O3. Land the super jump through the fuselage hoop (+2), and then the three additional jumps (3x +1) before leaving via the western ramp (+2).

Aim for: +20 multiplier or more.

STUNT RUNS

☐ 🏁 **1. LIGHTHOUSE PARTY**
Start Point: Patterson and 9th

☐ 🏁 **2. BRAVO, ENCORE!**
Start Point: 3rd and Lambert

☐ 🏁 **3. HANG 10**
Start Point: Lambert and 9th

☐ 🏁 **4. UNCONVENTIONAL**
Start Point: Andersen and Angus

☐ 🏁 **5. ELEVATION**
Start Point: 1st and Root

☐ 🏁 **6. OFFROAD PARKING**
Start Point: Lambert and Hall

☐ 🏁 **7. OVER CONSTRUCTION**
Start Point: Harber and Warren

☐ 🏁 **8. EXPRESS YOURSELF**
Start Point: South Mountain and South Bay Expressway

☐ 🏁 **9. ABOUT TOWN**
Start Point: Chubb and West Lake

☐ 🏁 **10. CLIFFHANGER**
Start Point: Chubb and Hans

☐ 🏁 **11. FALLING DOWN**
Start Point: North Mountain and Uphill

☐ 🏁 **12. NEAR THE EDGE**
Start Point: Nelson and Read

☐ 🏁 **13. BASE JUMPER**
Start Point: South Rouse and Ross

☐ 🏁 **14. RACK 'EM UP**
Start Point: East Lake and Rack

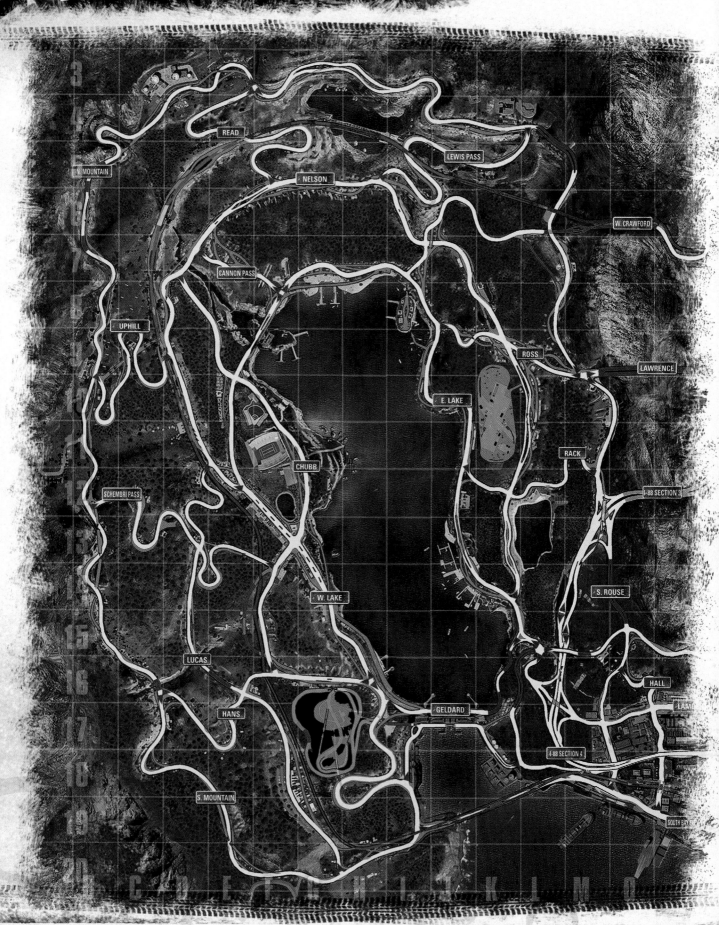

Paradise

READ
LEWIS PASS
N. MOUNTAIN
NELSON
W. CRAWFORD
CANNON PASS
UPHILL
ROSS
LAWRENCE
E. LAKE
RACK
CHUBB
SCHEMBRI PASS
I-88 SECTION 3
S. ROUSE
W. LAKE
LUCAS
HALL
HANS
LAMP
GELDARD
I-88 SECTION 4
S. MOUNTAIN
SOUTH BAY

W. CRAWFORD

NEWTON

E. CRAWFORD

NAKAMURA   SULLIVAN   MOORE   HAWLEY   HUDSON

9TH

I-88 SECTION 2

ROSS

LAWRENCE

PATTERSON

7TH

WATT

PARADISE

FRANKE

WEBSTER

RIVERSIDE

YOUNG

ANGUS WHARF

RACK

5TH

4TH

I-88 SECTION 3

3RD

ROOT

ANDERSEN

EVANS

FRY

GLANCY

2ND

S. ROUSE

HUBBARD

KING

I-88 SECTION 1

1ST

HARBER

HALL

LAMBERT

WARREN   MANNERS

PARR

SHEPHERD

I-88 SECTION 4

GABRIEL

SOUTH BAY EXPWY

ROAD RULES:
TIME AND SHOWTIME EVENTS

3
4
5
6
7
8
9
10
11
12
13
14
15
16
17
18
19
20

L M N O P Q R S T U V W X Y

ROAD RULES: TIME AND SHOWTIME EVENTS

OVERVIEW

The final two event types, which add up to a whopping 128 additional events, are the Road Rules Time, and Road Rules Showtime modes. In Road Rules Time, all you have to do is drive from one end of a marked road to the other, and beat the developer time. In Showtime, you begin a rolling crash in the road you want to score on, finish anywhere you like, and accrue more dollars in damage than the score you're beating. Simple!

MAP LEGEND

▼ START/FINISH

PART 1: GENERAL NOTES

Press ○ to begin Timed Road Rules Events. The best offline time is displayed. Press again, and the best online time is displayed. Press a third time, and you enter Showtime Road Rules Event mode. The best offline crash total is displayed. Press again, and the best online crash total is displayed.

NOTE

You know you've entered "Time" and "Showtime" mode as the road signs displayed at the top of your screen change color, as shown below:

(Usually) Green: The road sign during non–Road Rule gameplay.

Red: Roads you haven't attempted in Time or Showtime modes, or haven't beaten.

Silver: Roads you've taken in one mode (Time or Showtime), but not the other.

Gold: Roads you've completely beaten in both Time and Showtime modes.

NOTE

There are 64 different roads in Paradise City. This means there are 64 Timed Road Rule Events to complete, and 64 Showtime Road Rule Events to complete. Check the Appendices for details on what this unlocks!

PART 2: MAIN TACTICS AND NOTES (TIME)

1. Unlike Showtime Road Rules, Time Road Rules are played from the very start of a road to the very end. This means you must study the map, or learn from in-game driving, where each road begins and ends. You can start and finish a Time Road Rules from either end of a road.

2. Shortcuts can sometimes help you get a record time, but be careful not to take any that lead you away from the road you're attempting. Essentially, use only shortcuts that start on the road you're racing on, and finish on that same road.

3. Choose your vehicle carefully. Obviously, pick a fast car, but there are advantages of a Speed car or a Stunt car. Stunt cars are excellent on roads with ramps because you can use stunts to keep your boost going and your speed up. Speed cars are an obvious choice if you can chain Burnouts together, and there's no need for much braking.

4. Make sure you enter a road (and begin the Time Road Rules Event) with your vehicle at top speed, and with a full boost, to stand a chance of beating the listed records. Give yourself a good, fast run-up before you turn onto the road you're attempting.

5. Gas stations are another big help when it comes to keeping your speed up. Not all roads have them, but drive through them wherever possible. Your car does slow down slightly as it goes through, but the boost refill is usually worth it.

RECOMMENDED VEHICLES (TIME)

If you're more adept at Speed vehicles, choose ones with the fastest boost and speed in your collection. If you need a Stunt car to help with obstacles and to keep your boost up on longer courses, choose a Stunt car with the fastest boost and speed in your collection.

PART 3: MAIN TACTICS AND NOTES (SHOWTIME)

1. The Showtime technique is to begin the event, and when your vehicle comes to a halt, ground break to continue the rolling spin. The best plan is to simply tap this as you land, but not each time or you gain too much height and roll over vehicles you want to strike!

2. Don't spend too long stationary either, as the boost you're using to ground break depletes much more quickly than normal.

3. To gain a high score, combo vehicles you hit into other vehicles. Bounce into one so it strikes another, then look for a new vehicle to hit. Keep this up, but make sure you strike each vehicle with a dollar amount over it, so it wrecks and the dollar amount disappears (it is added to your total).

4. Showtime Road Rules are attached to the road you start on, but you can Showtime your car as far away from that road as you like. So, if you start on Hans Way in White Mountain, but finish somewhere along West Lake Drive, the Showtime score is counted for Hans Way.

5. If you're having difficulty, especially on a short road like Patterson, work out which are the most traffic-heavy connecting roads and plan a route that takes you from the low-scor-ing roads onto the higher-scoring roads. This is straightforward, because the wider the road, the more traffic it carries.

6. Remember, you can score off parked vehicles too. Check the parked vehicles locations on the map at the start of this section to help you work out where there's $-damage to be earned.

7. The following vehicles and structures are worth the following $-damage:

A. Cars: $1,000–$1,500

B. Small Trucks: around $1,500

C. Vans: $1,800–$3,000

D. Flatbed Trucks: $2,200–$3,000

E. Limousines: $5,000–$7,000

F. Buses: $6,500 +1 multiplier

G. Overhead District Signs: $10,000

8. The signs that hang over the road are worth the most ($10,000) if you can bounce through them. To do this, strike a vehicle and ground break with the momentum to spin your vehicle up. Bouncing onto buses then through signs is

an excellent plan. The highest-value vehicles are stretch limos, trucks, and buses, so if you see any of those driving past, give chase!

9. You can't afford to miss buses in Showtime. Hitting one adds one to your score multiplier. If you're struggling to beat a Showtime Road Rule, it's because you haven't been hitting enough buses. In fact, you may wish to begin a Showtime by looking for a bus, then starting Showtime. Also look for parked buses, such as the trio on Chubb Lane.

10. Lane discipline can help you. You'll usually score higher if you keep going forward, so if you must cross the road (for example, if you see a bus coming toward you) remember that oncoming vehicles can knock you backward into an area where you've already smashed all the traffic.

11. Usually, you should cross a road only if there's a gap in traffic ahead. Also try to stay in the middle of a road so you can move to either side while covering less distance.

12. Certain roads are excellent, such as the road islands of West Lake Drive. The narrow area on this main thoroughfare lets cars pile up easily. You can also try blocking a road where you know a stream of traffic will continue to arrive, such as near a jack-knifed bus on an interstate (such as the Lawrence Road Tunnel), and simply collect points in a single location. However, in most circumstances, moving forward is the recommended plan.

13. When you're running out of boost, try getting your car to the middle of a lane to maximize your chances of being hit by another vehicle and reviving your boost bar.

14. Use the right stick to look around. It's always worth making sure you're not missing a bus that's escaping behind you. Don't restrict yourself to the left stick for steering, either. Press forward on the left stick, and maneuver the right stick for your general direction.

ROAD RULES TIMES, SCORES TO BEAT, AND SHOWTIMES

15. Remember that the distance you travel is also important when your final score is tallied. The number of yards you travel is multiplied by 100, and this can account for as much as a third of your final total! Therefore, keep going as long as you can, as far as you can! Travel 1,000 yards, for example, and you receive an extra $100,000 in damage cash!

16. Finally, every 10th vehicle gives a boost bonus, so if you're grinding to a halt on 39 collisions, just one more smash can give you your second wind.

RECOMMENDED VEHICLES (SHOWTIME)

Any vehicle is fine for Showtime Road Rules, although you might want to find one that has a larger mass, such as the Takedown 4x4, to give you more surface area to hit vehicles with.

NAME OF ROAD	TIME TO BEAT (GAME, IN SECONDS)	SHOWTIME SCORE TO BEAT ($)
1ST STREET	34.9	700,000
2ND STREET	45.7	700,000
3RD STREET	38.4	700,000
4TH STREET	21.6	700,000
5TH STREET	29.8	700,000
7TH STREET	33.3	500,000
9TH STREET	35.6	700,000
ANDERSEN STREET	15.5	700,000
ANGUS WHARF	41.8	1,500,000
LEWIS PASS	34.4	250,000
CANNON PASS	13.5	250,000
CASEY PASS	26.1	250,000
CHUBB LANE	52.0	250,000
E. CRAWFORD DRIVE	44.8	1,500,000
E. LAKE DRIVE	71.3	500,000
EVANS BOULEVARD	23.7	700,000
FRANKE AVENUE	22.9	700,000
FRY AVENUE	14.1	700,000
GABRIEL AVENUE	13.4	500,000
GELDARD DRIVE	25.0	250,000
GLANCEY AVENUE	32.7	700,000
HALL AVENUE	26.9	500,000
HAMILTON AVENUE	44.0	1,000,000
HANS WAY	35.8	250,000
HARBER STREET	54.8	700,000
HAWLEY AVENUE	6.5	700,000
HUDSON AVENUE	8.1	700,000
I-88 SECTION 1	40.7	700,000
I-88 SECTION 2	51.0	700,000
I-88 SECTION 3	48.4	700,000
I-88 SECTION 4	67.6	700,000
KING AVENUE	21.5	700,000
LAMBERT PARKWAY	86.4	1,000,000
LAWRENCE ROAD	25.9	250,000
LUCAS WAY	61.4	250,000
HUBBARD AVENUE	61.7	500,000
MANNERS AVENUE	60.2	400,000
MOORE AVENUE	9.2	700,000
N. MOUNTAIN DRIVE	106.3	250,000
N. ROUSE DRIVE	78.4	250,000
NAKAMURA AVE	4.7	700,000
NELSON WAY	113.9	250,000
NEWTON DRIVE	24.9	700,000
PARADISE AVENUE	19.8	700,000
PARR AVENUE	17.5	500,000
PATTERSON AVENUE	8.2	700,000
RACK WAY	25.6	250,000
READ LANE	40.6	250,000
RIVERSIDE AVENUE	8.4	700,000
ROOT AVENUE	44.8	700,000
ROSS DRIVE	21.1	250,000
S. BAY EXPRESSWAY	52.7	1,500,000
S. MOUNTAIN DRIVE	81.3	250,000
S. ROUSE DRIVE	51.7	700,000
SCHEMBRI PASS	45.3	250,000
SHEPHERD AVENUE	12.9	500,000
SULLIVAN AVENUE	6.8	700,000
UPHILL DRIVE	32.4	250,000
W. CRAWFORD DRIVE	68.5	700,000
W. LAKE DRIVE	49.6	700,000
WARREN AVENUE	6.7	500,000
WATT STREET	5.8	700,000
WEBSTER AVENUE	32.9	1,000,000
YOUNG AVENUE	31.4	700,000

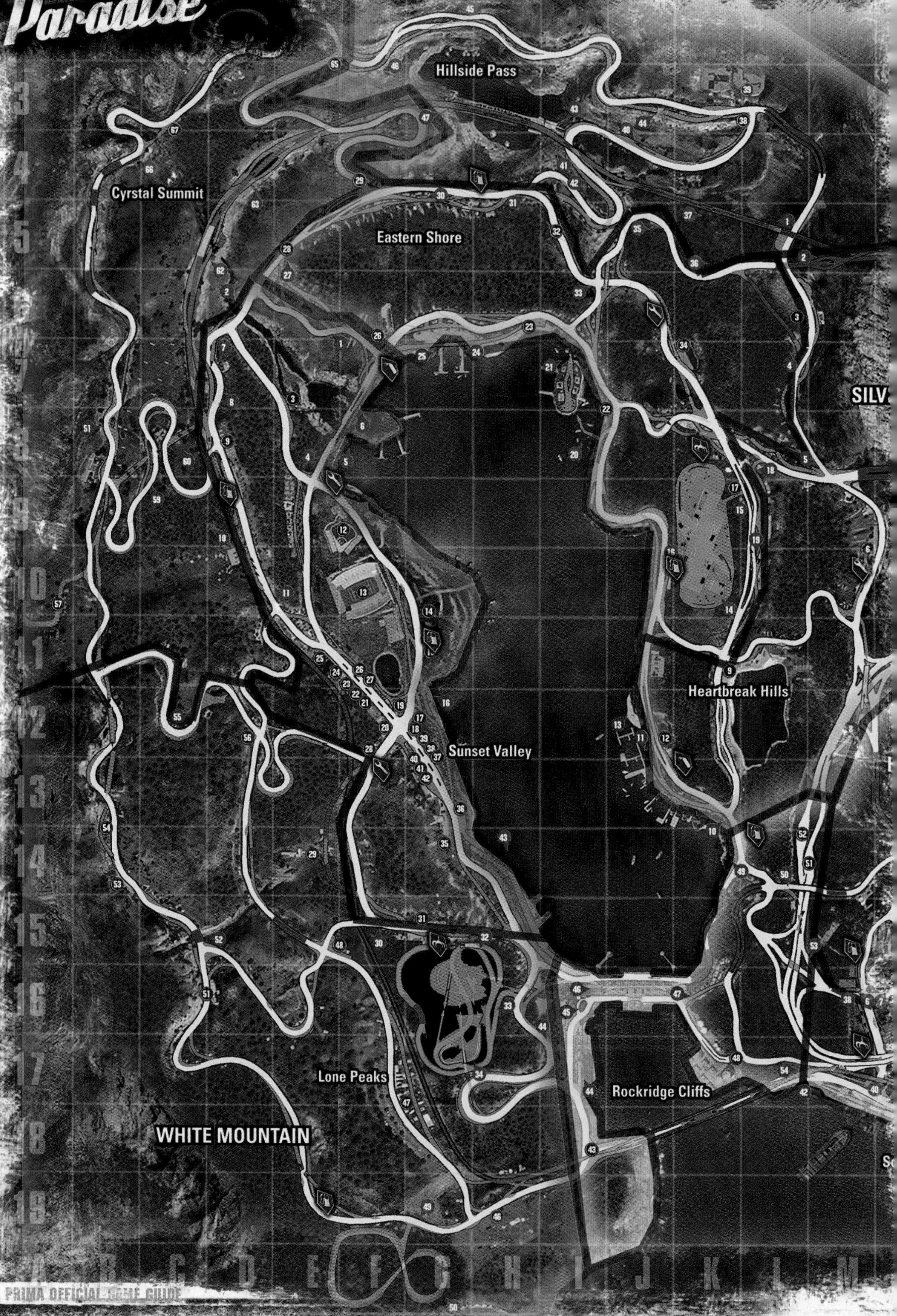

Paradise

Hillside Pass

Cyrstal Summit

Eastern Shore

SILV...

Heartbreak Hills

Sunset Valley

Lone Peaks

Rockridge Cliffs

WHITE MOUNTAIN

04: Tour of Paradise

Ocean View
PALM BAY HEIGHTS
Big Surf Beach
SILVER LAKE
Motor City
Twin Bridges
HARBOR TOWN
Park Vale
West Acres
Downtown
River City
Waterfront
DOWNTOWN PARADISE
Paradise Wharf
South Bay
M N O P Q R S T U V W X Y Z

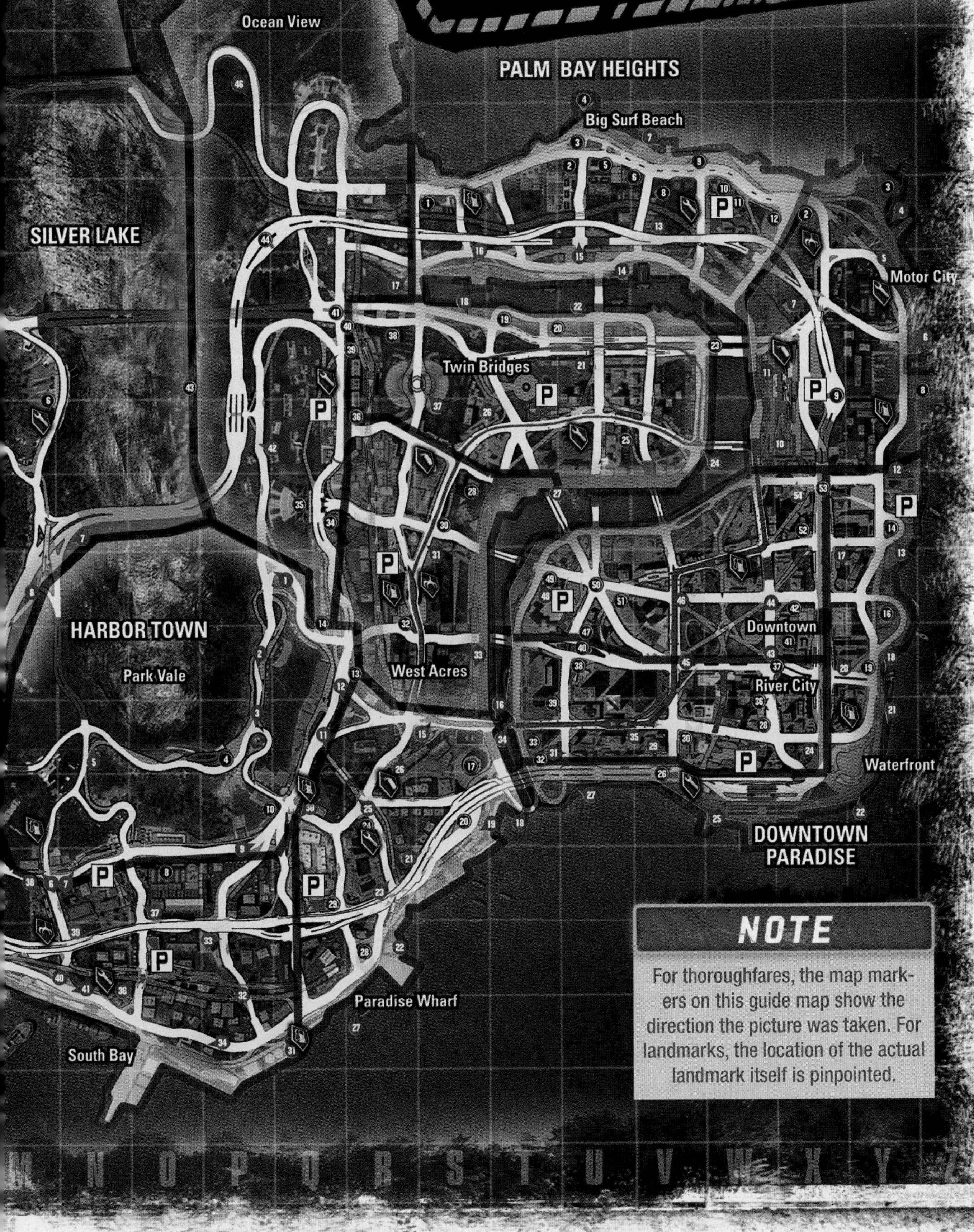

NOTE

For thoroughfares, the map markers on this guide map show the direction the picture was taken. For landmarks, the location of the actual landmark itself is pinpointed.

WELCOME TO PARADISE CITY!

Welcome to Paradise City; the home of the *Burnout* drivers! This chapter is all about discoveries, as well as a thorough examination of every single neighborhood down to the street level. Over the next five sub-sections, you'll find out all of the shortcuts, main thoroughfares, and every single super jump, billboard, and smash! Here's how it all breaks down:

OVERVIEW

This chapter begins with a map showing that Paradise City is, in fact, composed of five different neighborhoods. There are the beachfront hotels, apartments, and malls of Palm Bay Heights. There are the skyscrapers, fishing markets, and river bridges of Downtown Paradise. There are the naval base, train yards, and industrial cargo areas of Harbor Town. There are the pristine water and zigzagging rural roads of Silver Lake. And there are the extreme passes and rural hamlets of White Mountain.

Each neighborhood has between three and four districts. These are smaller areas with names that appear above your in-game map; learn them so you know exactly where you are. The following showcases the coolest information from each of these districts. Here's what to look for on the map:

▨ Main roads

▨ Main roads underground

▨ Shortcuts or off-road areas

▨ Shortcuts or off-road areas underground

▨ Shortcuts: Banked Turn (Stock Car Track)

▨ Off-road gravel and concrete

▨ Two or more roads or shortcuts above each other

▢ Interstate 88

▨ Train tracks or train yards

▨ Train tracks or train yards underground

▨ El-Train Track

▨ Covered El-Train Track

▶ Ramps and slopes*

▶ Drops**

● Landmarks

◖ Thoroughfares***

(* Blue arrows are small ramps that are placed on streets, slopes that allow you to become airborne, or drops from an insterstate.)

(**Black arrows are drops that can only be accessed in one direction; you'll hit a wall if you try to drive in the opposite direction.)

(***The direction and view from the photograph is shown for a thoroughfare.)

PART 1: NEIGHBORHOOD

This is the name of the neighborhood to be described. Notice that each one has a different colored border on the map, making it easy to see where each neighborhood begins and end.

PART 2: LANDMARKS AND THOROUGHFARES

Paradise pilots have flown countless sorties to photograph the most important landmarks and thoroughfares in every neighborhood. Each landmark or thoroughfare is shown on the city map at the beginning of this chapter. In the neighborhood sections, you'll find a photograph of the specific landmark or thorougfare, along with a description and tactics (such as how to reference a particular landmark or use a thoroughfare).

PART 3: DRIVETHRU AND PARKING STRUCTURE LOCATIONS

Next comes a small table, showing how many

> **NOTE**
>
> Drivethrus appear on your in-game maps when you drive through them. Parking structures don't, but they're useful for ascending to the rooftop ramps, which usually lead to a discovery or two.

auto repair shops, gas stations, paint shops, junkyards, and parking structures each district and neighborhood has. After that, a picture of each location is shown, under which is the road it is located on. Then comes a grid reference, so you can easily spot it on the strategy guide map.

PART 4: DISCOVERIES: SUPER JUMPS, BILLBOARDS, AND SMASHES

The final element of the neighborhood sections is a comprehensive location list of every single discovery in Paradise City! A map is presented, revealing all discoveries.

● Super jumps are shown in blue

● Billboards are displayed in red

▲ Smashes are revealed in green

Note that many discoveries can be approached in one of two directions, as opposed to only one direction. The arrow (or arrows) coming off each map icon shows you this. Then, a table lists the total number of super jumps, billboards, and smashes for each district and neighborhood. Next, all the super jumps in the neighborhood are listed, in the following order:

A picture of the super jump itself.

A check box so you can record this discovery.

The nearby road or roads.

The grid reference.

Whether the super jump allows you to barrel roll or not.

The direction(s) to head to complete the super jump.

And finally, a description of how to complete this discovery, and any other game tactics to use with this discovery.

Then, every billboard you can crash through in the neighborhood is shown, in the following order:

A picture of the billboard itself.

A check box so you can record this discovery.

The nearby road or roads.

The grid reference.

The direction(s) to head to complete the billboard crash.

And finally, a description of how to complete this discovery, and any other game tactics to use with this discovery.

Finally, all the smashes (fences you crash through) in the neighborhood are shown, in the following order:

The nearby road or roads.

The grid reference.

The direction(s) to head to complete the smash.

And finally, a description of how to complete this discovery, and any other game tactics to use with this discovery. Also, when groups of smashes are close to each other, they are shown together.

NEIGHBORHOOD 1: PALM BAY HEIGHTS

LANDMARKS AND THOROUGHFARES: BIG SURF

❶ MURCH FALL HOTEL

Marking the western end of the beachfront road (East Crawford Drive), this corner has a ramp ideal for heading into the stunt-filled beach promenade.

❷ BEACH VIEW HOTEL

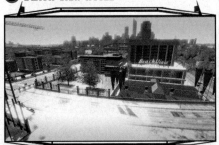

If you're looking for Moore Avenue and the northernmost area of Big Surf, head here. You're halfway down the beach drive at this point.

❸ MCDAIRMANT CONSTRUCTION SITE

There's a ramp on the east and west sides of this two-block construction site with East Crawford Drive on either side. This is the middle of the beach area.

❹ BIG SURF PIER

This landmark is visible from across town, giving you a large landmark to work from when you're concentrating on racing. You can't drive to the pier and Ferris wheel itself.

❺ OCEAN VILLA HOTEL

A useful landmark if only so you know you're coming to the corner of Moore and East Crawford. The concrete ramp into the construction site is just in front of this building. Moore Street is particularly important, as the interstate on-ramps are a block south of here.

❻ COAST VIEW AND PINE HOTELS

These two slightly more down-market places feature an open parking lot where you can stop and wait for your competitors or foes. These sit adjacent to Hawley Avenue.

❼ BEACHFRONT SHORTCUT

One of the largest areas for off-roading in the entire city, this location offers ramps, slopes, buildings, and another large promenade to the west. Chain stunts together in this location for massive points!

❽ PARADISE HOTEL (OPENING SOON)

On the other side of Hawley Avenue is the Paradise Hotel, which is another landmark you can use to gauge how far along East Crawford Drive you are.

❾ BEACHFRONT STORES

The 8-Ball Pool, Paradise City Surf, Beachfront Diner, and Daley's Donuts all face in from the ocean. A passage underneath them is part of the large beachfront shortcut.

❿ OCEAN VIEW HOTEL

Although this is on East Crawford Drive, the Ocean View is on the corner of Hudson Street, and locating this from afar can prepare you for hitting Hudson, where there's a parking structure and auto repair shop, as well as access one block to the south to the Downtown train yard.

11 BEACH VIEW HOTEL

The adjacent Beach View offers a ramped shortcut that allows access to and from the interstate; this is a very important shortcut to remember and perfect! You can also access it from the top of the parking structure on Hudson.

12 PALM HOTEL

On the corner of Patterson Street (part of the Downtown Paradise area), the Palm Hotel offers a raised area adjacent to the front, running to the Ocean View Hotel (Landmark #10), but this is also good to remember if you're heading to the Coast Guard HQ finishing place; it is just to the east.

13 INTERSTATE BRIDGE

This section of I-88 offers a couple of drops down to the southeast, onto the train tracks for a quick escape. You can also see the circular forecourt of the Lewis Mansions Apartment buildings. This open area cuts the corner if you're taking Hudson to or from 9th.

14 PARADISE BRIDGE (LOOKING SOUTHWEST)

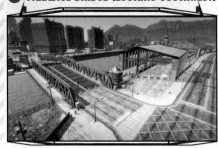

This is the quickest way to reach the Twin Bridges area. You need a run-up to sail over the gap, so approach at speed. Also, this is the eastern start of a long parallel shortcut running adjacent to 9th Street; an option if you're heading to the country club via this area.

15 INTERSTATE OFF- AND ON-RAMPS

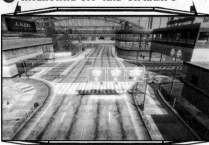

If you're heading in from I-88 to the west, or north from Downtown, and need to get off, this is an important area. Don't ignore the covered on-ramps either; Moore Avenue is the key to getting onto Section 2 of the I-88.

16 OFF-ROAD BRIDGE RAMP

One of the more entertaining parts of the shortcut that parallels 9th Street, this allows you to build up boost while keeping on-course for a destination.

LANDMARKS AND THOROUGHFARES: TWIN BRIDGES

17 CABLE SUSPENSION BRIDGE

This recognizable structure is the key to figuring out where you are. Hamilton Avenue cuts through this entire neighborhood from north to south, making this an often-traveled road, with excellent access to the small train yard and country club to the northwest.

18 SMALL PARK ON 7TH

Although this park can't be entered, the roads on either side show the large 7th Street, which splits up east and west all the way from the Twin Bridges themselves (Landmark #23) to the White Mountain tunnel all the way to the west. Remember you can cut between lanes in the gaps between the grassy areas.

19 TWIN LINKS SCULPTURE

This welcomes drivers heading east along 7th Street into the Twin Bridges area; if you spot this, the sunken highway is only a block away. Or, avoid this heavily trafficked area and take Root Avenue, which navigates around the northern riverfront area.

20 BRIDGE HOTEL

Most of the Twin Bridges area is composed of large brick apartment structures, and they can all look similar, so it's important to find distinguishing characteristics, like this hotel at the western end of the sunken highway.

21 SUNKEN HIGHWAY

Aside from Young, this is the other main route through here. This stretch offers access straight through to the Lawrence Tunnel (west) and Downtown northeastern corner (east), with a covered middle area devoid of traffic. Choose from three parallel routes here.

22 PARADISE BRIDGE (LOOKING NORTHEAST)

This is what the Paradise Bridge looks like from the Twin Bridges area. Approach from this area and you'll have a longer run-up, but once over, drift right so you don't slam into the parking lot.

23 THE TWIN BRIDGES

The area's eponymous landmark offers ample access to the city's northeastern corner and Downtown. Heading west, 7th Street becomes an exciting, lowered highway with jumps and a middle section that you can drive through to avoid traffic.

24 EL TRAIN TRACKS (SOUTHEAST EDGE)

This is the continuation of the El Train tracks from location #29. Beware of the roads (Young and Riverside) with the El Train over them; the many steel columns at the sides are great for shunting foes into!

25 DADO'S GYM

Remember the general location of this building, partly because it's off Young Avenue, where a gas station, shortcuts, and a parking structure are available, but mainly because there's a shortcut running below this structure, allowing access to 5th Street.

26 CIRCULAR MONUMENT AND PARK

Offering access via Franke Avenue to the alley and the large 7th Street sunken highway, this expanse of green can't be accessed, but the circular monument area is a good spot to lie in wait. Crash through that billboard after you find a flying ramp from the parking structure.

27 5TH STREET

The large, L-shaped roadways of Evans and 5th snake along the west and northern sides of the river that splits this district with Downtown to the east and south. If you're driving in this covered and straight road, you know you're near a bridge to Downtown.

LANDMARKS AND THOROUGHFARES: WEST ACRES

28 BOWL-A-RAMA

Although under most circumstances you will quickly zip past this, still watch out because you're between the El Train steel and the covered roadways of Evans Boulevard and 5th Street. If you need to reach the river, or get up from the river area, head along past this building.

29 EL TRAIN (NORTH)

This junction, where Young and 5th Street cross, is the gateway into the apartment block jungle of the Twin Bridges area, if you're heading northeast. Note that this section of El Train can't be driven on; only the southern section.

30 EAGLE MONUMENT

A flapping eagle flies atop a column on the corner of 3rd and Young. It isn't that visible, but the brick wall with the construction site gap in the middle to the east certainly is.

31 MEMORIAL TRIANGLE

The intersection of Hamilton, 3rd, and Young allows you to switch directions easily; a cunning plan during certain races. Here, you'll also find a nearby junkyard, gas station, parking structure, route into Downtown, and a ramp allowing access to the El Train tracks above Hamilton itself.

32 DISCO'S

This club on the corner of 2nd and Hamilton is a block south of the junkyard and gas station in West Acres; look for it for this reason alone. It also has a shortcut through the back parking lot, and offers great access via 2nd Street to the train tracks to the west, as well as the main Downtown bridges.

33 BUILDING SITE

Evans Boulevard runs in a tunnel-like enclosure, which then heads east, following the river, all the way to the Twin Bridges area. Some of the way, you can take a parallel underground tunnel, accessed from the Harbor Town area of Paradise Wharf. This offers excellent access up to Twin Bridges.

LANDMARKS AND THOROUGH-FARES: OCEAN VIEW

34 WEST ACRES MALL

Ironically located in Ocean View, the West Acres Mall runs south along Lambert. You can't drive through it, but it offers a shortcut and is the gateway into Harbor City's Park Vale area.

35 PARADISE AMPHITHEATER

With Hubbard Avenue behind this place, and Lambert in front, this is mid-way along both streets as they run north-south parallel to each other. You can head straight into Downtown from here on 3rd, and you're only a block from the north-south train yard and tracks.

36 FORT MONUMENT

Said to be constructed by the family of a mysterious driver known as the "Grand Master," this often-overlooked landmark sits on the corner of 5th and Hamilton. You'll notice the parking structure before this place.

37 TWIN BRIDGES MALL ON HAMILTON

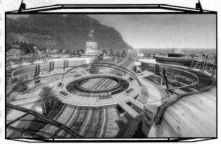

Although also a landmark, this road offers a couple of side shortcuts through the circular center, and quick access north and south. This is a great way to keep your speed up without worrying about too much traffic.

38 THE RADIO MAST

Although in the same general area as the Steakhouse (#39) and Guitar Records (#40), this tall structure is easier to spot from a distance, especially if you're heading northwest from the Twin Bridges area.

39 THE STEAKHOUSE

Harbor Town may have a rib shack, but the best steaks sizzle here, and the restaurant sits across from the looping northern end of Hubbard, as it intersects with Lambert.

40 GUITAR RECORDS STORE

The large guitars on the north and south walls of this landmark allow you to easily locate the entrances to the Lawrence Tunnel and the train yard.

41 OCEAN VIEW SIGNAGE

Between the separate sections of 7th Street, just before the Lawrence Tunnel, an arching sign shows you where you are. Your in-game map also has this information, so this is best used to ascertain the shortcuts you are near, such as the pond, and train yard entrances.

42 I-88 WESTERN BRIDGE

Head off Hubbard, either from Harbor Town or via the looping northern bend from Lambert, and you can easily reach the I-88 without resorting to shortcuts. Note the on-ramps on each side of the interstate bridge, and muddy shortcuts that let you cross to or from the bridge easily.

43 PARADISE CITY SIGN

The most gigantic landmark in all of the city, this sign is visible from three of the five neighborhoods. Use it from miles away to judge where you're heading. Note that the I-88 is below it. Most importantly, this sign is to the west; remember this!

44 I-88 TOLL BOOTHS

This is the widest road in the city. You needn't slow down for the toll, although it's sensible to steer to the extreme sides or line up a straight shot without any cars in the way to enter or exit this neighborhood. Don't forget the stunt-filled super jump leading down into the train yard if you're heading east.

45 MAPLEMOUNT COUNTRY CLUB

At the northern end of the Newton loop, this is the finishing place for any northern event. Be sure you're aware of the many alternate routes to take, including the tunnel from the beach and the winding road from Silver Lake.

46 THE WINDING ROAD FROM SILVER LAKE

You have three main choices if you're heading west into the mountains: the Lawrence Road tunnel (the continuation of 7th Street), I-88, or this road, West Crawford Drive. If you remember that East Crawford allows access to the beach, you're on your way to becoming spatially aware of the 64 roads in this city!

DRIVETHRU AND PARKING STRUCTURE LOCATIONS

DRIVETHRUS

DRIVETHRU TYPE	BIG SURF	TWIN BRIDGES	WEST ACRES	OCEAN VIEW	TOTAL
Auto Repairs	1	1	0	1	3
Gas Stations	1	0	1	0	2
Paint Shops	0	0	1	0	1
Junkyards	0	0	1	0	1
Grand Total	2	1	3	1	7

PARKING STRUCTURES

BIG SURF	TWIN BRIDGES	WEST ACRES	OCEAN VIEW	GRAND TOTAL
1	1	0	2	4

AUTO REPAIR SHOPS

☐ 1. BIG SURF

Hudson and E. Crawford
Grid Reference: V 7

☐ 2. TWIN BRIDGES

Young and Paradise
Grid Reference: U 10

☐ 3. OCEAN VIEW

Lambert and 5th
Grid Reference: Q 9

 GAS STATIONS

☐ 4. BIG SURF

Nakamura and E. Crawford
Grid Reference: S 7

☐ 5. WEST ACRES

Young and Hamilton
Grid Reference: R 12

 PAINT SHOPS

☐ 6. WEST ACRES

5th and Hamilton
Grid Reference: S 10

 JUNKYARDS

☐ 7. WEST ACRES

Young and Hamilton
Grid Reference: S 12

P PARKING STRUCTURES

☐ 8. PARKING STRUCTURE #1: BIG SURF

Hudson and E. Crawford
Grid Reference: W 7

☐ 9. PARKING STRUCTURE #2: TWIN BRIDGES

Young and Franke
Grid Reference: T 10

☐ 10. PARKING STRUCTURE #3: OCEAN VIEW (SOUTH)

Hamilton and Young
Grid Reference: R 12

☐ 11. PARKING STRUCTURE #4: OCEAN VIEW (NORTH)

Lambert and 5th
Grid Reference: Q 10

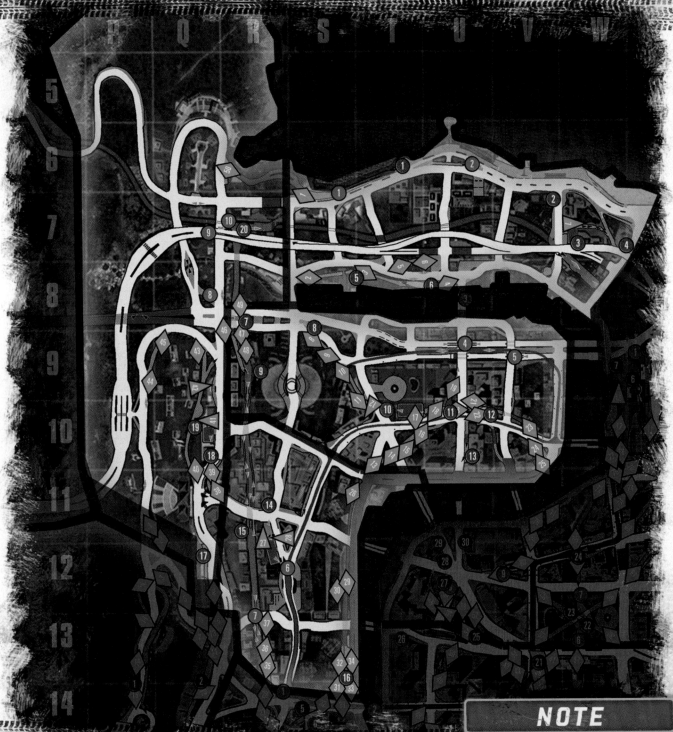

DRIVETHRU TYPE	BIG SURF	TWIN BRIDGES	WEST ACRES	OCEAN VIEW	TOTAL
● Super Jumps	2	3	2	3	10
● Billboards	6	7	3	4	20
△ Smashes	7	18	12	13	50

● SUPER JUMPS: BIG SURF

☐ 1. BEACH FRONT JUMP

Shortcut north of East Crawford
Grid Reference: T 6
Barrel Roll Available: No
Heading: East
Description: Drop down from the road or off-road tunnel, onto the beach promenade. Keep to the right, increasing your speed over the ramp, and land on the roof of the overhang. Keep your speed up, so you don't fall short.

☐ 2. OVER CONSTRUCTION

East Crawford and Moore
Grid Reference: U 6
Barrel Roll Available: No
Heading: West
Description: Accelerate along East Crawford, heading west toward the construction site surrounded by road, with the beach to your right. Hit the ramp at speed to land on the building, rather than hitting the steel floor.

● SUPER JUMPS: TWIN BRIDGES

☐ 3. PARADISE BRIDGE: MIND THE GAP!

Paradise and Root
Grid Reference: U 8
Barrel Roll Available: No
Heading: North or south (north shown)
Description: A great way to speed northward is along Paradise, and leap across the river via the bridge, as long as you mind the gap. Skid right after you land so you don't crash into the parking lot! Approaching heading south is trickier, as there's less of a run-up. This is a good way to reach Big Surf.

☐ 4. FLYING OVER 7TH (WEST)

7th
Grid Reference: U 9
Barrel Roll Available: No
Heading: East or west (east shown)
Description: Avoid traffic and increase your speed by heading up the long ramp in the middle of the northern section of 7th. Obviously, driving east to west is easier, due to the same-way traffic.

☐ 5. FLYING OVER 7TH (EAST)

7th
Grid Reference: V 9
Barrel Roll Available: No
Heading: West
Description: Start your run from the bridge near Riverside, and power down the dropped road, into oncoming traffic. Smash through lampposts if you need to. Stay in the middle, and launch over Root, landing on 7th afterward.

● SUPER JUMPS: WEST ACRES

☐ 6. EL TRAIN RAMP

El Train tracks above Hamilton and Young
Grid Reference: R 12
Barrel Roll Available: Yes
Heading: North
Description: Locate Parking Structure #3, and the large ramp on the road next to it. Accelerate up it, heading south, landing on the El Train tracks, then spin 180 degrees. Now accelerate to the super jump, landing on Hamilton.

☐ 7. TRAIN YARD ROAD LEAP

Shortcut south of 2nd
Grid Reference: R 12/13
Barrel Roll Available: No
Heading: North or south (north shown)
Description: Either at the beginning (as shown) or end of the train yard run, head for the ramp and leap over 2nd Street. Watch your speed if you're heading south, and steer left out to exit. You can also slow right down, ignoring the super jump, and move out onto 2nd.

● SUPER JUMPS: OCEAN VIEW

☐ 8. POND SKIM

Junction of 7th, Lambert, and Newton
Grid Reference: Q 8

Barrel Roll Available: No
Heading: Northwest or southeast (northwest shown)
Description: This super jump needs a run-up, while avoiding the traffic. Attempt this either via a race up 7th (as shown), or by heading south along Newton, crossing the gap, and skimming the pond from this direction.

9. SECTIONED

I-88 Section 2
Grid Reference: Q 7
Barrel Roll Available: No
Heading: Northeast
Description: A perfect start to a Stunt Run, drive through the toll booths, then efficiently straighten your vehicle for the jump. Landing is more difficult, so try heading off the interstate, onto the train yard area, or through Billboard #20.

10. ALL-NEW ON-RAMP

Train yard north of 9th
Grid Reference: Q/R 7
Barrel Roll Available: No
Heading: West
Description: If you need to quickly reach Section 2 of I-88, this is a great place to try it; land in the lanes where the traffic is heading in the same direction as you. This is a great place to start a Stunt Run.

● BILLBOARDS: BIG SURF

1. LOOK-OUT RAMP

Shortcut north of East Crawford
Grid Reference: T 6
Heading: West
Description: Just west of the construction site where Super Jump #2 is located, travel at speed near the semicircular lookout, and use the ramp next to it to fly into the billboard, and land on the beach shortcut afterward.

2. DROP NEAR THE CHOP SHOP

Parking Structure #1 on Hudson
Grid Reference: V 7
Heading: Northwest
Description: Drive through Smash #7, and ascend to the roof, then spin and face northwest. Boost and accelerate, off the ramp, so you land near the auto repair shop sign, facing north, having fallen through the billboard.

3. FREEWAY FREEFALLING

Parking Structure #1 on Hudson
Grid Reference: W 7
Heading: Southeast
Description: Drive through Smash #7, ascend to the roof, and spin to face southeast. Accelerate and boost up the ramp in the corner, fall through the billboard, and land on Section 2 of the I-88.

4. SECRET INTERSTATE ACCESS

Parking Structure #1 roof, or shortcut off E. Crawford
Grid Reference: W 7
Heading: Southeast or northwest (southeast shown)
Description: Destroy this sign from one of three places. The eastern ramp from Parking Structure #1 leads to a shortcut that you can also access up a ramp from East Crawford. Or, steam through from the interstate itself; this is a good racing shortcut.

5. BRIDGE RAMP ON THE WAREHOUSE RUN

Shortcut south of 9th Street
Grid Reference: S 8
Heading: East or west (west shown)
Description: The open bridge, accessed via the shortcut near Smash #3 or at the western end of the warehouse run (Smash #2), has this billboard between the bridge ramps.

6. WAREHOUSE RUN ROOFTOP

Shortcut south of 9th Street
Grid Reference: T/U 8
Heading: East or west (west shown)
Description: During the warehouse run shortcut, beginning with Smash #2 or #4, use one of the interior warehouse ramps to reach the open-air roof where the billboard is.

⬤ BILLBOARDS: TWIN BRIDGES

☐ 7. PLANNING ON THE PLINTH

7th, near the junction with Lambert
Grid Reference: R 8
Heading: East
Description: This billboard is tricky to destroy. Drive south down Lambert toward the junction with 7th Street, swing left (avoiding traffic) toward the plinth (the large stepped area), and launch off the northeastern corner of it, as shown.

☐ 8. RAMP FLYING NEAR THE RADIO MAST

7th and Hamilton
Grid Reference: R/S 8
Heading: West
Description: Drive west along 7th, and look for the radio mast landmark ahead and left. Hit the ramp at the junction with Hamilton to crash through the billboard.

☐ 9. TRAIN YARD RAMP

Train yard south of 7th
Grid Reference: R 9
Heading: South
Description: Enter the train yard via Smashes #46, 47, or 48 (#47 is recommended) and drive up the ramp cut into the concrete. At the southern end of

this concrete mass is the billboard. Note that this is on the border of Twin Bridges and Ocean View.

☐ 10. PARKING STRUCTURE #2 (WEST)

Parking Structure #2, north of Young
Grid Reference: T 9/10
Heading: West
Description: Ascend to the top of Parking Structure #2, hitting Smash #17, and position yourself facing west. Drive onto and over the ramp, pointing straight down the middle of the ramp itself so you hit the billboard and land on Franke Avenue.

☐ 11. PARKING STRUCTURE #2 (EAST)

Parking Structure #2, north of Young
Grid Reference: U 10
Heading: East
Description: Ascend to the top of the parking structure, through Smash #17, and make a run-up to the ramp on the eastern side. Land on the lower parking lot, drive into the billboard, and onto Paradise.

☐ 12. PARKING LOT DROP

Shortcut north of Young
Grid Reference: U/V 10
Heading: East
Description: Hit the fence at Smash #21, heading east, as this allows you access to an upper concrete

passage; at the end is a gap with the billboard to fall through. Land, and exit over Smash #23.

☐ 13. YELLOW GATE DROP

Shortcut at corner of Young and Paradise
Grid Reference: U 10
Heading: South
Description: Half a block east of the auto repair shop is a shallow ramp with two yellow barred gates. Head through, up into and out of a parking lot, and ram the billboard as you drop onto Paradise, and into the tunnel section.

⬤ BILLBOARDS: WEST ACRES

☐ 14. DOUBLE RAMP DROP

Parking structure on Hamilton and 3rd
Grid Reference: R 11
Heading: North
Description: Enter Parking Structure #3 (Smash #28), drive up to the roof, and hit the southern ramp (Smash #27). Carefully land, line up a second ramp, and boost off, hitting the billboard on Hamilton and 3rd.

☐ 15. TRAIN YARD CARRIAGE

Train yard just south of 3rd
Grid Reference: R 11
Heading: South

Description: Head south down the train tracks, and locate the ramp (which isn't a super jump) that rises up to 3rd Street. Take it, crossing 3rd and landing on the train carriage roof, and hit the billboard after driving over the carriages.

16. MAINTENANCE TUNNEL DROP

Shortcut north of 1st, west of Evans
Grid Reference: S 13
Heading: North
Description: Enter the building site via the smash in Harbor Town. Pick up speed so you launch from the slope and land on the top wooden floor, so you can crash through the billboard. You'll land in front of Smash #33.

● BILLBOARDS: OCEAN VIEW

17. LEAPING NEAR LAMBERT

Shortcut west of Lambert
Grid Reference: Q 12
Heading: North
Description: Enter via the smash in the Park View area of Harbor Town, and immediately keep to the left, as there's a precarious ledge to the left of the lower Lambert Parkway. Stay on the ledge, up the ramp, and through the billboard, dropping back onto Lambert.

18. PARKING STRUCTURE #4 (SOUTH)

Parking structure west of Lambert and 5th
Grid Reference: Q 10
Heading: South
Description: Enter the parking structure (Smash #41) and ascend to the roof. There are four ramps, but ignore all but the southern one. Accelerate over the south ramp, staying straight, and land on the lower roof. Crash through the billboard, and land back on Lambert.

19. PARKING STRUCTURE #4 (NORTHWEST)

Parking structure west of Lambert and 5th
Grid Reference: Q 10
Heading: Northwest
Description: Ascend the parking structure. The two ramps to the east simply lead back down to Lambert, so point northwest, accelerate over the ramp and through the billboard, and land in the semicircular area midway through the Lambert-Hubbard shortcut (Smashes #40 and 43).

20. BRIDGE FALL

I-88 Section 2
Grid Reference: Q/R 7
Heading: Northeast
Description: Whether you've just completed Super Jump #9 or not, avoid the oncoming traffic, point your vehicle at the billboard, and fall through it, onto the tracks below.

▲ SMASHES: BIG SURF

1. TUNNEL ENTRANCE/EXIT
Shortcut north of East Crawford
Grid Reference: S 6/7
Heading: East or west (west shown)
Description: Crash through this fence, either after using the underground tunnel (a shortcut to the country club north finishing point) or after emerging from it, onto the beachfront shortcut. Smash #50 is at the western end of this tunnel.

2. WAREHOUSE RUN (WEST)
9th and Hamilton
Grid Reference: S 8
Heading: East or west (east shown)
Description: Access the western end of the warehouse run south of 9th Street from the junction with Hamilton Avenue, or after you finish the run. If you're heading east, the next discovery is Billboard #5.

3. WAREHOUSE RUN (MIDDLE)
9th and Sullivan
Grid Reference: T 8
Heading: East or west (east shown)
Description: Access the middle of the warehouse run south of 9th Street from 9th Street itself, or after you finish the run if you're moving from east to west.

4. WAREHOUSE RUN (EAST)
9th and Paradise
Grid Reference: U 8
Heading: East or west (west shown)
Description: The beginning (or end) of the warehouse run south of 9th Street is easily accessible at the corner of Paradise Avenue. Smash through the fence at the warehouse.

5, 6. EASY I-88 ACCESS
Shortcut north of 9th Street
Grid Reference: T/U 7/8
Heading: East or west (east shown)
Begin your run through this shortcut (which allows excellent interstate access to the off- and on-ramps during races) by smashing this long fence. Speed through the fence at the opposite end of this paved shortcut a second later. You'll be on Moore, and can easily reach the interstate (or speed from it to a nearby finishing place if you're heading west).

7. PARKING STRUCTURE #1
Hudson and East Crawford
Grid Reference: W 7
Heading: North or south (south shown)
Drive up Hudson, and swing into Parking Structure #1 near the auto repair shop. Note that if you look through the windows as you ascend to the roof, you can spot both Billboards #2 and 3.

▲ SMASHES: TWIN BRIDGES

8, 9, 10, 11. OFF 7TH STREET, INTO THE BACK ALLEY
Shortcut south of 7th
Grid Reference: S/T 9
Heading: Northwest or southeast (southeast shown)
Description: Speed along 7th (or Franke if you're heading northwest), and quickly steer into the first of three smashes.
Head under the El Train track above, and cut the corner. This is a well-used shortcut when you're racing to or from the Downtown area.

Continue down an alley running parallel to Franke Avenue itself, which cuts the corner effectively. The last part of the alley allows access onto (or from) Franke Avenue, where you can continue your southeast (or northwest) racing.

12. CORNER-CUTTING

Franke and Young
Grid Reference: T 10
Heading: Southwest

Description: This is an excellent shortcut to take after Smash #11 if you want to take Young Street south. Hit the fence and drop off onto Young; you can't try this the other way around!

13, 14, 15, 16. SHORTCUT TO THE AUTO REPAIR SHOP

Shortcut between Evans, Franke, and Young
Grid Reference: T 10
Heading: Northeast or southwest (northeast shown)

Description: This is an excellent shortcut if you need to reach the auto repair shop on Young, or head into West Acres and the tunnels and bridges there. Smashes #13 and #14 are on the edge of West Acres, so your in-game map may show this. Drive diagonally from Evans, through both fences. Simply speed diagonally through Franke, and into the next fence, which leads to a second paved shortcut.

The last gate is right next to the auto repair shop. Or, you can head onto Young, or continue into Smash #18 if you need to quickly reach the raised bridge to the north.

17. PARKING STRUCTURE #2

Young
Grid Reference: T 10
Heading: North

Amid the many smashes in this area is an entrance to a parking structure, accessible from Young Avenue, near the auto repair shop. Head to the top to access Billboards #10 and 11.

18, 19. UNDERGROUND AT THE CORNER

Shortcut near Young and Paradise
Grid Reference: U 9/10
Heading: Northeast or southwest (northeast shown)

Description: This can be maneuvered into after Smash #16, or as the beginning of a run to the southwest (from Smash #19). Assuming you're heading northeast, head into the low parking garage. Billboard #12 is on the roof, and there's a series of shortcuts to the east. However, exit onto Paradise Avenue to set up a massive run to Super Jump #3 over the broken bridge.

20, 21, 22, 23. PARKING LOT SHOT

Shortcut near Young and Paradise
Grid Reference: U/V 10
Heading: East or west (west shown)

Description: There are some snaking concrete

shortcuts just east of Paradise Avenue, via the fence at Smash #20 as you emerge from the low parking garage near Smash #18.

Cross Paradise, head up the sloping ground, over the triangle of grass, and into a narrow concrete passage. A gap ahead allows you to smash through Billboard #12.

Or, if you're approaching from Young, enter this passage via a lower curved entrance (this is the exit if you're heading east to west).

You miss the Billboard if you enter via Smash #22. Escape back onto Young via this Smash, emerging under the El Train, and positioned to hit Smash #24.

24, 25. APPROACHING THE RIVER

Shortcut between Young and 5th
Grid Reference: V 10
Heading: Northwest or southeast (southeast shown)

Description: For the final two smashes in the run, begin at Smash #13, and move in a curved path criss-crossing Young. This allows swift access to the tunnels and the bridges south to Downtown.

You can also start a shortcut route from Smash #25, all the way back to #13, heading onto main roads at any time to shorten your progress to one of the finishing places.

⚠ SMASHES: WEST ACRES

26. MAINTENANCE TUNNEL (NORTH)

Shortcut south of Evans and 5th
Grid Reference: S/T 11
Heading: North or south (north shown)

Description: Find the single northern exit of the maintenance tunnel running along Evans here, near the junction with 5th Street. Or, enter this tunnel here for a great shortcut heading south, exiting at 1st.

27. PARKING STRUCTURE #3 ROOF

Parking Structure #3, off Hamilton
Grid Reference: R 11/12
Heading: North

Description: Complete Smash #28 first, head to the roof, and make an accelerating run into the ramp facing south, landing on the lower roof to the north. Line yourself up for the billboard, too. The other ramps allow access down to the road (east), or onto the El Train (north).

28. PARKING STRUCTURE #3

Hamilton and Young
Grid Reference: R 11/12
Heading: West

Drive up or down Hamilton until you reach the parking structure near the ramp that allows you to leap to the El Train. Ascend to the roof, where Smash #27 and Billboard #14 can be destroyed.

29. MAINTENANCE TUNNEL (SOUTH)

Shortcut south of Evans and 3rd
Grid Reference: S 12
Heading: North or south (north shown)

Description: Use this to enter the maintenance tunnel, which stretches back south to Smash #33, to head parallel to Evans. Exit (or enter) at Smash #26. Note that the tunnel continues south just after this gate, but you need to spin 180 degrees to your left.

30. MAINTENANCE TUNNEL (ALSO SOUTH)

Shortcut south of Evans and 3rd
Grid Reference: S 12
Heading: North or south (north shown)

Description: Just to the left of Smash #29 is this fence, which is accessed via the tunnel itself, rather than being adjacent to Evans Boulevard. It is north of the building site, where Smashes #31–34 are found.

31, 32. BUILDING SITE TO MAINTENANCE TUNNEL (WEST)

Shortcut north of 1st, west of Evans
Grid Reference: S 13/14
Heading: North or south (north shown)

Description: This assumes you took the western entrance to the building site from 1st Street (in Paradise Wharf of the Harbor Town Neighborhood); follow the passage into this fence.

A second later, hit this second fence as the maintenance tunnel begins, and you're on your way to Smash #30. Note that there's another fence (#34) right next to this one, and an exit onto Evans.

33, 34. BUILDING SITE TO MAINTENANCE TUNNEL (EAST)

Shortcut north of 1st, west of Evans
Grid Reference: S 13/14
Heading: North or south (north shown)

Description: Drive up from Harbor Town's Paradise Wharf, and slow down as you head up the slope. If you're too fast, you'll land on the upper corridor leading to Billboard #16.

Instead, slow down, pass through Smash #33 and under the billboard, and into the next fence, which is adjacent to Evans. Another fence (#32) is right next to this one. The maintenance tunnel now begins.

35, 36, 37. INTO (OR OUT OF) THE TRAIN YARD

Shortcut south of 2nd
Grid Reference: R 13
Heading: North or south (north shown)

Description: If you're heading north, the initial fence is accessed via Paradise Wharf in Harbor Town. Drop down to the first of two fences near the southern entrance/exit to the train yard.

The second fence is just north of the train yard entrance. You can start a very quick northern

race up toward the country club from here.

Or, exit onto 2nd Street via the final of the three fences. This is a good shortcut because you can reach two main north-south thoroughfares, or get onto the train tracks.

⚠ SMASHES: OCEAN VIEW

38, 39. AMPHITHEATER ANTICS
Shortcut south of 2nd
Grid Reference: Q 11
Heading: Northwest or southeast (northwest shown)
Description: Drive along 3rd to the junction with Lambert, next to the amphitheater, and drift right, into the fence to avoid the junction and gain a good shortcut north.

A second later, the shortcut is over. Smash through the fence (#39) and continue north, all the way up to the country club. Or, zoom southeast and accelerate into Ocean View.

40. SOUTHERN ENTRANCE/EXIT
Lambert/Hubbard Shortcut
Grid Reference: Q 11
Heading: North or south (north shown)
Description: One of the longest off-road areas links Lambert and Hubbard to the west of Parking Structure #4. The southern entrance (or exit) offers a quicker route to Hubbard.

41. PARKING STRUCTURE #4
Lambert and 5th
Grid Reference: Q 10
Heading: West
Description: Although you can come in from 5th heading west, or north/south from Lambert, the entrance to this parking structure is west of the junction. There are two billboards (#18 and 19) to leap to when you reach the roof.

42. GRASSY KNOLL TO LAMBERT
Lambert/Hubbard Shortcut
Grid Reference: Q 9
Heading: North

Description: If you're heading north from Smash #40, passing the rear of Parking Structure #4, ignore Billboard #19 and watch for a fence along the low white wall to your right. This leads to a drop back down to Lambert; good when shaking off pursuers!

43. NORTH ENTRANCE/EXIT
Lambert/Hubbard Shortcut
Grid Reference: Q 9
Heading: North or south (north shown)
Description: The opposite end of the shortcut to Smash #40 is onto the long looping corner of Hubbard Avenue.

44, 45. HUBBARD CORNER
Shortcut east of Hubbard
Grid Reference: P/Q 9
Heading: Northeast or southwest (northeast shown)
Description: If you're heading for the I-88 on-ramp west of Hubbard, or you want a quicker way around the looping north bend onto Lambert, take this shortcut.

The shortcut has two sets of smashes to hit; this shortcut may not seem too exciting, but it quickens your pace to the nearby auto repair shop if you're heading northeast!

46. ROAD ENTRANCE TO TRAIN YARD (WEST)
7th and Lambert
Grid Reference: R 8/9
Heading: South
Description: One of the three entrances into the long train yard shortcut area is via this sloping tunnel, accessed via 7th Street on the south side, near the guitar sign. Drop off the long ledge as you emerge, onto the tracks below, just right of Smash #47.

47. TRAIN YARD EXPEDITION (SOUTH)
Train yard under 7th
Grid Reference: R 8/9
Heading: North or south (south shown)
Description: If you're heading south, enter on 9th, accelerate through Smash #49, and once under 7th Street, exit to the train yard and dodge the ramp, or head up it to crash into Billboard #9.

48. ROAD ENTRANCE TO TRAIN YARD (EAST)
7th and Lambert
Grid Reference: R 8/9
Heading: South
Description: One of the three entrances into the long train yard shortcut area is via this sloping tunnel, accessed via 7th Street on the south side. Drop off the ledge as you emerge, onto the tracks below, just left of Smash #47.

49. TRAIN YARD EXPEDITION (NORTH)
Train Yard under 7th
Grid Reference: R 8
Heading: North or south (south shown)
Description: This is one of three entrances into the train yard, if you're heading south, or the main exit north, allowing you access up to the country club. Enter via 9th Street if you're heading south.

50. TUNNEL ENTRANCE/EXIT
Newton Drive
Grid Reference: R 6
Heading: Northwest or southeast (southeast shown)
Description: This makes an excellent shortcut if you're heading to or from the Big Surf area and want to catch opponents before they reach the country club. This leads to a tunnel; Smash #1 is on the other side.

NEIGHBORHOOD 2: DOWNTOWN PARADISE

LANDMARKS AND THOROUGH-FARES: MOTOR CITY

⚑ 1. COAST GUARD HEADQUARTERS: FINISHING PLACE

Make sure you learn this location quickly, especially as the finish is just southeast of Patterson Avenue. If you take this road, you'll need a final sharp right turn. Look at the shortcuts both here and in Palm Bay Heights when plotting a course.

❷ COAST GUARD CONSTRUCTION SITE

Just next to the finishing place is a large building under construction. It is actually the new Coast Guard HQ. Spot this from a distance to tell exactly where you are.

❸ Coast Guard Lighthouse

At the very northeastern edge of the city, the lighthouse itself can't be reached, but it's still an excellent landmark. Don't forget the shortcuts near the container yards nearby.

❹ CONTAINER YARD OFF-ROAD AREA

Three shortcuts wind through the container yard south of the Lighthouse, and these are useful during Stunt Runs and cutting final corners to reach the Coast Guard HQ finishing place.

❺ CONTAINER YARD: RAMPS

The ramps in the container yard are your main methods of increasing Stunt Run points, but they're also large obstacles if you don't line your jumps up precisely.

❻ CONTAINER YARD: WATT AND ANGUS WHARF

This junction allows access all the way south along Angus Wharf, and also features a couple of corners to cut during a race. Watch for heavy parked vehicles in this area.

❼ I-88 BILLBOARD DROP

Billboard #4 is here, and this is one of the few methods of descending from I-88. There are three other ramped points at the bridge over Webster right next to this point.

❽ PARADISE FERRY TERMINAL

You can drive alongside but not into this large, modern building when you're on Angus Wharf. Use it to pinpoint your location; you're just north of the gas station here.

❾ I-88 TOLL BOOTHS

The I-88 is full of tooth booths, and Motor City is no exception. Be careful not to hit the barricades as you speed through. The tunnel to the south is the entrance to the underground road, under Webster.

❿ TRAIN YARD (LOOKING NORTH)

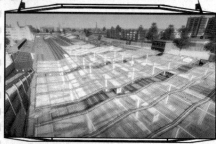

Spend some time exploring this playground. Crash into three billboards here (two accessed from the parking structure to the east), and attempt some major leaps, stunts, and shortcuts.

⓫ TWIN BRIDGES

The district in Palm Bay Heights was named after this double road. Look for this entrance for quick access west (or east), into Palm Bay Heights.

LANDMARKS AND THOROUGH-FARES: WATERFRONT

12 PARKING LOT ROOF (LOOKING SOUTHWEST)

One of the most difficult jumps in the city—the leap from Parking Structure #2 onto the roof of the parking lot roof opposite—is shown here. You're only a block away from the Waterfront Plaza finishing place.

13 PARKING LOT ROOF (LOOKING NORTH)

This is the parking lot roof from a different direction. You can land atop here, and then figure out four different exits (ramps, a super jump, and a glass-roofed corridor exit) as well as the ground-level shortcut.

14 SYMBOL OF THE CITY

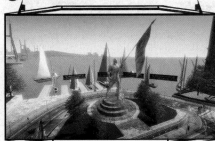

This giant statue provides you with an excellent way of spotting the Waterfront Plaza finishing place when the red sign is obscured; the finish line is slightly south of this point.

15. WATERFRONT PLAZA: FINISHING PLACE

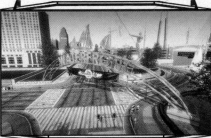

This finishing place has the most roads connecting to it. Immediately trace back all the possible ways to get here, including the shortcuts through Downtown; some stretch back a few city blocks!

16 RAYFIELD GRAND HOTEL

Locate this as a main marker during north-south (or vice versa) Waterfront district runs. Not only is this a shortcut to the finishing place, but it is wider than usual shortcuts, too.

17 PARKING LOT (SEALED)

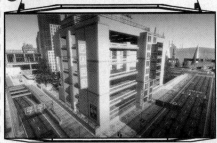

If you're traveling in the Webster Avenue area and searching for the road to the eastern finishing place, find this parking lot (which you can't enter), which serves as an excellent marker for finding Andersen Street. Also look for the construction zone, large hotel, and other markers at this intersection.

18 SCAFFOLDING AND PARKING LOT SHORTCUT

Only accessible heading south, this should be the start (or continuation) of a Stunt Run throughout this part of the city. It also allows easy access around the southeastern corner of the Wildcats Baseball Stadium.

19 THREE STONE FOUNTAIN

This fountain is a good example of a corner with a brief shortcut. There are loads of them throughout this neighborhood, and finding them all on the guide map could give you that crucial extra second during a race!

20 INTERSTATE UNDERPASS AND MALL TUNNEL

Spend some time figuring out the layout of this area. There are two thoroughfares: Webster Avenue and I-88 underneath. Access the latter via ramps on either side of Webster. Use the ramps in the middle of I-88 to launch up here, and figure out which parts of the middle section of Webster have ramps and which feature low walls. Remember that you can speed south down here, on the Interstate, and launch up a middle ramp and land near the Wildcats Baseball Stadium finishing place!

21 WILDCATS BASEBALL STADIUM (FACING SOUTHWEST)

Although a major landmark in this part of the city, the Wildcats Baseball Stadium is actually open, and the two gates allow you into and out of the grassy area.

22 WILDCATS BASEBALL STADIUM (FACING NORTH)

This is simply a good method of cutting the corner if you're heading north or west. Don't head into here if you're closing in on the finishing place because it is outside the stadium!

23 WILDCATS BASEBALL STADIUM: FINISHING PLACE

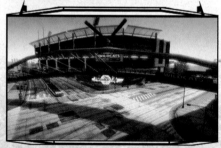

Carefully note the various roads that intersect here (Angus Wharf, Webster Avenue, and 1st Street), and remember them, even when you're far away. First Street is a great example of a road you can take all the way from a different neighborhood!

24 EXHIBIT HALL

Nestled west of the Wildcats Baseball Stadium, between that and the waterfront suspension bridge, this is the place to avoid the Interstate, merging onto Webster (which is important for reaching the finishing place). The southern off-road area is great for stunts!

25 WATERFRONT SUSPENSION BRIDGE

Stretching over most of the Waterfront district's southern area, this offers quick access to and from Downtown Paradise. Check the shortcuts to the east of the bridge, allowing access to Webster. Also, remember that Harber Street runs underneath it.

26 SUSPENSION BRIDGE TOLL BOOTH

The toll booth is troublesome if you don't have a racing line and hit one of the barricades here. Also note the ramp area allowing you to drop onto Harber below. You can also reach this area from a rooftop to the northeast, but only after a parking structure climb.

27 SUSPENSION BRIDGE ON/OFF-RAMP

The western end of the suspension bridge offers a few choices; for example, the looping on/off-ramp can set you up for a good run north along King Avenue near the river. Locate this area if you need quick access onto the Interstate.

LANDMARKS AND THOROUGH-FARES: RIVER CITY

28 THE STONE CIRCLE (MODERN ART)

This piece of modern art is on 1st, a block away from the finishing place. It is just north of Parking Structure #2, and a block south of the park. Knowing this helps your spatial awareness.

29 ROOFTOP JUMPS

This exciting series of maneuvers only really comes into play during the location and destruction of Billboard #16, as you must head up to the roof of Parking Structure #2, which isn't really a cunning plan during a race. Be sure you know which shortcuts are like this, and which are easily accessible.

30 THE DOUBLE HELIX (MODERN ART)

Located at the corner of 1st Street and Root Avenue, this is another good landmark. You're close to the El Train, a block south of the park, and you're on the same road (1st) as the finishing place.

31 PARKING LOT THOROUGHFARE

On the corner of Harber Street and Fry, this offers not only a corner-cutting opportunity, but the option of heading into the covered mall (to the east), or driving all the way into Paradise Square (north along Fry).

32 THE SUNDIAL (MODERN ART)

On the border of Waterfront and River City, with a smash that's actually accessed in Harbor Town, this sundial is in the southwestern corner of Downtown Paradise. The shortcut offers good access into this area.

33 THE MARBLE PLAZA

You can easily see this large skyscraper from Harbor Town. Use this to locate the broken bridge and the southwestern part of Downtown Paradise.

34 THE BROKEN BRIDGE

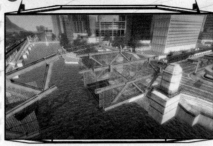

Offering exciting (or embarrassing, if you're not fast enough) jumps across the river, this is the only partially constructed bridge in this neighborhood. It offers easy access to 1st Street, and a straight shot to the Wildcats Baseball Stadium finishing place!

35 EL TRAIN STATION

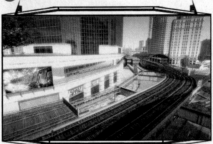

This is an important area if you're driving from west to east. Locate the ramp under the El Train to land on the tracks above (watch the hole in the ground between the two ramps), and then drop off this ramped end, gaining boost on a dash east to the finishing place!

36 MUSEUM OF ART

Nestled behind trees and a cool shortcut area with ramps and a drop is this imposing building, which is located just south of the park on Glancey Avenue.

37 FAN BRIDGES

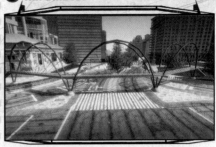

Located at the junction of Glancey and 2nd Street, this marks the southeastern corner of the park area, and is a block west of Webster/I-88.

38 PARADISE CITY POLICE HEADQUARTERS

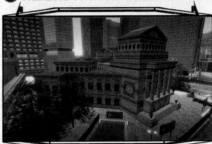

Over on the western side of River City, near the "Urban Ocean Liner" on Fry and 2nd, is the Police HQ, with a shortcut through its underground parking lot.

39 MUSEUM OF NATURAL HISTORY

Flanked by two imposing obelisks, and featuring a small shortcut in the southeastern corner at the junction of Fry and 1st, this is another great landmark.

40 THE URBAN OCEAN LINER

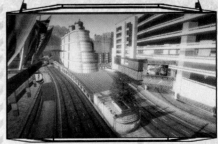

This effectively splits 2nd Street in two, just before the bridge to the west, into Palm Bay

Heights. Remember that Fry runs through the middle of this structure, allowing quick access to and from Paradise Square.

LANDMARKS AND THOROUGHFARES: DOWNTOWN

41 MUSEUM

This grand building overlooks the park along the eastern edge, on Glancey. Note the shortcut in the northwestern corner of this block.

42 THE SPINED SHARK (MODERN ART)

This sculpture is easy to spot, and just north of the museum. From here you're a block south, and a block and half west of the Waterfront Plaza finishing place.

THE CITY PARK

The following four views show the impressive urban park in the middle of Downtown Paradise. Note that the main paths run diagonally across this area; anywhere else is simply for discoveries or just plain fun!

43 CITY PARK (LOOKING NORTHWEST)

44 CITY PARK (LOOKING SOUTHWEST)

45 CITY PARK (LOOKING NORTHEAST)

46 CITY PARK (LOOKING SOUTHEAST)

47 CIRCLES (MODERN ART)

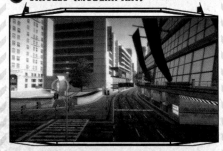

Look for this smaller sculpture if you're traveling east along 2nd Street and want to find the fourth parking structure. Remember, you're a block south of Paradise Square.

48 COVERED RIVER BRIDGE

Most bridges are easily seen, but this one is covered. The gateway into Palm Bay Heights, it also offers a great racing line to and from adjacent neighborhoods.

49 THE CAFFEINE HIT

Find this shop on the ground floor of this tall building. Keeping a mental note of where it is helps you navigate through or around the glitzy Paradise Square area.

50 PARADISE SQUARE

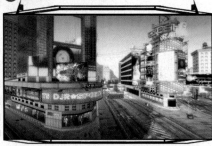

The intersection of Fry Avenue, Paradise Avenue, 3rd Street, and Franke Avenue is the largest junction in the city. The wide roads mean you can adjust your racing direction easily, except for the traffic congestion.

51 HAMILTON'S DEPARTMENT STORE

Use this building, and the others coated in neon signs, as landmarks during a race.

52 DOLPHIN FOUNTAIN

Over on the eastern part of Downtown is this quiet fountain area. Finding it means you're only a block west of the Waterfront Plaza finishing place!

53 THE RED FOX (MODERN ART)

This obstacle is on the border between Waterfront and Downtown, near the train station. Think of this as the northern end of the Webster/I-88 thoroughfare.

54 PARADISE CITY TRAIN STATION

This grand building has a couple of small shortcuts in front. The two shortcuts on either side running north to south allow you access into and out of the train yard, making them excellent ones to try!

DRIVETHRU AND PARKING STRUCTURE LOCATIONS

DRIVETHRUS

DRIVETHRU TYPE	MOTOR CITY	WATERFRONT	RIVER CITY	DOWNTOWN	TOTAL
Auto Repairs	1	1	0	0	2
Gas Stations	1	1	0	1	3
Paint Shops	1	0	0	0	1
Junkyards	1	0	0	0	1
Grand Total	4	2	0	1	7

PARKING STRUCTURES

MOTOR CITY	WATERFRONT	RIVER CITY	DOWNTOWN	TOTAL
1	1	1	1	4

AUTO REPAIR SHOPS

1. MOTOR CITY

Angus and Watt
Grid Reference: Y 8

2. WATERFRONT

Harber and Root
Grid Reference: V 14/15

GAS STATIONS

3. MOTOR CITY

Angus and 4th
Grid Reference: Y 10

4. WATERFRONT

Angus and Webster
Grid Reference: Y 14

5. DOWNTOWN

Andersen and Glancey
Grid Reference: W 12

PAINT SHOPS

6. MOTOR CITY

7th and Webster
Grid Reference: X 9

JUNKYARDS

☐ 7. MOTOR CITY

East Crawford and Angus
Grid Reference: X 7/8

[P] PARKING STRUCTURES

☐ 8. PARKING STRUCTURE #1: MOTOR CITY

Webster
Grid Reference: X 9/10

☐ 9. PARKING STRUCTURE #2: WATERFRONT

Angus and 4th
Grid Reference: Y 11

☐ 10. PARKING STRUCTURE #3: RIVER CITY

1st and Glancey
Grid Reference: W 14

DISCOVERIES

DISCOVERY TYPE	MOTOR CITY	WATERFRONT	RIVER CITY	DOWNTOWN	GRAND TOTAL
● Super Jumps	2	3	1	4	10
● Billboards	8	9	4	9	30
△ Smashes	16	15	19	30	80

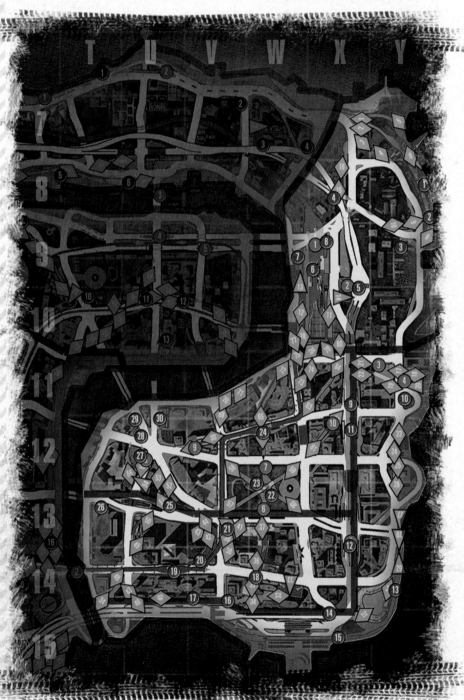

NOTE

Some of the super jumps, billboards, and smashes are on the border between two different areas, and may appear in one or the other (or different from this guide) on your in-game map.

⬤ SUPER JUMPS: MOTOR CITY

☐ 1. TRAIN YARD LEAPING

Train yard south of 7th
Grid Reference: X 9
Barrel Roll Available: No
Heading: Northeast
Description: Drop down onto the train yard from any of the entrances, and locate the ramped area on either side of 7th Street. Swing your vehicle around to head north, and accelerate to the concrete ramp with the flashing cones. Steer northeast, make the super jump, and land near the paint shop.

☐ 2. PARKING STRUCTURE #1 TO INTERSTATE

Parking structure off Webster
Grid Reference: X 9
Barrel Roll Available: No
Heading: Northeast
Description: Crash through Smash #14, and drive all the way up to the roof itself. Back up to the southwest corner, and point your vehicle northeast. Accelerate around the middle of the structure, and onto the ramp. Land on the I-88 Section 2, heading north.

⬤ SUPER JUMPS: WATERFRONT

☐ 3. PARKING LOT LEAP

Parking lot near 4th and Webster
Grid Reference: X 11
Barrel Roll Available: No
Heading: West
Description: Complete the insane Super Jump #4 first. Now that you're on the rooftop of the parking lot, head northwest, toward Smash #22, and drop through it, toward the super jump overlooking the intersection of 4th Street and Webster Avenue. Take the super jump ramp and land the vehicle without crashing. Note that the ramps on the parking lot roof don't lead to a discovery.

☐ 4. PARKING STRUCTURE SPEED

Parking structure off Angus
Grid Reference: Y 11
Barrel Roll Available: No
Heading: West
Description: This is a slightly insane super jump, as you must fly off the ramp at the top of Parking Structure #2 (having entered via Smashes #18 and 19), and then locate the ramp with Smash #20 at its base. Accelerate hard, and make a loop around the eastern edge of the roof to gain even more speed. Boost quickly as you head toward the ramp (picture 1) and through Smash #20. Fly across Angus Wharf, and land on the parking lot (picture 2) opposite. Smash #22 and Super Jump #3 are accessible from this new rooftop.

☐ 5. UNDERGROUND INTERSTATE

I-88 Section 1
Grid Reference: X 13
Barrel Roll Available: No
Heading: South
Description: Enter the I-88 underpass, underneath Webster Street, either after the waterfront suspension bridge, or near Parking Structure #1 (or any entrance on Webster Street). Travel south until you spot this ramp with the flashing cones. Other ramps aren't the super jump. Accelerate up the ramp, and land on the raised middle roadway of Webster (you can crash through Billboard #12, too).

⬤ SUPER JUMPS: RIVER CITY

☐ 6. INTO THE CENTER OF THE PARK

Shortcut north of 2nd
Grid Reference: W 13
Barrel Roll Available: No
Heading: North or south (north shown)
Description: Ideally, attempt this after crashing through Smash #37 heading north (as shown); you have the additional speed to hit the pile of dirt, and fly up, and land just before the central bridge. Ignore Billboard #22 and try aiming for Super Jump #7 instead.

Paradise

● SUPER JUMPS: DOWNTOWN

☐ 7. OUT OF THE CENTER OF THE PARK

Shortcut south of 3rd
Grid Reference: W 12
Barrel Roll Available: No
Heading: North
Description: This super jump requires a massive accelerated run-up, as you must land on the raised shortcut just north of 3rd Street. Accelerate under the park bridge, hit the pile of dirt, fly through the air, and land on the concrete ramp down to 4th street, then crash through Smash #65.

☐ 8. PARADISE SQUARE: PARKING STRUCTURE SCAFFOLD RAMP

Scaffold ramp on Fry
Grid Reference: U/V 12
Barrel Roll Available: No
Heading: Northeast
Description: This is deceptively simple. Head up Fry Avenue, passing the entrance to Parking Structure #4 (Smash #54), and hit the ramp leading into the scaffolding. Make sure you're traveling quickly enough to cover the initial gap. Then continue to boost up the ramp, and fly off, landing in Paradise Square. The trick is to remain intact as you land; there are many vehicles here!

☐ 9. PARADISE SQUARE: TWO-TIER PLAZA LEAP

Shortcut on El Train above Andersen
Grid Reference: U 12
Barrel Roll Available: No
Heading: West
Description: Drive onto the El Train, ideally by using the ramp and crashing through either Billboard #19 or 24. Then move west along the track above Andersen until you reach the corner without any barriers (picture 1). Jump across, into the upper mall, and continue to accelerate off the other end (picture 2). Land on 3rd, or steer right as you jump, so you can destroy Billboard #30.

☐ 10. CONSTRUCTION SITE STRAIGHT SHOT

Shortcut near Webster and Andersen
Grid Reference: X 12
Barrel Roll Available: No
Heading: Northeast

Description: Not only is this a spectacular super jump, but it allows you to make a deft racing attack for the Waterfront Plaza finish line! Enter from Smash #61, steering left (picture 1) so you don't head down to the ground exit (Smash #62), and race off the edge of the steel girders (picture 2).

● BILLBOARDS: MOTOR CITY

☐ 1. RAMPED CONTAINER SHORTCUT (NORTH)

Shortcut off East Crawford
Grid Reference: Y 8
Heading: North or south (south shown)
Description: If you're heading south, two shortcuts merge just before you reach this set of containers, with a ramp at each end. You can drop under the middle container if you're not traveling fast enough, but a better plan is to increase the speed, hit the ramp straight, and sail into the billboard.

☐ 2. RAMPED CONTAINER SHORTCUT (SOUTH)

Shortcut off East Crawford
Grid Reference: Y 8
Heading: North or south (south shown)
Description: Just like Billboard #1, this is a set of containers with a ramp at each end. Above the middle container (which you can drop under if you're not fast enough) is the billboard. Accelerate off the ramp and crash through the billboard. Remember to land properly and adjust your racing line for the next billboard, or exit.

3. WATT A JUMP!

Shortcut at Watt and Angus
Grid Reference: Y 9
Heading: Northwest
Description: The intersection of Watt Street and Angus Wharf has a small concrete off-road area to the southwest, and a ramp that leads to this billboard. The trick here is to drive north up Angus, across the bridge, and then swing left (getting enough speed) up the ramp to hit the billboard. Have you tried barrel rolling through it?

4. INTERSTATE FALLING

Shortcut off I-88
Grid Reference: X 8
Heading: Southeast
Description: If you're driving at speed along Section 2 of I-88, prepare yourself for an impromptu exit just after the three signs reading "Downtown." Swerve left, through the billboard, and land on the junction of East Crawford and Watt.

5. TOLL BOOTH TROUBLE

Shortcut off Webster
Grid Reference: X 9/10
Heading: South
Description: This billboard requires a good run-up, and top speed. Begin at the intersection of Watt and East Crawford, and drive south, onto the open parking lot east of Webster. Hit the ramp near the parking structure (picture 1), and fly through the air. Keep your vehicle straight as you hit the ramp so your landing is accurate. Drop onto the roof of the toll booth, where the billboard is (picture 2).

6. ROOFTOP RAMPAGE (PART 1)

Rooftop west of Webster
Grid Reference: X 9
Heading: Northwest
Description: Crashing through this billboard requires skill. First, enter Parking Structure #1 via Smash #14, and at the top, make a fast run-up to the ramp that's pointing northwest. Hit the ramp, sail over Webster (picture 1), and land on the roof of the train yard building. Brake hard, position yourself heading northwest, and boost forward. Don't go too slowly, or you drop through the hole in the train yard roof building. Ignore the platform sections leading to this billboard in the yard below; this is the only way to crash into this billboard!

7. NORTHWEST TRAIN YARD EXIT

Train yard near 7th and Glancey
Grid Reference: W 9
Heading: North
Description: Exit the train yard via the northwest sloped exit, through a couple of open warehouse areas. Begin by crashing through Smash #13, and continue north, through the billboard, and drop down into the busy intersection, near the Twin Bridges.

8. ROOFTOP RAMPAGE (PART 2)

Rooftop west of Webster
Grid Reference: X 9
Heading: North
Description: This billboard requires cunning to destroy. First, enter Parking Structure #1 via Smash #14, and at the top, make a fast run-up to the ramp that's pointing northwest. Hit the ramp, sail over Webster (picture 1) and land on the roof of the train yard building. Brake hard, and swing your vehicle to head north. Accelerate along the roof section adjacent to Webster (picture 2), and drop off the end, crash through the billboard, and land near the paint shop.

BILLBOARDS: WATERFRONT

9. WEBSTER BILLBOARD BARRAGE (NORTH)

Webster and Andersen
Grid Reference: X 11
Heading: North or south (south shown)
Description: Drive onto Webster (access this from the side streets, or even the underground Interstate), and then head up and onto the central raised area. Use the ramp at 4th or Andersen, and then drive through the billboard. You can crash into Billboards #11 and 12 farther along this road.

10. PARKING STRUCTURE #1 ROOF

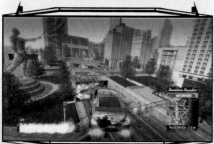

Parking structure off Angus
Grid Reference: Y 11
Heading: South
Description: Travel into Parking Structure #1 by crashing into Smashes #17 and 18. Once on the roof, back up to the northeast corner, and point your car southwest. Accelerate, steer into the southern ramp (picture 1), launch off, and strike the billboard at the base of the statue (picture 2). This may take a few tries!

11. WEBSTER BILLBOARD BARRAGE (MIDDLE)

Webster and Andersen
Grid Reference: X 12
Heading: North or south (south shown)
Description: This can be destroyed just after hitting Billboard #9 or 12. Use the ramp at the intersection of Webster Avenue and Andersen Street, and head up onto the ramp and into the billboard. You can also access this raised area heading north at Webster and 3rd Street.

12. WEBSTER BILLBOARD BARRAGE (SOUTH)

Webster and 2nd
Grid Reference: X 13
Heading: North or south (south shown)
Description: This can be crashed through after (or before) smashing Billboards #9 and 11. Stay on Webster, avoiding the barrier in the mall tunnel (between 3rd and 2nd) and steer onto the raised middle ramp at Webster and 2nd. Or, if you're heading north, enter the raised area via the ramp at the Wildcats Baseball Stadium finishing place.

13. OUT OF THE PARKING LOT

Shortcut near Angus
Grid Reference: Y 14
Heading: South
Description: You must destroy Smashes #27 and 28 first, using the ramp to drive up into the parking lot, drop out of the southern end, through the billboard, and land in the off-road area east of the stadium. Keep your speed up. Next stop is Billboard #15!

14. FALL NEAR THE EXHIBIT HALL

Shortcut near Webster and Glancey
Grid Reference: X 15
Heading: West
Description: Attempt this after exiting the Wildcats Baseball Stadium via Smash #30. This lines you up to cross the intersection of Webster Avenue and Glancey Avenue, and up these steps (picture 1). A second later, you're flying into the billboard, and over the entrance to the I-88 underpass (which tunnels below Webster), en route to the waterfront suspension bridge (picture 2).

15. EXHIBIT HALL EXHIBITION

Shortcut near Webster
Grid Reference: X 15
Heading: West
Description: A rather exciting off-road rampage is called for here. Head around the southeastern corner of the Wildcats Baseball Stadium, keeping near the perimeter wall (to your left), and then launch up the steps at speed or you won't make the gap. Crash through the billboard, go over a couple of humps, and land near Webster, behind the auto repair.

16. ROOFTOP DROPS

Rooftops southwest of Parking Structure #3
Grid Reference: V 14
Heading: Southwest
Description: An exciting and precise series of maneuvers is needed here. First, enter Parking Structure #3 through Smash #32, get to the roof, and launch off the southwest ramp, through Smash #33. Continue heading southwest, and accelerate over this alley (picture 1; you're passing over Smash #36). Land on the next roof and straighten your racing line so you're heading directly for the left ramp (picture 2). Boost off it, through the billboard, and land on the suspension bridge.

17. DOWN FROM THE MALL

Shortcut near Harber and Root
Grid Reference: V 14
Heading: East
Description: You can only access this billboard heading east. Enter the covered mall via the steps just north of Harber and east of Fry, and steer left so you don't head down the exit steps. Instead, crash through the billboard, landing at the junction of Harber Street and Root Avenue.

● BILLBOARDS: RIVER CITY

18. DROP FROM PARKING STRUCTURE #3

Parking Structure #3 south of 1st
Grid Reference: W 14
Heading: West
Description: This is another billboard that's only accessible if you fly off a parking structure roof. Begin by entering the structure via Smash #32, and race to the roof. Back up to the eastern side, and accelerate toward the ramp in the northwestern corner (picture 1). When you fly off, make sure you land on the lower roof and bounce off, into the billboard, before landing on 1st Street.

19. EL TRAIN GROUND RAMP (SOUTH)

El Train track above 1st
Grid Reference: U 14
Heading: East or west (east shown)
Description: Simply boost along 1st until you spot this ramp in the middle of the road. Drive up it, through the billboard, and optionally continue off the end of the El Train, landing back on 1st with a full boost. This is a great technique if you're heading directly for the Wildcats Baseball Stadium finishing place. You can also crash into this billboard if you drove onto the El Train via Billboard #20 or 24.

20. MALL TO EL TRAIN

El Train track above 1st
Grid Reference: U/V 14
Heading: Southwest
Description: This billboard is visible from the El Train, but you can only crash through it if you enter the mall (ideally via Smashes #44, then 43), and drive up the interior stairs, swerve right, and head down the corridor (pictured) and through the billboard, landing on the El Train.

21. RAMPED INTERIOR TO EL TRAIN

Construction site near Root and 2nd
Grid Reference: V 13
Heading: North
Description: Enter the construction site near the corner of Root Avenue and 2nd Street via Smash #38, and immediately turn left, striking Smash #39 and driving up the concrete ramp, through this billboard, and land on the El Train track, heading north with the park to your right.

● BILLBOARDS: DOWNTOWN

22. PARK BILLBOARD (EAST)

Park between 2nd and 3rd
Grid Reference: W 13
Heading: Southwest
Description: Enter the park via Smash #59, under the arched monument, and increase your speed along the main straight pathway (picture 1). As you head up to the bridge area, turn left and keep your speed up, and drop down (picture 2), catching the bottom right corner of the billboard as you land. If you miss, adjust your steering at the turn, and quicken your pace!

23. PARK BILLBOARD (WEST)

Park between 2nd and 3rd
Grid Reference: W 12/13
Heading: Northeast
Description: Enter the park via Smash #57, under the iron arch and pillars, and increase your speed along the main straight pathway (picture 1). As you head up to the bridge area, turn left and keep your speed up, and drop down (picture 2), catching the bottom right corner of the billboard as you land. If you miss, adjust your steering at the turn, and quicken your pace!

24. EL TRAIN GROUND RAMP (NORTH)

Andersen
Grid Reference: W 12
Heading: East or west (east shown)
Description: This billboard allows you to reach the El Train track via the ramp on Andersen Street, near Smashes #65 and 66. Of course, you could have accessed the El Train at the ramp or mall exit near Billboards #19 and 20. Remember that you can continue east, and drop off one of two areas; depending on whether you want a straight shot to the Waterfront Plaza finish, or to head northeast into the long alley (Smash #63).

25. PARADISE SQUARE: OVERGROUND, NOT UNDERGROUND

Shortcut between 3rd and 2nd
Grid Reference: U 13
Heading: South
Description: The first part of this billboard takedown is to locate Smash #53, and head through it from 3rd Street, and then take the overground, interior passage to the billboard and drop onto 2nd.

26. PARADISE SQUARE: FROM THE WALKWAY

2nd and Fry
Grid Reference: T 13
Heading: West

Description: Perhaps the easiest billboard to shatter in this neighborhood, simply drive along 2nd until you spot the junction with Fry; there's a walkway to the west you can drive onto, into the billboard, and off, onto 2nd. This is a great place for a vertical takedown and boost improvement, too!

27. PARADISE SQUARE: FROM PARKING STRUCTURE #3 (NORTHEAST RAMP)

Parking structure above Paradise Square
Grid Reference: U 12
Heading: North
Description: This is actually rather straightforward. Enter the parking structure via the ground entrance (Smash #54), head up to the roof, and take the northeast ramp, through Smash #56. Land on the next section of roof, and drive up the ramp straight ahead.

28. PARADISE SQUARE: FROM PARKING STRUCTURE #3 (NORTHEAST RAMP)

Parking structure above Paradise Square
Grid Reference: U 12
Heading: North
Description: Return to the roof of the parking structure, using the route you already tried during Billboard #27's run. Take the northeast ramp as before, but keep left, passing the ramp to Billboard #27, and speed up, aiming directly for the ramp ahead and left. You need a lot of speed and boost, as you must clear the road below and crash into the billboard on the opposite building.

29. PARADISE SQUARE: FROM PARKING STRUCTURE #3 (NORTHWEST RAMP)

Parking structure above Paradise Square
Grid Reference: U 11/12
Heading: North
Description: Time for a more tricky set of maneuvers. Scale the roof of the parking structure, and this time take the northwest ramp, landing on a thin sliver of roof (picture 1). Accelerate quickly, aiming at the ramp, and jump the road below. Land on the next sliver of roof, and drive to the end of this passage, turning left hard so you drop off the end (picture 2), flying through the billboard, and landing on Franke Avenue.

30. PARADISE SQUARE: SCAFFOLD BILLBOARD

Area above 3rd and Paradise
Grid Reference: U 11/12
Heading: West, then north
Description: This is one of the trickiest billboards to shatter in the whole of the city! Begin by accessing the El Train, and journeying west, above Andersen Street. At the corner without the barrier (picture 1), boost across and land on the mall's upper floor. Continue to boost, all the way to Super Jump #10, and turn right just as you lift off (picture 2). Aim for the scaffolding and brake sharply as you land. Then swing right (picture 3), and drop off the northern end of the scaffolding, claiming the billboard as you fall.

▲ SMASHES: MOTOR CITY

1. LIGHTHOUSE SHORTCUT (WEST)
Shortcut off East Crawford
Grid Reference: X 7
Heading: East or west (east shown)
Description: This is one of three nearby fences (along with #2 and 3) that lead to three separate shortcuts in the coast guard and container yard area. Be sure you know which one is which; this leads to Smash #5.

2. MIDDLE SHORTCUT (NORTH)
Shortcut off East Crawford
Grid Reference: X 7
Heading: East or west (west shown)
Description: Whether you're traveling to the Coast Guard HQ finishing place (seen just past the fence in this picture), or traveling toward Angus Wharf through the container yard, this offers a slightly quicker route than the lighthouse shortcut, and leads to Smash #6.

3, 4. WAREHOUSE SHORTCUT
Shortcut off East Crawford
Grid Reference: X/Y 7/8
Heading: North or south (south shown)
Description: One of the first shortcuts to find, this gives you a quicker route from East Crawford to Angus Wharf. Batter down this fence, and choose a racing line; either through the ramped area of the warehouse, or along the ground. This gives you a straight shot onto (or away from) Angus, and the nearby gas station. Your initial junkyard is only a block away, too.

---

5. LIGHTHOUSE SHORTCUT (EAST)
Shortcut off East Crawford
Grid Reference: Y 7
Heading: Northwest or southeast (southeast shown)
Description: Accelerate along this shortcut, which joins up with another shortcut at Smash #6, and crash through this fence by the lighthouse. The lighthouse road itself cannot be accessed.

6. MIDDLE SHORTCUT (SOUTH)
Shortcut off East Crawford
Grid Reference: Y 7/8
Heading: North or south (north shown)
Description: This shortcut leads to/from Smash #2 near the Coast Guard HQ finishing place, and merges with the lighthouse shortcut (seen to the right in the picture above). This offers a slightly quicker route than the lighthouse shortcut.

7. LIGHTHOUSE SHORTCUT (SOUTH)
Shortcut off East Crawford
Grid Reference: Y 7/8
Heading: North or south (south shown)
Description: The last of the lighthouse shortcut's fences is here, just by the merging of this and the middle shortcut route, and north of the ramped containers and Billboards #1 and 2.

8. CONTAINER YARD ENTRANCE/EXIT
Shortcut at Angus and Watt
Grid Reference: Y 9
Heading: North or south (south shown)
Description: Whether you've traveled south from the Coast Guard HQ, or you're heading that way from the junction of Watt Street and Angus Wharf, the large fence makes entering this area easy.

9, 10. CUTTING CORNERS
Shortcut at Angus and Watt
Grid Reference: Y 9
Heading: East or west (west shown)
Description: If you need to cut the corner and avoid the busy Watt and Angus intersection, use the shortcut through these containers. The eastern smash (#9) is just south of the auto repair shop. As you exit, beware of the concentration of parked cars and the low ramp—great for stunts and crashes, but not so good when racing. That billboard to the west (#4) can only be accessed via the Interstate.

11. INTO THE TRAIN YARD
Webster
Grid Reference: X 10
Heading: North or south (south shown)
Description: If you haven't entered the train yard from the tracks to the north or the access on 7th Street, you can find this fence opposite Parking Structure #1. You can continue south, up through the small tunnel to Smash #80, or head north up here as a shortcut to avoid the covered area of Webster, near 4th.

12. OUT OF THE TRAIN YARD

Train yard
Grid Reference: W 10
Heading: South

Description: Exit the train yard (as shown). Note that this isn't part of the cluster of Smashes (#75–78) near 4th Street; you actually drive up to a drop down onto Glancey Avenue, just north of the 4th Street intersection.

13. NORTHWEST EXIT OF THE TRAIN YARD

Train yard adjacent to Glancey
Grid Reference: W 9
Heading: North

Description: This is at the opposite end of the open warehouse from Smash #12. Travel north to this point from the cluster of Smashes (#75–78), and steer left, into the fence, and then continue toward Billboard #7.

14. INTO PARKING STRUCTURE #1

Webster
Grid Reference: X 10
Heading: East

Description: This smash is easy to find. Simply head along Webster, and with the train yard at one side, look for the parking structure on the other. Swerve in and make a super jump, and take a ramp to the train yard roofs!

15, 16. JUNKYARD RAMP TO/FROM I-88

Shortcut at I-88 and East Crawford
Grid Reference: X 8
Heading: North or south (north shown)

Description: The first available smash—#16—is just south of your initial junkyard location. However, the two-fence shortcut allows access to, or (in this case) from the I-88 section. If you're racing and using the Interstate to gain speed, line yourself up with this exit, head down onto the off-road area by the junkyard, and steer onto East Crawford and through the finishing place at Coast Guard HQ!

⚠ SMASHES: WATERFRONT

17, 18. INTO PARKING STRUCTURE #2

Shortcut near Angus and 4th
Grid Reference: Y 11
Heading: East

Description: Ready yourself for some insane jumping, but only after you swerve east along Angus, just north of the Waterfront Plaza finishing place, and head into the short off-road path to the parking structure. A second later, swerve right, into the parking structure building itself, through this fence. Continue all the way to the roof, where you find the very difficult Super Jump #4, and is also how you discover Smash #20!

19. UNDER THE PARKING LOT: 1

Parking lot by Angus
Grid Reference: Y 11
Heading: East or west (west shown)

Description: Although there's activity on this parking lot roof, via the super jump from Parking Structure #2, you can enter the base of the building from Angus Wharf (or Webster Street). This provides a good shortcut, especially if you're heading east, then southeast to the Waterfront Plaza finishing place. The smash at the opposite end of this shortcut is #21.

20. SUPER JUMP SMASH

Parking Structure #2 roof
Grid Reference: Y 11
Heading: West

Description: Enter the parking structure on Angus Wharf near the Waterfront Plaza finishing place, and ascend to the roof. Of the three ramps up here, take the one directly west. This is Super Jump #4, but the smash is at the base of the ramp—an easy discovery!

21. UNDER THE PARKING LOT: 2

Parking lot by Angus
Grid Reference: X 11
Heading: East or west (west shown)

Description: The smash at the opposite end of this underground shortcut is Smash #19. This brings you out onto Webster (if you're heading west), or onto Angus Wharf heading south (if you enter heading east).

22. PARKING LOT DROP

Parking lot roof near Webster and 4th
Grid Reference: Y 11
Heading: West

Description: Reach this parking lot roof (Super Jump #4) and drive northwest toward this fence. Ignore the ramps because they don't lead to discoveries. Drop through Smash #22; this sets you up for Super Jump #3. The passage across the rooftop, with the glass-roofed area, simply leads to Webster.

23, 24, 25, 26. RAYFIELD GRAND SLAMS

Shortcut east of Angus
Grid Reference: Y 12/13
Heading: North or south (south shown)

Description: This series of four smashes allows you to head through the forecourts of two hotels. The southern one is the Rayfield Grand. Simply line yourself up with the incoming fence and crash through it. A second later you're through the next gate. Attempt this in either direction. Is it saves you steering around Angus and is excellent if you're heading to the northeast or southeast finishing places.

The final fence is accessible, and if you're traveling south you can line yourself up with the next set of smashes as you head up into a parking lot area (Smash #27).

27, 28. PARKING LOT ROOF (HEADING SOUTH)

Shortcut east of Angus
Grid Reference: Y 13
Heading: South

Description: This allows you to attempt some stunt-filled fun up through a long ramped scaffold that leads to a parking lot. Accelerate and make sure your racing line is straight.

The second smash is just as you enter the parking lot. Remember to keep your speed up so when you exit, you fall through Billboard #13. Note that you can head up a ramp inside this parking lot if you head north through Smash #29.

29. PARKING LOT ROOF (HEADING NORTH)

Shortcut east of Angus
Grid Reference: Y 14
Heading: North

Description: This is useful if you need a boost (although the nearby gas station is a better bet), but during a Stunt Run, definitely try heading out of the Wildcats Baseball Stadium (through Smash #30), head north into the base of the parking lot, through this fence, and up the ramp. You land just south of the Rayfield Grand Hotel.

30, 31. INTO AND OUT OF WILDCATS BASEBALL STADIUM

Shortcut southeast of Angus
Grid Reference: X/Y 14/15
Heading: Northeast or southwest (southwest shown)

Description: This isn't a particularly recommended shortcut because the corner of Webster just west of here offers quicker passage in this area, and the finishing place is at the junction of Webster, Angus, and 1st.

However, the stadium is great fun for messing about in or attempting a Freeburn Challenge or two. Crash in via the north gate, and out via the southwest gate. Or try it the other way around. Heading north sets you up well for Smash #29.

⚠ SMASHES: RIVER CITY

32, 33. INTO PARKING STRUCTURE #3

Parking structure off 1st and Glancey
Grid Reference: W 14
Heading: South and southwest

Description: This parking structure is easily located if you head along 1st Street, and then swing south through the fence at the entrance. Head up to the roof.

There are two ramps of interest up here. The northwest one leads to Billboard #18, but the southwest one leads to a series of exciting roof jumps and Billboard #16. Get a good run-up, crash through this smash, and land on the roof.

34, 35, 36, 37. TWO BLOCKS TO THE PARK

Shortcut north of Harber, or south of 2nd
Grid Reference: V/W 13/14

Heading: North or south (north shown)

Description: For a quick route into (or from) the mark in the middle of Downtown Paradise, locate the entrance beneath the waterfront suspension bridge, and head north.

The next smash occurs at 1st Street, and you can break off the shortcut here (if you need to get to the parking structure or Wildcats Baseball Stadium finishing place to the east, for example).

Or, you can continue across 1st Street, and into the next shortcut, which curves slightly so you're heading directly north.

Crash through the final fence onto 2nd Street. Watch for cross traffic! You can now use the pathways in the park, including the curved path heading northwest, allowing you to flee Downtown Paradise in seconds! Or, continue over Super Jumps #6 and 7, and continue the northern shortcuts to Smash #65!

38, 39, 40. GROUND LEVEL CONSTRUCTION SITE

Shortcut near Root and 2nd

Grid Reference: V 13/14

Heading: Northeast or southwest (northeast shown)

Description: Although you can approach in both directions, if you want to shatter Smash #39, try a northeastern heading. Drive up Root Avenue, and as the El Train crosses above you, steer right, into the construction site.

A millisecond later, there's this fence to your left. It leads up a ramp to Billboard #21, and a landing on the El Train. Take this route only if you want this to be your destination.

Or exit, having cut the Root Avenue and 2nd Street corner, onto 2nd and think about heading into the park. Remember you can approach heading southwest if you wish.

41. UPPER LEVEL CONSTRUCTION SITE

Shortcut from El Train, near Root and 2nd

Grid Reference: V 13

Heading: Northeast

Description: It takes a little time to realize that this construction site has more than one floor, and the upper one is only accessible (aside from the ramped exit through Billboard #21) via the El Train tracks. Get up here (from Billboard #19, for example), and drive off this small ramp (picture 1), into the construction site. From here, accelerate out through the fence (picture 2), and drop down to 2nd.

42, 43, 44. MALL CRASH

Shortcut near Root and 2nd

Grid Reference: V 13

Heading: Northeast or southwest (#42; northeast shown); north or south (#43 and 44; south shown)

Description: Two of these smashes (#42 and 44) are useful if you want to cut the corner of Root Avenue and 2nd Street. Smash #42 is in the side of the mall, under the El Train.

Once inside however, think about crashing into Smash #43 too. It leads south, up some steps and allows access onto the El Train, and to Billboard #20.

The northern exit allows better access into the mall if you want to reach Smash #43. This shortcut is useful for quick access to Root, or (if heading north) toward Franke, and into Palm Bay Heights.

45, 46, 47. "HARBERING" A SHORTCUT

Shortcut near Harber and Fry

Grid Reference: U 14

Heading: East or west (west shown)

Description: This trio of fences is located at the base of a parking lot near the southwestern edge of this district, and it is useful for quick access north or east (north in this case).

Assuming you want to head north on Fry, approach the first Smash (#45) via the covered mall area, heading away from Billboard #17. Crash into the parking lot, then make a split-second decision: swerve back onto Harber…

…or crash through this fence (#47) and skid onto Fry Avenue, and begin to head north into the River City district.

48. HERE COMES THE SUN(DIAL)

Shortcut near Harber and Fry

Grid Reference: T 14

Heading: Northeast or southwest (northeast shown)

Description: This shortcut can begin on the southeastern tip of Harbor Town. Crash through the smash there, by the sundial, then head over the low ramp and through the exit smash, onto Fry Avenue near 1st. This is a good shortcut if you're exiting or entering this neighborhood.

49, 50. COP A LOAD OF THIS!

Shortcut near Fry and 2nd

Grid Reference: U 13

Heading: North or south (north shown)

Description: The short tunnel beneath the Paradise City Police Department allows quicker access to and from 2nd Street, which is excellent if you're coming in from the southwest, heading northeast.

Steer right, into the tunnel, and head out the other side. You can line yourself up with the off-road areas of the park (Smash #57) if you're heading north.

⚠ SMASHES: DOWNTOWN

51, 52. PARADISE SQUARE: UNDERGROUND, NOT OVERGROUND

Shortcut between 2nd and 3rd

Grid Reference: U 12/13

Heading: North or south (north shown)

Description: If you require a curved underground passage to and from 2nd and 3rd Streets, try this entrance, underneath Billboard #25.

You emerge (if heading north) near Paradise Square, and can head into the two-tier mall (at Smash #68) to continue your progress.

53. PARADISE SQUARE: OVERGROUND, NOT UNDERGROUND

Shortcut between 3rd and 2nd

Grid Reference: U 12

Heading: South

Description: You must approach this shortcut heading south. It's easy to miss because it's right next to Smash #52. Once through, you tear through the above-ground interior, and into Billboard #25.

54, 55, 56. PARADISE SQUARE: PARKING STRUCTURE #4

Parking structure on Fry

Grid Reference: U 12

Heading: West and north

Description: Locate the last parking structure in Downtown, and drive west, through the fence at the base of the building. Then ascend the structure to the roof. Three ramps are up here.

The ramp facing southeast simply lands you back on the ground near 2nd, so choose one of the other two ramps. This one (northwest) leads to a narrow rooftop, a leap, and a maneuver into Billboard #29.

This ramp (northeast) leads to a segment of roof, and the choice of driving into two Billboards (#27 and 28). Be sure you have a reasonable speed, and that you're heading straight into the ramps as you hit them.

57, 58, 59, 60. INTO (OR OUT OF) THE PARK

Shortcut park between 2nd and 3rd

Grid Reference: V/W 12/13

Heading: Northeast, northwest, southeast, southwest (all shown)

Description: In the midst of the massive skyscrapers and metal El Train track, this area provides a different kind of playground, and includes two billboards and super jumps.

You can enter each of the park's four corners through a fence, as the four associated pictures show you. As you can see on the map, there's a straight route directly through the park.

This means you can head from the northwest to southeast corner, and the northeast to southwest corner (or vice versa) in a straight line. Or, you can turn in the middle section, where the two billboards are located.

Take a look at the guide map and you'll see the shortcuts continue after the park, such as the construction site to the northeast (Smash #61). Plan racing shortcuts through here because it's quicker than 90-degree turns at main road corners!

61. CONSTRUCTION SITE SOUTHWEST ENTRANCE/EXIT

3rd and Glancey
Grid Reference: W/X12
Heading: Northeast or southwest (southwest shown)

Description: The construction site has a couple of secrets to reveal. The first is easy to spot if you're coming in from the park (exiting via Smash #59), or heading southwest from Smash #62. Exit this fence. Heading northeast is a fantastic plan; you can access Super Jump #10 and have a straight shot to the Eastern Waterfront Plaza finishing place!

62. CONSTRUCTION SITE NORTHEAST ENTRANCE/EXIT

Webster and Andersen
Grid Reference: X 12
Heading: Northeast or southwest (southwest shown)

Description: The entrance/exit at the opposite end of the construction site from Smash #61 is a ground-level access point. Take the route heading southwest, and you merge along the shortcut before hitting Smash #61. This is a great way to reach the park from the northeastern parts of Downtown Paradise.

63, 64. TENEMENT BLOCK SHORTCUT

Glancey and Andersen
Grid Reference: W/X 11
Heading: Northeast or southwest (northeast shown)

Description: Like Smashes #61 and 62, this provides a diagonal route to cut out an intersection. Head into here, either via the ground, or jump down from the El Train track.

The exit, through a narrow, debris-filled alley, brings you out at the corner of Webster and 4th. This is useful if you're heading to or from Webster or the train yard.

65, 66. CROSSING ANDERSEN

Shortcut across Andersen
Grid Reference: W 11/12
Heading: North or south (north shown)

Description: Whether you're continuing from Super Jump #7 (as shown) or not, this stretch of shortcutting allows access to a long, thin mall pavement area, after you cut across Anderson Street.

Once through the fence on the road's northern side, keep your speed up into this shortcut, allowing you to reach the junction of Glancey and 4th, and crash through Smash #72. Remember, if you're heading south, you can drop down into the park.

67, 68. TWO TIER MALL, INTO/OUT OF PARADISE SQUARE

Shortcut near Andersen and Root
Grid Reference: V 12
Heading: East or west (east shown)

Travel under the El Train line to the junction of Andersen and Root Avenue, and head straight through the ground floor of the two-tier shopping mall.

Accelerate out the other side, into the neon glitz of Paradise Square. In either direction, this shortcut is excellent for getting across Downtown, especially to and from 3rd Street.

69, 70, 71. CINEMA SIGN SHORTCUT

Shortcut near Root and 4th
Grid Reference: V 11
Heading: Northeast or southwest (northeast shown)

Description: There's a shortcut by the vertical "cinema" sign on the corner of Root and 4th, and this is an excellent spot to cut this intersection out of your travels.

Once inside the shortcut, you can immediately head out to the corner, if you only want a small shortcut.

Or, you can continue and exit further along 4th Street. When heading southwest, this entrance/exit gives you a better racing line.

72. ONTO THE MALL PAVEMENT

Shortcut near Glancey and 4th
Grid Reference: W 11
Heading: Northeast or southwest (southwest shown)

Description: Use this shortcut for a quick access to the park and beyond. Drive into the mall pavement area, shoot across Andersen (through Smashes #65 and 66), and drop down onto 3rd. Coming the other way, you can easily access the train yard if you shoot out of here heading northeast.

73, 74. MUDDY CORNER CUTTING

Glancey and 4th
Grid Reference: W 11
Heading: North or south (north shown)

Description: If the train station courtyard, and the train yard itself, is your target, cut the corner on Glancey and 4th and head into the construction yard.

Immediately head out the other side, leading (if you're headed north) to 4th Street and a straight shot to Smash #79 at the train yard. If you're heading out of the yard, use this shortcut so you don't need to brake sharply. Cut across 4th and enter Smash #74 instead.

75, 76, 77, 78. TRAIN STATION AREA: THOROUGHFARE

Shortcut near Glancey
Grid Reference: W/X 10/11
Heading: East or west (west shown)

Head through Smash #75 first to reach this western part of the interior train station courtyard. This is an option to avoid traffic when racing along 4th. It also allows quicker access to the three additional smashes.

Much as you can access the small interior path near Smash #75, you can hit the eastern side of this area from this location, and set yourself up for the smash cluster (#77, 78) to the west.

The last two fences are just feet apart from each other, and land you on Glancey Avenue, or (if you're starting this crashing run from west to east) enable access into the train station courtyard.

You exit onto Glancey, which has a lot of traffic and the steel columns of the El Train to avoid.

79. TRAIN YARD ENTRANCE (WESTERN COURTYARD)

4th and Glancey
Grid Reference: W 10
Heading: North or south (north shown)

Description: This stone arched entrance allows you into the train yard, and gives you a straight shot toward Smash #13. When heading north or south, use this excellent shortcut to avoid Glancey and the congestion near the Twin Bridges intersection with 7th Street.

80. TRAIN YARD ENTRANCE (EASTERN COURTYARD)

4th and Webster
Grid Reference: X 10
Heading: North or south (north shown)

Description: Access the eastern corner of the courtyard through this fence. When smashed, it allows you to enter the train yard, and head toward a ramp and Smash #11. This is a good way to avoid Webster and the covered area of that road.

NEIGHBORHOOD 3: HARBOR TOWN

LANDMARKS AND THOROUGHFARES: PARK VALE

❶ JUNCTION OF HUBBARD AND 2ND

The main north-south thoroughfare between Harbor Town and Palm Bay Heights. Check the shortcut to the east of the main junction.

❷ HUBBARD AVENUE LOOKING SOUTH

The massive White Mountain splits this neighborhood from Silver Lake to the west. A few shortcuts run parallel to this main road.

❸ JUNCTION OF HUBBARD AND HARBER

Harber Street winds east and is a good route to the interstate and Downtown. Hubbard continues west, toward the mountains. Note that the shortcut running north-south (on the left of this picture) leads to a drop; try driving north into it and you'll hit a wall.

❹ PARK VALE OBSERVATORY

The Park Vale Observatory faces south and is inaccessible. Hubbard Avenue runs below it. A tunnel runs directly under the observatory dish, too.

❺ LOG CABIN CORNER

The intersection of Hubbard and South Rouse Drive allows easy access northward, through the tunnel and into the Silver Lake I-88 section. Or, continue west to the Rockridge interstate area. Or, turn south, accessing all of South Bay's numerous shortcuts.

❻ THE GIANT PIPES

Just south of the gas station are a set of huge pipe pieces, and to the west is an interstate entrance (and ability to reach the upper railroad). To the east is the beginning of one of the main arterial routes: Lambert Parkway.

❼ LAMBERT PARKWAY (WEST)

Lambert Parkway snakes through much of this neighborhood, and it is important to check out the off-road possibilities running parallel, such as this ramp and rooftop shortcut to the north. This is excellent when performing stunts or when you need boost. You can see Parking Structure #1 from here, too.

❽ NAKAMURA CAR PLANT

Farther east along Lambert, if you look south into South Bay, you'll spot the entrance to the massive Nakamura Car Plant. A shortcut runs parallel to the road, but the building itself can't be entered.

❾ LAMBERT JUNCTION

It is important to note this large junction, where Lambert Parkway crosses Harber Street (it runs north-south). Parr and Gabriel also merge into Lambert here, and this is an important access point during events. That grassy knoll is a great shortcut, too.

⑩ PARK VALE RACK'S RIBS

Home for decades to the best ribs in Paradise, this corner restaurant is there purely so you know exactly where you are without taking your eyes off the road.

⑪ WEST ACRES CONSTRUCTION SITE

This neighborhood contains various sites under construction, and most offer great shortcuts, such as this off-road path south into Paradise Wharf.

⑫ OBELISK TRIANGLE

Near the landmark Hotel Paradise City, this expanse of triangular greenery allows two split sections of 1st Street and Lambert to join. This is the place to reach if you quickly need to race to or from Downtown. Note that the triangular island can't be entered.

⑬ HOTEL PARADISE CITY

One of the oldest and grandest structures in

town, this large hotel provides excellent reference when racing; you know 2nd Street is coming up if you're traveling north, or the Obelisk Triangle if racing south.

⑭ THEATRICAL ARTS CENTER

The TAC provides support for struggling actors, and also a good reference for drivers who want to know where 2nd Street is, as they race up toward Hubbard. This is also a good measure of where the neighborhoods merge, as this is on the cusp of Palm Bay Heights. Note the shortcut to the east, and the Paradise City sign behind.

LANDMARKS AND THOROUGH-FARES: PARADISE WHARF

⑮ EL TRAIN AND MORE CONSTRUCTION

This area of Paradise Wharf is basically a road that gets you quickly to or from the broken bridge leading into Downtown. You can drive onto the El Train if you use a ramp up in Palm Bay Heights. Otherwise, there are a couple more construction shortcuts to the north.

⑯ THE BROKEN BRIDGE

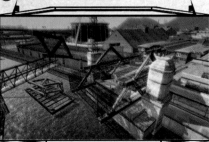

Currently under repair, this bridge linking Paradise Wharf to the Downtown neighborhood is still accessible if you drive off 1st Street quickly enough! Or, use the underpass heading south to quickly reach the interstate overpass and numerous junctions.

⑰ PARADISE CITY FILM SCHOOL

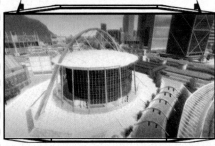

An unusual cylindrical building should give you all the information you need on your whereabouts when traversing this area. Notice the shortcut to the south of the building, the numerous interstate access points, and Harber Street under the I-88 itself.

⑱ I-88 RAMPS

Take some time to study this map, and drive around this area of Paradise Wharf so that you understand the layout of the off- and on-ramps onto the I-88. Then make sure you learn that you can fly off the interstate on numerous ramps, fleeing from foes or winning races in the process!

⑲ FISH MARKET WAREHOUSES

If you need to travel quickly between Downtown and the south, southwest, or west, definitely use this section of shortcuts to shave seconds off your time.

⑳ PARADISE CITY SEAFOOD WHOLESALERS

The wholesalers itself offers a couple of narrow shortcut passageways, but there's also an interesting ramp that enables you to quickly head north onto I-88— perfect for a cunning getaway!

21 INTERSTATE 88

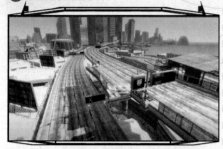

A quick look at the interstate in this part of Harbor Town shows that for speed, you can't beat boosting along this overpass. However, you should study the map, and roam the area yourself, to locate the ramps allowing you to drop down to Manners Avenue, which runs under the interstate.

22 THE SMALL WAREHOUSE

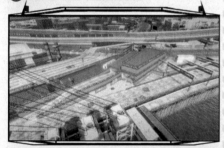

Offering more than just a collection of fences to smash, this shortcut allows you (if you're quick enough) to land on the interstate, and head through and across Manners toward a shortcut east of Warren Avenue. This is a good alternative if you're heading south down Warren, too.

23 WARREN AVENUE WAREHOUSE

The warehouse at the south end of Warren Avenue is a great shortcut whether you're heading north or south, as it allows you to reach the main four-way intersection to the north, or escape it and head south quickly and effectively.

24 D BALL'S B BALL COURT

Although completely enclosed, this piece of Harbor Town history offers a slight shortcut on its northern edge (if you're heading onto or from Harber Street, for example). Otherwise, this is good to use as a visual cue.

25 FOUR-WAY INTERSECTION AND CONSTRUCTION SITE

Warren, Harber, and Hamilton meet at this junction in the center of the Paradise Wharf area. There's a fifth entrance (or exit) too: the southern end of the construction site first mentioned at Waypoint #11 (previously).

26 HAMILTON SECRETS

Hamilton is a main road in this area, but it has a two-way warehouse to the southeast (on the right of this picture) offering great shortcuts to and from Downtown or Palm Bay Heights. To the left (on this picture) is a shorter off-road area allowing access into the Palm Bay Heights train tracks.

27 A WATERY RAMP

Moving to the south end of Shepherd Street, you can see (in the middle of this picture) that you can cut the corners at the south end of this street. In the foreground is a ramped jump over the pier; access this via the oceanside shortcuts from west or east.

28 PARADISE DINER

A fine dining establishment if you wish your cuisine to be caked in grease, but for drivers, this offers a great reference point; you can easily know where Shepherd begins without looking at onscreen prompts.

29 DALEY'S DONUTS

A block north of the diner, next to the parking structure, is a small donut shop. It isn't open, but it does allow you to check your location, especially if you're driving westbound along I-88.

30 BUILDING SITE

On the edge of Paradise Wharf, near the ribs restaurant (Landmark #10), there's a half-built building, offering multiple entrances and exits both on the ground and in the area. For a quick escape to or from Gabriel Street, this is an excellent plan. Don't forget the shortcut down from the parking structure on Manners!

LANDMARKS AND THOROUGH-FARES: SOUTH BAY

31 GAS TOWER SHORTCUT

Just past the gas station, at the south end of Parr Avenue, is a small ground-level parking lot that's a good shortcut, and Parr Avenue itself is a good choice for a direct path north. Don't forget the three entrances to oceanside shortcuts along the south side of the expressway, though!

32 TRAIN YARD (EAST END)

Parr Avenue isn't that eventful in its southern area, but it does offer two chances to drive onto the train tracks. These can take you all the way west to the expressway bridge and beyond! Or, they offer a quick shortcut northwest, toward Hall Avenue.

33 I-88 EXITS AND ENTRANCES

The massive I-88 offers two floors of quick racing east or west, and while getting off the interstate via one of the ramped drops is easy,

getting on might prove tricky. Make sure you remember the off- and on-ramps to the east, on Gabriel Street. Associate Gabriel with interstate access and remember it!

34 FORT LAWRENCE NAVAL SHIPYARD

South of the expressway, along the shoreline, is a massive frigate. This ship is open and you can travel from east to west (or vice versa), and also enter via a shortcut just west of this concrete sign. Quicken your pace and use this east-west shortcut!

35. FORT LAWRENCE FINISHING PLACE

This is the southern finishing point for all relevant events. It is just east of Hall Avenue, on the expressway, so plan your final routes to en-compass either of these main roads. The Events section has specific route information.

36 TRAIN YARD (WEST) END

The western end of the main train yard offers a bridge over Hall Avenue, and a couple of billboards to destroy. Otherwise, use this to gain access east a couple of blocks, west all the way to the expressway bridge, or try a cunning route from the railroad to the southern finish place (Waypoint #35).

37 BUILDING SITE DROPS

Farther north, up Hall Avenue, is a building site on your left. The series of drops through the partially constructed building leads to Billboard #14, but otherwise, this isn't a useful shortcut.

38 DROPS TO THE SUPER JUMP

One of the most entertaining off-road antics is to drive down the giant stepped drops from Lambert to the ramp above the junkyard, and land on the interstate; this is an option if your vehicle is weighty.

39 SOUTH BAY INTERSTATE

A quick glance at this section of interstate shows ample opportunities to change lanes both laterally, and vertically! Consult the map and seek out the ramp arrows to find all places you can drive off.

40 OFF-ROAD ONTO TRACKS

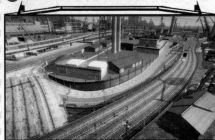

South Rouse, as well as the railroad itself, offers another way to head west (to the expressway bridge) or east (to the train yard) from this loca-tion. Note that the off-road area splits into two.

41 CONTAINER SHORTCUTS

Just to the south of the gas station on the expressway is the continuation of the naval yard shortcut, a maze of containers that are actually simple to negotiate, and provide incredible potential both in races, and more importantly, during Stunt Runs.

LANDMARKS AND THOROUGH-FARES: ROCKRIDGE CLIFFS

42 SOUTH BAY EXPRESSWAY BRIDGE

The quickest way into the mountains and the southwestern area of Paradise City is via this long bridge, which offers ramps up to the train tracks. If you're heading east, you can drop down at any time, or stay on the tracks, and use a ramp to leap to the interstate.

43 ROCKRIDGE CLIFFS SIGN

Before you head into the wilds, get your bearings by learning the location of this stone sign, on the corner of the expressway and South Mountain Drive. There's a small corner shortcut behind it.

44 GAS TANK CONSTRUCTION ZONE

Technically, the southern part of this area is in the Lone Peaks area of White Mountain, but the billboard and ramps bring you back into Rockridge Cliffs. This is a quick and spectacular alternate route to the base of the dam.

45 BASE OF ROCKRIDGE DAM

A gigantic Rockridge Dam is spectacular and useful, as you can use this to maneuver toward the interstate, or back from the interstate into White Mountain. Don't forget to find the secret tunnel exit from the quarry that's in White Mountain, and not on your in-game map!

46 TOP OF ROCKRIDGE DAM

If you're steaming in from White Mountain (or the tunnels to the east), along Geldard Drive, you can stay on the dam road and leap the concrete ramps, or (more spectacularly) head off the drops to the catwalk halfway down, then drop onto Casey Pass. This takes precision driving!

47 ELECTRIC SHORTCUT

The eastern corner of the dam base on Casey Pass offers a shortcut that allows quick access to the interstate, and even Hubbard Street, which is useful if you're racing across town. Drive up this tunnel. Similarly, drive down to reach the dam if you're heading southwest and don't want to chance the dam drop.

48 ROCKRIDGE HYDRO STATION (ENTRANCE)

This is the ground-level, eastern entrance to the dam area, or exit onto Manners Avenue, taking you toward the junkyard in South Bay.

49 OVERLOOKING SILVER LAKE

The northwestern edge of Rockridge Cliffs offers access north into Silver Lake, and it is important to learn the lakeside tunnels leading to and from the top of the dam, as well as the nearby junction toward the interstate.

50 PASSING OVER THE INTERSTATE

This is the western end of Hubbard, and it offers no direct route onto the interstate, but does allow access to the tunnel junction, and Silver Lake to the northwest. If you need to use the interstate, drop off the dirt drop, through the billboard shown in the picture.

51 NORTHBOUND TOLL BOOTHS

There's access to and from the southbound section of the I-88 near this toll booth. Otherwise, use this to speed north (or south if you want to chance the oncoming traffic!). A quick route to your destination is assured!

52 SOUTHBOUND TOLL BOOTHS

Similarly, the southbound toll booth offers you the chance to head directly into the South Bay area and cover great distances quickly. But watch the narrow gaps as you negotiate the booth itself.

53 LAMBERT PARKWAY OFF-RAMP

Another vital place for you to join or get off the interstate is this junction, which allows you to take Lambert, either east toward Park View area, or west, up toward Silver Lake. Don't forget this useful intersection!

54 RAILROAD RAMP

This is extremely useful if you're on the railroad section of the expressway bridge. You can leap onto the interstate and gain incredible speed over your foes, or drop down onto the junkyard area, and quickly reach the southern finish point.

DRIVETHRU AND PARKING STRUCTURE LOCATIONS

DRIVETHRUS

DRIVETHRU TYPE	PARK VALE	PARADISE WHARF	SOUTH BAY	ROCKRIDGE CLIFFS	TOTAL
Auto Repairs	0	1	1	0	2
Gas Stations	2	0	1	1	4
Paint Shops	0	1	0	0	1
Junkyards	0	0	1	0	1
Grand Total	2	2	3	1	8

PARKING STRUCTURES

PARK VALE	PARADISE WHARF	SOUTH BAY	ROCKRIDGE CLIFFS	TOTAL
1	1	1	0	3

AUTO REPAIR SHOPS

1. PARADISE WHARF

Warren Avenue
Grid Reference: R 15

2. SOUTH BAY

South Bay Expressway and South Rouse
Grid Reference: N 17

 GAS STATIONS

3. PARK VALE (WEST)

Lambert and South Rouse
Grid Reference: M 15

4. PARK VALE (EAST)

Lambert and Harber
Grid Reference: Q 15

5. SOUTH BAY

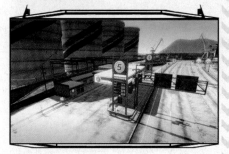

South Bay Expressway
Grid Reference: Q 18

6. ROCKRIDGE CLIFFS

East Lake and Hubbard
Grid Reference: K/L 14

PAINT SHOPS

7. PARADISE WHARF

Harber and Hamilton
Grid Reference: R 15

JUNKYARDS

8. SOUTH BAY

Manners and South Rouse
Grid Reference: M 17

P PARKING STRUCTURES

9. PARK VALE

Lambert and Hall
Grid Reference: N 16

10. PARADISE WHARF

Manners and Shepherd
Grid Reference: Q 16

11. SOUTH BAY

Hall and Manners
Grid Reference: O 17

DISCOVERY TYPE	PARK VALE	PARADISE WHARF	SOUTH BAY	ROCKRIDGE CLIFFS	TOTAL
● Super Jumps	0	3	4	3	10
● Billboards	4	7	9	5	25
△ Smashes	25	28	32	5	90

NOTE

Some of the super jumps, billboards, and smashes are on the border between two different areas, and may appear on one or the other (or different from this guide) on your in-game map.

● SUPER JUMPS: PARADISE WHARF

NOTE

There are no super jumps in Park Vale.

1. EL TRAIN TRACK

1st and Hamilton
Grid Reference: R 14
Barrel Roll Available: Yes
Heading: South
Description: Use the ramp at the corner of Hamilton and 3rd (in Palm Bay Heights neighborhood outside the parking structure), and race south on the El Train track to the super jump. Land on Hamilton Avenue.

2. BROKEN BRIDGE

1st and Evans
Grid Reference: T 14
Barrel Roll Available: No
Heading: East
Description: Accelerate down 1st Street and leap the broken bridge leading to Downtown (1st and King).

3. WATERY GAP

Shortcut south of South Bay Expressway and Shepherd
Grid Reference: R 17
Barrel Roll Available: No
Heading: East or west
Description: Drive either east or west through the shortcut near the water's edge, and leap the ramped gap at speed. Land your vehicle (don't sink into the ocean!).

● SUPER JUMPS: SOUTH BAY

4. ONTO THE I-88

Manners and Gabriel
Grid Reference: Q 16
Barrel Roll Available: No
Heading: Southwest
Description: Enter Parking Structure #2 (through Smash #54), ascend, and use the ramp in the southwest corner. The parking structure is half in South Bay, but the entrance is in Paradise Wharf.

5. PARKING ROOF RIDE

Hall and Manners
Grid Reference: O 17
Barrel Roll Available: No
Heading: Northwest
Description: Drive up to the roof of Parking Structure #3 on Hall and take the northwest ramp. Back up to the southwest corner and take a run-up.

6. FREEWAY FALLING

Shortcut south of Lambert and South Rouse
Grid Reference: M 17
Barrel Roll Available: No
Heading: South
Description: Take the shortcut on Lambert (through Smash #62), and descend down three drops to the super jump, and launch either onto the I-88, or land near the junkyard below.

7. SHORELINE CRANE JUMP

Shortcut south of South Bay Expressway and South Rouse
Grid Reference: M 17
Barrel Roll Available: No
Heading: East
Description: Leap the gaps between the containers at the western end of the crane yard run; the gap over the crane is just after you destroy Billboard #18.

● SUPER JUMPS: ROCKRIDGE CLIFFS

8. SOUTH BAY BRIDGE (EAST)

South Bay Expressway (Bridge)
Grid Reference: L 17
Barrel Roll Available: No
Heading: West or east
Description: Approach the small ramp in the middle of the road from either direction (head-

ing west is shown). Simply land your vehicle and optionally continue to the second super jump (below).

9. SOUTH BAY BRIDGE (WEST)

South Bay Expressway (Bridge)
Grid Reference: J 18
Barrel Roll Available: No
Heading: West or east
Description: Approach the small ramp in the middle of the road from either direction (heading west is shown). Simply land your vehicle, and optionally continue to the second super jump (above).

10. DOWN ON THE DAM BASE

Casey Pass
Grid Reference: J 16
Barrel Roll Available: No
Heading: West or east (east shown)
Description: Drive to the base of the dam, and jump across the middle of Casey Pass. Stay in the middle, as there are watery gaps on either side.

● BILLBOARDS: PARK VALE

1. SHORTCUT DROP

Shortcut West of Hubbard
Grid Reference: P 13
Heading: South
Description: After rampaging through Smash #15, continue south along the shortcut, and when

Paradise

you hit the drop down, sail through the air, into the billboard, and land on Hubbard Avenue. Watch that you don't overshoot Smash #16.

2. ROOFTOP DROPS

Shortcut north of Lambert Parkway
Grid Reference: Q 14
Heading: South
Description: After hitting Smash #7, speed down the concrete shortcut, on the roof of the low-lying buildings with a parking lot to your right. The billboard is above the final drop, near Smash #12.

3. NARROW LEDGE LAUNCH

Shortcut off north end of Harber
Grid Reference: P 15
Heading: Southeast
Description: Head in from the shortcut starting at Smash #3, or south from the start of Harber Street, and head left into the narrow shortcut which ends in a drop from a ledge, through the Billboard to Harber Street below.

4. ROOF LEDGE LARKING

Shortcut north of Lambert Parkway
Grid Reference: O 15
Heading: East
Description: Locate the ramp to the roof at the junction of Hall and Lambert, and drive onto the warehouse roof. Stay on this structure as you

accelerate east, and drop off the end, through the billboard.

BILLBOARDS: PARADISE WHARF

5. EL TRAIN TRACK ATTACK

El Train above Hamilton and 1st
Grid Reference: S 14
Heading: West
Description: Land on the train tracks like you did to reach Super Jump #1 (use the ramp at the parking structure on the corner of Hamilton and 3rd). Stay on the track and head east, then spin 180 degrees around, and accelerate off the drop, landing on 1st Street.

6. WAREHOUSE RUN TO 1ST

Shortcut northeast of Hamilton
Grid Reference: S 14
Heading: Northeast
Description: Hit the fence (Smash #29) on Hamilton, just north of the paint shop, and keep left as you enter a warehouse. There's a drop to boost over at the northeastern end. Land through the billboard, on 1st.

7. MARKET STALL MADNESS

Shortcut east of Manners
Grid Reference: S 15/16
Heading: Northeast

Description: Hit the fence (Smash #41) and stay on the left side of the market stall warehouse, and then accelerate over the ramp, crashing through the billboard. Land and continue through Smash #42.

8. LOW CLEARANCE

South Bay Expressway and Manners
Grid Reference: R 16
Heading: North
Description: Approach this heading north from the expressway, through Smash #36, and keep left, up and over the humped road at speed, so you clear the "low clearance" chevrons, and land on the roof shortcut. Smash the billboard under the interstate jump.

9. WEST ACRES CONSTRUCTION EXIT

Shortcut north of 1st Street junction
Grid Reference: R 15
Heading: Southeast
Description: Take the shortcut into the construction site, ideally from Smash #53. Drive into the site and through Smash #52, into the small snaking passage that leads to a steep ramp and billboard. Last in the junction.

10. PARKING STRUCTURE #2 ROOF RAMP

Manners and Warren
Grid Reference: R 16
Heading: East

ation of the shortcut you took (or will reach) leading through Smashes #1 and 2. Head to the side of 2nd, through the fences.

If you take the ramp almost immediately afterward at speed, it launches you over the exit fence (either #5 or #6 depending on your heading). Either slow, or swerve to the side (as shown) to guarantee your smash.

Cross 2nd (assuming you're heading south) and boost through another fence (Smash #7) that allows access to a shortcut north of Lambert Parkway, and rooftop access to Billboard #2. Smash #10 is just east of #7; don't confuse the two.

8, 9, 10, 11. FOUR FENCE FRACAS

Shortcut north of Lambert, across 2nd
Grid Reference: Q 13/14
Heading: North or south (south shown)

Description: Start in Palm Bay Heights (although the map says this smash is in this neighborhood, it is counted in Harbor Town). Approach the paved shortcut to the right.

Once you've hit Smash #8, continue up the paved shortcut, and exit onto 2nd Street. The next fence (Smash #9) is here.

Simply continue your run south, into Smash #10, after crossing 2nd. Watch for cross traffic. Note that this smash is slightly down from Smash #7. Don't get them confused!

You'll know you're correct if you exit quickly onto Lambert, via this final smash.

12. ACCESS TO LAMBERT

Shortcut to the north of Lambert
Grid Reference: Q 14
Heading: Southwest, southeast, or northeast (southeast shown)

Description: Ideally, take this if you're on Lambert Parkway and you want to use the parallel shortcut north of this arterial road. Also take it if you're already on the shortcut and need to head northeast onto Lambert to avoid the wall with Billboard #2 under it. The picture here shows a third option—continuing the shortcut from Smash #7—but you must slow down after the drop to reach this fence.

13. PARALLEL SHORTCUT ENTRANCE (AND EXIT)

Shortcut to the northwest of Lambert
Grid Reference: Q 14
Heading: North or south (north shown)

Description: Continue to drive south from Billboard #2, Smash #12, or (in this case) head north from the building site, gas station, and Harber Street, and there's a fence to the side of Lambert. Crash into it!

14. THE LOOKOUT (SOUTH END)

Shortcut west of Hubbard
Grid Reference: P 13
Heading: Northwest or southeast (southeast shown)

Description: Along the large mountain to the west of Hubbard is a small curved shortcut allowing you to pass by a "Lookout" sign. Hit the smash at the entrance or exit (as shown).

15, 16, 17, 18. PARK VALE HILLSIDE SHORTCUTS (PART 1)

Shortcuts west and north of Hubbard
Grid Reference: O/P 13/14
Heading: North or south (south shown)

Description: This section of Park Vale has a load of smashes; head south down Hubbard to complete them all in a single run. Begin with Smashes #4, then #14 to the north, before heading through this smash as another shortcut appears.

This leads to a short jump and Billboard #1. Make sure you slow down so you don't fly over the exit Smash (#16). Then continue on Hubbard, keeping to the right.

Just after the junction with Harber Street, stay to the right and look for the tunnel in the mountain wall. This is directly under a large satellite dish that you can use as a landmark.

The tunnel shortcut swings to the southwest, and also splits into two narrow paths that merge again a second later. Smash through the exit fence (#18).

19, 20, 21, 22. PARK VALE HILLSIDE SHORTCUTS (PART 2)

Shortcuts north of Hubbard, to South Rouse
Grid Reference: N/O 14
Heading: East or west (west shown)

Description: After exiting the tunnel (Smash #21), continue along Hubbard, optionally hitting the low ramp, then steer right toward the small dirt shortcut of earth. There's a smash fence here. Stay along the northern wall, as you can easily drop back onto Hubbard if you hit the edge of the shortcut. Smash the fence at the base of the hillock.

Instead of heading through the road junction with South Rouse, make a drifting skid to the south. You'll pass a log cabin between the shortcut and the junction.

The last section of this smash selection is the exit fence, which places you heading south on South Rouse. Remember that you can approach from here if you wish.

23, 24. PARK VALE HILLSIDE SHORTCUTS (PART 3)

Shortcuts east of South Rouse and Hall
Grid Reference: N 15
Heading: North or south (south shown)

Description: Either continue your hillside shortcuts (beginning in Part 1), or start them from Smash #24, heading in the opposite direction. This shortcut avoids the South Rouse/Hall junction. Head through the fence, drift toward the exit fence, and head out onto Hall itself. This saves time, and heading south sets you up easily for Smash #25.

25. UP ON THE ROOF

Shortcut northeast of Lambert and Hall
Grid Reference: O 15
Heading: South

Description: Approach the final part of the hillside shortcuts (starting with Smash #15) heading south on Hall, then steer left onto the shortcut and rooftop drop, which lands you at the Lambert-Hall junction.

⚠ SMASHES: PARADISE WHARF

26, 27, 28. HAMILTON AVENUE SHORTCUT

Shortcut west of Hamilton
Grid Reference: R 14
Heading: North or south (north shown)

Description: This shortcut shaves time if you're heading south from the train yard run in Palm Bay Heights, or swinging in from 1st. Or, you can zip north toward either of these two thoroughfares. Assuming you're heading north, shatter the first fence, entering the tunnel (#26). A second later, exit the tunnel, onto 1st Street. Here you have a good racing line (if you steer left) toward the triangle junction to the west, or you can continue to Smash #28.

Cross 1st, and blast through the long fence. Here you can head down onto the train yard run and into Palm Bay Heights if you wish. Usually, you strike Smash #28 upon exiting that route.

29, 30. HAMILTON AVENUE WAREHOUSE (SOUTH-NORTH)

Shortcut east of Hamilton, south of 1st
Grid Reference: R/S 14
Heading: Northeast or southwest (northeast shown)

Description: Four smashes close together are easily accessed from Hamilton if you keep right as you head north, passing the paint shop. Hit the first fence soon after.

The brightly lit "24 Hour Towing Service" sign sits above the next smash. Stay to the left, or you'll hit a wall, and smash through, into the warehouse. Once inside, increase speed and hit Billboard #6. Exit onto 1st.

31. HAMILTON AVENUE WAREHOUSE (NORTH-SOUTH)

Shortcut east of Hamilton, south of 1st
Grid Reference: S 14
Heading: Southwest

Description: To cut the 1st-Hamilton junction, steer to the left while heading west, skidding southwest into the shortcut, and keep left. Enter the warehouse and speed up, jetting over the ramp and landing near Hamilton, heading south.

32. WEST ACRES CONSTRUCTION (INTO WEST ACRES 1)

Shortcut north of 1st and Evans

Grid Reference: S 14

Heading: North or south (north shown)

Description: This allows access to the shortcuts leading to the southern part of West Acres, in Palm Bay Heights. Approach from Palm Bay Heights, or drive north off-road from 1st Street.

33. WEST ACRES CONSTRUCTION (INTO WEST ACRES 2)

Shortcut north of 1st and Evans

Grid Reference: S 14

Heading: North or south (north shown)

Description: This also allows access to the shortcuts leading to the southern part of West Acres, in Palm Bay Heights. Approach either from Palm Bay Heights, or drive north off-road from 1st Street.

34. INTO (OR OUT OF) DOWNTOWN

Shortcut near Harber and King

Grid Reference: T 14

Heading: Northeast or southwest (northeast shown)

Description: Near the Rayfield Hotel billboard, just northeast of Harber and King, is a shortcut that leads straight into (or out of) Downtown. Watch for the low ramp afterward, if you approach from the northeast.

NOTE

Technically, Smash #34 is outside the boundary of Paradise Wharf, but it's still counted toward this total.

35. INTO (OR OUT OF) THE OCEANSIDE SHORTCUT

Shortcut south of the South Bay Expressway, near Shepherd

Grid Reference: R 17

Heading: West or east (west shown)

Description: This smash is under a large graffiti billboard and is the start of the shortcut drive if you're heading east to west. It leads almost immediately to Super Jump #3. If you're heading west (as shown), hit Smash #84 next.

36, 37, 38, 39, 40. MIND YOUR MANNERS

Shortcut east of South Bay Expressway and Manners

Grid Reference: R 16/17

Heading: Northeast or southwest (northeast shown)

Description: This is one of the best ways of cutting the expressway and Manners junction,

whether you're heading to or from Downtown. Employ these shortcuts with the ones to the northeast (Smashes #41–47). Steer right as you approach Manners.

Once through Smash #36, you have three options. For the first option, increase your speed, stay left, and jump the ramp through Billboard #8. Or, reduce your speed, sneak under the small warehouse roof, and slam through Smash #37. Smash #37 is left of the concrete column. However, you can choose Smash #38 to the right instead. Double back to destroy both fences though; they each count as a smash.

The second main option is to ignore the small humped ramp and destroy Smash #39, which leads to the right side of the small warehouse interior, and out, under the interstate, onto Manners. Smash #38 is just beyond.

The last plan is to ignore the cluster of fences, and keep to the far right (or left if you're traveling southwest), and crash through the fence that's a straight shot from Smash #36.

41, 42, 43, 44. FISH MARKET JUMPS

Shortcut east of Manners

Grid Reference: S 15/16

Heading: Northeast or southwest (northeast shown)

Description: This is one of the most useful shortcuts to reach the expressway or Downtown. The inner route through the two market warehouses has four fences to destroy. The first occurs as you enter the building. This sets you up to hit Billboard #7.

The remaining three smashes are all in the general area of the white, concrete warehouse that's just south of Manners Avenue. The next one (assuming you're heading northeast) is at the warehouse entrance.

A gap leads onto Manners Avenue, just to the side of this warehouse, allowing you access to Smashes #42, 43, and 44 if you didn't approach from the fish market. The next fence is at the warehouse exit.

A small shortcut passage leads out onto Harber Street. This is a great place to begin a Stunt Run along the shortcuts all the way to the naval yard and the expressway bridge (if you're heading southwest).

45, 46, 47. SEAFOOD WHOLESALERS SHORTCUT

Shortcut between Manners and Harber

Grid Reference: S 15

Heading: Northeast or southwest (northeast shown for #45 and 47)

Description: Between Manners and Harber is a seafood wholesaler with a narrow shortcut with two entrances on the south, leading to one (Smash #47) to the north. This is the left one. This is the right one, but heading southwest, exiting into Manners.

This is the exit onto Harber. Notice the ramp? This allows you access onto the interstate, which is an excellent shortcut during races, or if you want to flee from a pursuer.

48, 49, 50. WARREN AVENUE ALLEY

Shortcut east of Warren

Grid Reference: R 15/16

Heading: North or south (north shown)

Approach these two smashes from either end of the alley east of Warren Street. In this example, we took the warehouse entrance on the corner of Warren and Manners.

The second smash is at the other end of the warehouse, which (if you're heading north) allows access into a long alley east of Warren Avenue. Exit to Harber Street, near the three-way intersection. If you steer left slightly as you exit, you can line up the building site shortcut that leads to 1st Street (Smashes #51–53). Or, if you're heading south, attempt that shortcut first.

51, 52, 53. WEST ACRES CONSTRUCTION

Shortcut between Hamilton and 1st

Grid Reference: Q/R 14/15

Heading: Northwest or southeast (northwest shown)

Description: From the intersection (if heading north), head northwest into the building site with the "West Acres Construction" sign to the left of it. The first smash (#51) is at the entrance.

The second is available only if you're heading southeast, or you spin 180 degrees during your run northwest. This leads to an underground passage below the southern entrance (and Smash #51), and allows you to break Billboard #9. The smash at the northern end of the building site allows easy access to 1st Street; steer to the right as you emerge to keep a good racing line.

⚠ SMASHES: SOUTH BAY

54, 55. PARKING STRUCTURE #2

Manners and Shepherd

Grid Reference: Q 16

Heading: North

Description: Drive along Manners either east or west until you come to this parking structure, located under the interstate overpass. Destroy Smash #54 to enter, and ascend to the roof. On the roof, there are three ramps, and all lead to discoveries (the east ramp to Billboard #10, the southwest ramp to Super Jump #4). Smash #55 is in the northwest corner. Drive up the ramp, land, and enter a roof run toward Billboard #11.

NOTE

Smashes #56–70 are on the border between Park Vale and South Bay. They have been included in the South Bay section because they are all south of Lambert Parkway, which borders the two areas. However, sometimes your in-game map (and the screenshots in this guide) may show Park Vale.

56, 57. BUILDING SITE ON GABRIEL (WEST)

Lambert and Gabriel
Grid Reference: Q 15
Heading: Northeast

Description: It is preferable to drive north along Gabriel (or exit via Smash #70) to get a good racing line into this fence. Smash through, into the multi-level building site.

Drive under the steel building above, and stay left. There's a ramp on your right, allowing you to fly over Harber Street, into the gas station. However, you want the ground-level smash. This is a good shortcut to take if you're heading south.

58, 59, 60. BUILDING SITE ON GABRIEL (EAST)

Lambert and Gabriel
Grid Reference: Q 15/16
Heading: North or south (north shown)

Description: This smash looks very similar to the western entrance on Gabriel (#56). Enter it heading north to efficiently locate Smash #59. You have a choice of exits, each with a smash to complete. Smash #59, easily accessible if you're heading north, is just after #58. The fence leads you into the building site, and a drop onto the junction with Harber, above Smash #57. The other smash is to the north, leading to and from Harber Street. Approach it after hitting Smash #58, heading south from Harber Street itself, or on a continuous path from the warehouse roof and Billboard #11.

61. INTO THE PIPES

Shortcut off Lambert, near South Rouse
Grid Reference: M 16
Heading: East

Description: Drive down Lambert until you spot the dirt road and giant pipes, and hit the fence to enter this shortcut. Your next target should be Billboard #12.

62. ROOF RUN FUN

Shortcut off Lambert, near South Rouse
Grid Reference: M 16
Heading: South

Description: Just south of the pipes and Smash #61 is a line of fencing leading to a series of roof run drops, just west of South Rouse. They lead to Super Jump #6.

63, 64. PARKING STRUCTURE #1

Lambert and Hall
Grid Reference: N 16
Heading: South

Description: Travel east or west along Lambert Parkway to locate the parking structure entrance, and head south, smashing through the fence. Note that the entrance to this structure is in Park Vale, but the roof is on the border between Park Vale and South Bay.

Atop the parking structure, you can pick from three ramps. The one to the southeast has the fence you're looking for, and it leads through a building site to Billboard #14. The west roof ramp leads to Billboard #13. The third ramp simply allows a quick return to the ground.

65. OUTSIDE THE CAR PLANT (WEST)

Shortcut south of Lambert Parkway, east of Hall
Grid Reference: O 16
Heading: West

Description: Accelerate west along Lambert, looking left for the car plant. Steer left, onto the forecourt, and enter the fence that leads to a ramp allowing you to land on the Hall-Lambert intersection.

66. OUTSIDE THE CAR PLANT (EAST)

Shortcut south of Lambert Parkway, east of Hall
Grid Reference: O 16
Heading: East

Description: Accelerate east along Lambert, looking right for the car plant. Steer right, onto the forecourt, and pass the low concrete wall, into the fence smash. Continue down the drops to Smashes #67 and 68.

67, 68. WAREHOUSE RUN (CAR PLANT GROUNDS)

Shortcut south of Lambert Parkway, west of Parr
Grid Reference: P 16
Heading: East

Description: After destroying Smash #66, enter the series of drops leading to the warehouse along the shortcut south of Lambert. Enter the warehouse by hitting Smash #67.

Exit by smashing the second fence (#68), and fly over the low wall, landing on Parr Avenue. Note that you can steer left and get back on Lambert too, or line up Smashes #69 and 70.

69, 70. PARSING PARR AVENUE

Shortcut between north ends of Parr and Gabriel
Grid Reference: P 16
Heading: East or west (east shown)

Description: Although you can take these easily spotted smashes from either direction, heading east makes most sense as you can line up the cluster of smashes (#56–60) inside the building site. Quickly slam through both smashes at speed, arriving quickly in Gabriel, and then access either entrance to the building site (Smashes #56 or 58) if you wish.

71, 72. PARKING STRUCTURE #3

Hall and Manners
Grid Reference: O 17
Heading: East

Description: Travel north or south along Hall Avenue, until you spot the parking structure near Manners, and swing through the fence, into it. Get to the roof for Smash #72.

There are three ramps on the roof. The one with the flashing cones to the northwest leads to Super Jump #5. The one to the south allows difficult access to Billboard #16. Instead, drive off the southeast ramp with the fence. It leads to a high shortcut to Billboard #15.

73, 74. ONTO THE RAILROAD

Shortcut off South Rouse (or Manners) and South Bay Expressway
Grid Reference: N 17
Heading: East or west (east shown)

Description: You can exit from the railroad, too. However, the easiest way to spot this is to head south down South Rouse Drive, and scoot down the curved shortcut.

This leads to a dual alley. Stay to the right, on the ground, rather than investigating the upper shortcut (that leads to Billboard #10) to the left. Drive through this fence (#74), and onto the railroad tracks.

75, 76, 77. WAREHOUSE DASH

Shortcut off South Rouse (or Manners) and South Bay Expressway
Grid Reference: M 17
Heading: East or west (west shown)

Description: Approach from Manners or South Rouse (as shown). Skid into the warehouse grounds and execute Smash #75 at the warehouse entrance.

Continue through the warehouse, up the ramp, and destroy Smash #76 halfway through.

Exit via the small ramped garage door, and into Manners. Billboard #19 is available to destroy here; this is preferable than approaching from the east.

78. START OF THE CONTAINER RUN

Shortcut east of the South Bay Expressway Bridge

Grid Reference: M 17

Heading: East

Description: Either make a U-turn on the South Bay Expressway while heading west, just before the bridge, or keep right as you exit the bridge. This is the start of the stunt-filled container run, where Billboards #17 and 18, and Super Jump #7 are available.

79. END OF THE CONTAINER RUN

Shortcut south of the South Bay Expressway

Grid Reference: N 18

Heading: East

Description: Ideally, after landing Super Jump #7 (or you can access this fence from the Expressway), enter and accelerate up the narrow ramp.

80. INTO (OR OUT OF) THE NAVAL YARD (WEST)

Shortcut south of the South Bay Expressway

Grid Reference: O 18

Heading: West or east (west shown)

Description: This smash is almost directly underneath Billboard #20. Either approach after driving through the naval ship (as shown), or from the expressway just east of the auto repair shop.

81. INTO (OR OUT OF) THE NAVAL YARD (NORTH)

Shortcut south of the South Bay Expressway

Grid Reference: O 18

Heading: North or south (south shown)

Description: More easily seen and driven through via the expressway, this zigzag ramp leads into the naval ship. Slow down to take this tight series of turns. This isn't a well-used shortcut.

82. INTO (OR OUT OF) THE NAVAL YARD (EAST)

Shortcut south of the South Bay Expressway and Parr

Grid Reference: P 18

Heading: Southwest or northeast (southwest shown)

Description: This is easy to spot, as the Fort Lawrence sign is prominent if you're heading southwest from the expressway. Smash through the entrance gate, or use this as an exit after driving through the ship.

83. INTO (OR OUT OF) THE WAREHOUSE

Shortcut south of the South Bay Expressway

Grid Reference: P 18

Heading: Northwest or southeast (northwest shown)

Description: If you're exiting the warehouse (Smashes #84–85), you can drive back onto the expressway via this exit, which peels off to the right of the main shortcut leading into the naval yard.

84, 85. UNDER THE WAREHOUSE

Shortcut south of the South Bay Expressway

Grid Reference: Q 18

Heading: West or east (west shown)

Description: This fence is under the main west-east shortcut path, and easy to miss. It's easier to find if you're heading west, from Smash #35. Strike Smash #85 first (the second picture), and then drive under the warehouse, into Smash #84 (the first picture). If you approach from the east, Smash #84 is easy to miss as you jump over it.

⚠ SMASHES: ROCKRIDGE CLIFFS

86. SECRET QUARRY EXIT

Shortcut from quarry, below South Mountain Drive (to Casey Pass)

Grid Reference: I 16

Heading: East

Description: Enter the off-road quarry area (the two entrances are shown in the White Mountain Tour section), exit via the tunnel in the base of the eastern wall, and drive back into Harbor Town, out and onto Casey Pass.

87. TOP OF DAM EXIT (WEST)

Shortcut west of Geldard Drive

Grid Reference: I 16

Heading: West (shown) or east

Description: After crossing the top of the dam (as shown), or heading in from the White Mountain area, break this fence and enter the shortcut to (or from) South Mountain Drive.

88. TOP OF DAM EXIT (NORTHWEST)

Shortcut north of Geldard Drive

Grid Reference: I 16

Heading: Northwest (shown) or southeast

Description: After crossing the top of the dam (as shown), or driving the tarmac shortcut by the lake, bust open these fence sections. You'll enter (or come from) White Mountain.

89, 90. DAM TUNNEL

Shortcut between Casey Pass and Manners

Grid Reference: K 16

Heading: Northeast (shown) or southwest

Description: Either route is just as feasible. From the base of the dam (and Super Jump #10), drive through the arrow chevrons, into the tunnel, and into Smash #89.

The last smash in Harbor Town is at the upper end of the tunnel, as you merge onto Manners.

NEIGHBORHOOD 4: WHITE MOUNTAIN

LANDMARKS AND THOROUGHFARES: SUNSET VALLEY

1 FRANKIE'S CAMPGROUND (SOUTH ENTRANCE/EXIT)

This campground's northern area is in Silver Lake, but this area provides great access onto Nelson Way from Cannon Pass, and there are multiple paths to choose from, including a drop you can only access heading north.

2 BASE OF THE VISTA

This is the base of the gigantic mountain you can zoom to the top of. A small river empties out into Silver Lake, and Nelson Way continues southwest. Head up here to reach Uphill Drive, and the way to the Wind Farm.

3 PARADISE WOODS

This peaceful and quaint water mill, with housing among the trees, is near the base of the vista. Chubb Lane stretches southeast to Lone Peaks Quarry, Hans Way, and the junkyard.

4 CHUBB LANE CHALETS

It's difficult to make out the line of wooden chalet-style homes above these shortcut paths that enable you to cut the corner of Chubb and West Lake Drive. The stadium is just east of here.

5 FIRST STEEL BRIDGE AND PROMONTORY

West Lake Drive, before you reach the junction of Cannon Pass where the road becomes East Lake Drive and heads into Silver Lake, has two steel bridges. It's important to remember that the first (western) one has one span.

6 SECOND STEEL BRIDGE

The second steel bridge has two spans, and a rickety bridge on the eastern side. You can access the top of the bridge, but only if you're heading southwest and take one of the two ramps.

7 VISTA RUN (NELSON WAY TO UPHILL DRIVE)

This section shows the lower reaches of the vista, with the wind turbines just visible. Cruise up or down here if you want to reach the train tracks and the start of Uphill Drive, or you're heading down towards Frankie's Campground.

8 BASE OF UPHILL DRIVE

Uphill Drive is a series of severe switchbacks, and the base can be seen on the top left of this picture. The train tracks heading north or south make an excellent shortcut. The billboard on the right of this picture is at the bottom of a series of drops—the quickest and most spectacular method to descend from the Wind Farm!

9 GRACE'S NORTH LAKE BAIT SHOP

Instead of looking at the map, and perhaps messing up your turn onto Uphill Drive, check the eastern side of Nelson Way. The giant trout atop this fishing shop is your cue to swerve and head west, up the switchbacks.

10 END OF THE TRAIN TRACKS

Make preparations to drop onto Nelson Way, either via a super jump over the gas station, or by driving over the tracks and off the wall before you reach the carriages blocking your path. You can rejoin the train tracks at the Lone Stallion Ranch to the southwest.

⓫ LUCAS WAY JUNCTION

This junction is used relatively frequently if you're trying to quickly reach the Lone Stallion Ranch. Look for the gray bridge (the train tracks can't be accessed) as a landmark.

⓬ SUNSET VALLEY BASEBALL PARK

This baseball park is the first of two large landmarks that you cannot access in Sunset Valley. It's near the junction of West Lake Drive and Chubb Lane.

⓭ SUNSET VALLEY STADIUM

This is the other large landmark that you can't drive into. This stadium indicates that you're halfway along this section of Chubb Lane (to the east) or West Lake Drive (to the west). Try the shortcut running by the eastern perimeter.

⓮ SILVER LAKE MOBILE HOME PARK

You can't access this old mobile home park with stunning views of Silver Lake, but you can spot

the trailers as you speed along Chubb. The gas station is just south of here.

⓯ KWIKI 24 HOUR MART

This serves the patrons of the trailer park just to the north, and is also attached to the gas station. It's out of the way, and one of the buildings you encounter throughout Sunset Valley.

⓰ LAKESIDE RAMPS AND DROPS

Access these three jumps via a shortcut along West Lake Drive to the south. They can increase your boost and cut the intersection of Chubb and West Lake. Remember that there are two jumps northward, and only one southward.

NOTE

Landmarks 17–28 provide Sunset Valley's inhabitants with a variety of goods and services. They are all shown so you can easily spot where you are, and how far you are from a road or shortcut you need to reach.

⓱ SUNSET VALLEY: KING LAM'S BBQ GRILL

⓲ SUNSET VALLEY: 8-BALL POOL HALL

⓳ SUNSET VALLEY: WAR MEMORIAL (UNDER CONSTRUCTION)

⓴ SUNSET VALLEY: PARADISE CITY DINER

㉑ SUNSET VALLEY: LAKE VIEW HOTEL

㉒ SUNSET VALLEY: TAD'S CAR RENTAL

23 SUNSET VALLEY: PARADISE CITY MOTEL AND BARRY'S LIGHT FITTINGS

24 SUNSET VALLEY: PENNEN'S POWER TOOLS

25 SUNSET VALLEY: NORTH LAKE LODGE

26 THOMASSEN'S HARDWARE AND ADDIS CAMPING SUPPLIES

27 SUNSET VALLEY: MURCH SECURITY SERVICES AND MAXIE'S DINER

28 SUNSET VALLEY: THE BOAT HOUSE

29 TINDLE'S MINE

Although not exactly a shortcut along the southern area of Chubb Lane, the mine workings to the west allow a slightly better racing line if you follow the off-road areas from and to Hans Way (south) and Schembri Pass (north).

30 THE OLD STATION

Remember this old building so you know where you are. The patch of earth it sits on is surrounded by an intersection and a train track you can't drive on.

30 SUNSET VALLEY: NICOLA'S NATURE STORE

A small row of terraced houses and some stores are on the other side of the road from the junkyard.

32 LONE PEAKS QUARRY: LOOKING SOUTH

The Lone Peaks Quarry is the biggest of all the "hidden" areas that aren't visible on your map. From this view, you can see the quarry is a large playground with a looping circular perimeter path.

33 LONE PEAKS QUARRY: LOOKING WEST

This view is just above the entrance, which is on South Mountain Drive. If you look closely, you'll see a second entrance/exit, and a river segmenting the quarry into two different zones.

34 LONE PEAKS QUARRY: LOOKING NORTH

This is perhaps the most useful view of the quarry, as you can see the two towers you can leap through, the ramps on either side of the river, and much of the perimeter road. Note that there are three ways to exit this place, and two to enter (which are revealed in the Discoveries section).

35 RD DINER

West Lake Drive has a large number of stores, but the RD Diner is just south of them, as you're about to head into Sunset Valley. Don't forget the shortcut behind the houses, just north of here.

36 HILLS HOTEL

This small hotel is on the western side of the road opposite the RD Diner. Cut through the large front parking lot when traveling to or from the lakeside route to the top of the dam.

> **NOTE**
>
> Landmarks 37–42 provide the inhabitants of the area with a variety of goods and services. They are all shown so you can easily spot where you are, and how far you are from a road or shortcut you need to reach.

37 SUNSET VALLEY: NEWTON'S AND TOURIST BOARD

38 SUNSET VALLEY: HUNTLEY'S TOOL SHACK AND GOODWIN GOODS

39 SUNSET VALLEY: CROPPERS COMMUNITY HOUSE

40 SUNSET VALLEY: PARADISE CITY PIZZA AND THE CAFFEINE HIT

41 SUNSET VALLEY: BAKER'S HOME IMPROVEMENTS AND SHIRE'S SHOE REPAIRS

42 SUNSET VALLEY: LIBRARY AND CONSERVATION MUSEUM

43 SOUTH OVER SILVER LAKE

This unnamed road runs parallel to West Lake Drive and offers a quicker way to maneuver between West Lake just south of Sunset Valley's town and the Rockridge Dam in Harbor Town.

LANDMARKS AND THOROUGHFARES: LONE PEAKS

44 CLIFFTOP PLUNGE

As revealed in the Discoveries section, this part of South Mountain Drive road offers not only a shortcut to the base below, but prime barrel rolling opportunities! This is a key shortcut!

45. LONE STALLION RANCH FINISHING PLACE

This is the southwestern finishing place for all of your racing events. Note the location of the red sign, east of Lucas Way and just off the shortcut leading from the train tracks.

46 THE LONE STONE STALLION

The actual stone statue of the stallion at the Lone Stallion Ranch is just west of the finishing place. Keep going west from here to reach the stock car grounds.

47 LONELY ACORNS TRAILER PARK

Although you aren't initially aware of this, the trailer park just north of the Lone Stallion Ranch finishing point overlooks the quarry, but you can't reach it from here. However, the shortcut is excellent to take if you're accelerating south on Lucas Way toward the finish!

48 PARADISE DINER

Another Paradise Diner, this one is at a little-used intersection that allows access from Lucas to Hans Way, and the main South Mountain Drive route to and from the Wind Farm or Schembri Pass.

49 PARADISE CITY STOCK CAR TRACK (LOOKING SOUTH)

White Mountain is full of secrets, and this one is an entire mud-filled, figure-eight stock car track! Head here to test your car's drifting abilities.

50 PARADISE CITY STOCK CAR TRACK (LOOKING NORTHWEST)

Looking at this hidden area to the north, you can see the small "8" section. This track only has one entrance and exit, and it's used for simply messing about on, and for online Free-burn Challenges.

51 WHITE MOUNTAIN LOOKOUT: ADAM'S WATCHTOWER SIGN

Although Adam's Watchtower is never seen, this sign is the real entrance to the most mountainous drive in Paradise City. It is also close to the junction with Hans Way.

52 MOUNTAIN BARN

You can drive through this barn, on the northern side of the junction with Hans Way, but don't forget the shortcut to the left, which increases your boost with a ramp, too.

53 TOURIST CENTER AND DINER

This is one of the few dotted buildings along the massive winding South and North Mountain Drive, which scales the entire north/south part of the western area of Paradise City.

54 CANNON'S CAVERNS

The caverns aren't open, but you can fly through one of the natural openings if you take the four separate ledge drops from Schembri Pass all the way to the ledge behind this building.

55 SCHEMBRI PASS LOOKOUT

Heading down Schembri Pass is much quicker than ascending it if you drive off this tarmac vista point and then drop down onto the pass itself.

56 THE BED AND BREAKFAST

This quaint Victorian building is at the junction of Lucas Way and Schembri Pass, and close to another jump down to the base of Schembri Pass, to the east.

LANDMARKS AND THOROUGH-FARES: CRYSTAL SUMMIT

57 WHITE MOUNTAIN SKI RESORT

Over on South Mountain Drive, the winding road continues and passes this ski resort, which cannot be entered. However, you can take a shortcut leading to and from the Wind Farm for a quick boost and a quicker route.

58. WIND FARM FINISHING PLACE

This finishing place has three separate roads that meet it: North and South Mountain Drives, and the infamous Uphill Drive itself. As you can see, planning your racing route here is of paramount importance!

59 UPHILL DRIVE DROPS (UPPER)

Study the two sets of drops carefully. They allow you to descend Uphill Drive to the train tracks below in incredible, record time! However, you must enter the top drop in a straight line.

60 UPHILL DRIVE DROPS (LOWER)

After the first set of drops, you land on the road itself, but you can quickly drop off the gap in the barrier to another set of drops and make your escape. Stunt action is assured!

61 WIND FARMS GAP

Just north of the Wind Farms finishing place is a gap in a rocky outcrop that's great for collecting more boost, especially if you're driving south and you're about to hit the finish line.

62 YELLOW STEEL BRIDGE

This bridge has a billboard accessed via a ramp to the north, and on the east side is a rough road with a super jump gap. This is part of the

train route throughout White Mountain, which stretches all the way into Silver Lake to the east.

63 DOUBLE BILLBOARD JUMP

Just northeast of the yellow bridge, but west of the suspension bridge in Silver Lake, are a couple of large shacks and a small carriage yard. Avoid the carriages, or choose either jump if you need the boost.

64 CLIFF JUMP TO TRAIN TRACKS

One of the key reasons for driving up the winding Read Lane is the monstrous super jump you can take off it, onto the train tracks below. You can then head southwest or east.

65 READ LANE RADIO MAST

This small radio mast area is at the junction of Read Lane, North Mountain, and North Rouse. Use it to remember that this is the three-way junction, and that you're near the observatory.

66 DEAD MAN'S JUMP

This fearsome gap allows you to avoid the looping road of North Mountain Drive (which you should at every opportunity). Approach at speed, because falling short leads to an embarrassing plummet!

67 RD DINER

This RD Diner is perched precariously over the eastern part of Dead Man's Jump. Use it as a marker to aim for before you can properly see the jump itself.

CRYSTAL SUMMIT OBSERVATORY: FINISHING PLACE

This is your northwestern finishing place. The observatory is above the road itself, but off-road trails (see map) allow you to take different paths to this goal. Remember this!

DRIVETHRU LOCATIONS*

DRIVETHRUS

DRIVETHRU TYPE	SUNSET VALLEY	LONE PEAKS	CRYSTAL SUMMIT	TOTAL
Auto Repairs	2	0	0	2
Gas Stations	2	1	0	3
Paint Shops	1	0	0	1
Junkyards	0	1	0	1
Grand Total	5	2	0	7

*There are no parking structures in White Mountain

5. LONE PEAKS

South Mountain Drive
Grid Reference: E 19

AUTO REPAIR SHOPS

1. SUNSET VALLEY (NORTH)

West Lake and Chubb
Grid Reference: E 8/9

2. SUNSET VALLEY (SOUTH)

Schembri Pass and Chubb
Grid Reference: F 13

GAS STATIONS

3. SUNSET VALLEY (NORTH)

Nelson Way, in front of train tracks
Grid Reference: D 9

4. SUNSET VALLEY (SOUTH)

Chubb Lane
Grid Reference: G 11

PAINT SHOPS

6. SUNSET VALLEY

West Lake and Cannon Pass
Grid Reference: F 7

JUNKYARDS

7. LONE PEAKS

Hans Way, Grid Reference: G 15

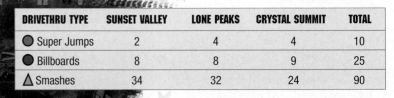

DISCOVERIES

DRIVETHRU TYPE	SUNSET VALLEY	LONE PEAKS	CRYSTAL SUMMIT	TOTAL
● Super Jumps	2	4	4	10
● Billboards	8	8	9	25
△ Smashes	34	32	24	90

NOTE

Some of the super jumps, billboards, and smashes are on the border between two different areas, and may appear in one or the other (or different from this guide) on your in-game map.

● SUPER JUMPS: SUNSET VALLEY

☐ 1. ACROSS THE BROKEN BRIDGE

Shortcut east of West Lake
Grid Reference: F 8
Barrel Roll Available: No
Heading: Northeast or southwest (southwest shown)
Description: Crash through either Smash #8 or 9, and drive parallel to the red steel bridge, until you reach the broken area just east of the structure. Simply accelerate and land without incident.

☐ 2. UP ON THE ROOF

Train tracks west of Nelson Way
Grid Reference: D 8/9
Barrel Roll Available: No
Heading: Southeast
Description: Head south, along the railroad tracks, under the Uphill Drive junction with Nelson Way. Once under that bridge, keep left, head up the narrow ramped path, and launch over the building, passing over the gas station. Keep your speed up and land on the parking lot, then set yourself up for Billboard #3.

SUPER JUMPS: LONE PEAKS

3. LONE PEAKS QUARRY: RAMP SPECTACULAR

Quarry north and west of South Mountain
Grid Reference: H 16
Barrel Roll Available: Yes
Heading: West
Description: Crash through Smash #40 or 41, and stay in a straight line heading west, toward the ramp, and fly off it. You can spend seconds in the air, dropping into this massive, off-road quarry! Don't forget to try barrel rolls off this ramp; it's one of the best places in the entire City to perfect this technique!

4. BEST BARREL ROLL IN THE CITY!
South Mountain

Grid Reference: I 17
Barrel Roll Available: Yes
Heading: Southeast
Description: If you want sheer terror, or the thrill of falling hundreds of feet (while optionally barrel rolling!), head south along South Mountain Drive, and locate the super jump off the cliffs. Remember that you must land the jump to claim the super jump! This is not only a fantastic shortcut, but one of the best places of all to try barrel rolls. How many can you do?

5. SOUTH MOUNTAIN JUMPS

South Mountain
Grid Reference: B 13
Barrel Roll Available: No
Heading: South
Description: To achieve this, you must first complete Billboard #15 and 16. Land on the ledge just after crashing through Billboard #15, and drive to the end of it, where the super jump is. Stay at top speed, because you must fly through the hole in the mountain and land on the final ledge opposite for this jump to count. Then drop off the ledge onto South Mountain Drive itself.

6. SOARING OVER SCHEMBRI PASS

Lucas and Schembri
Grid Reference: E 12

Barrel Roll Available: No
Heading: East
Description: One of the least-used roads is the winding Schembri Pass, but don't let that put you off taking this super jump, which is well-hidden on a path just north of the junction with Lucas Way. Swerve east at the billboard (#17), accelerate over the lower portion of the pass, and land on the rough dirt path (picture 2). This is the only time you'll ever drive on this, because you drop off lower down and can't drive back onto it without taking the super jump again.

SUPER JUMPS: CRYSTAL SUMMIT

7. DOWNHILL ON UPHILL: SUPER JUMP

Uphill
Grid Reference: C 8
Barrel Roll Available: No
Heading: Northeast
Description: Crash through Smash #71, and begin a couple of nasty drops. Keep your vehicle at speed but heading straight, and land the jump with the flashing cones. Drop onto the gap between Smashes #73 and 76.

8. DEAD MAN'S CURVE

Shortcut off North Mountain
Grid Reference: C 4

Barrel Roll Available: No
Heading: Northeast or southwest (northeast shown)
Description: This exciting and terrifying jump is slightly easier if you approach heading southwest from the observatory (this gives you more height when you leap). Simply accelerate like a maniac, shoot off the stone ramp—ignoring the switchback to the west—and hope you have enough speed to land on the opposite side!

9. BROKEN BRIDGE BY YELLOW BRIDGE

Train tracks north of Nelson
Grid Reference: D 5
Barrel Roll Available: No
Heading: North or south (south shown)

Description: On the opposite side of the tracks is a ramp to the top of the bridge and Billboard #23, but on the eastern side is a gap in the road next to the bridge that must be jumped. You can attempt it from either direction.

10. TRAIN TRACK DESCENT

Train tracks west of Read
Grid Reference: E 3/4
Barrel Roll Available: Yes
Heading: West
Description: You must be travelling along Read Lane, either from the junction with Nelson Way, or down from North Rouse and North Mountain.

Approach the middle of Read Lane and look for the jump, with two barrel roll ramps on either side (picture 1). You don't need to be traveling quickly, but you do need to land the super jump with all four wheels on the ground, on the train tracks below.

● BILLBOARDS: SUNSET VALLEY

1. BASE OF THE VISTA POINT

Ramp near Nelson and Chubb
Grid Reference: D 6
Heading: Northeast or southwest (southwest shown)
Description: Attack this ramped area at the base of the Vista Point section of Nelson Way in either direction. You need to hit Smashes #13 and 14 to enter and exit.

2. RAMP ONTO BRIDGE

Bridge along West Lake Drive
Grid Reference: F 7
Heading: Southwest
Description: This billboard is unique because there are two separate ramps in the same direction that you can take to reach it. The first is the overhanging ramp on the shortcut north of West Lake Drive. Zoom off it (picture 1) and land on the bridge. The second ramp is on West Lake itself (picture 2). Hit the ramp head-

ing southwest, land on the bridge, and head through the billboard. Watch out! This ramp is only available on the north side of the bridge!

3. PARKING LOT LAUNCH

Shortcut between Nelson and the tracks
Grid Reference: D 9
Heading: Southeast
Description: After you make Super Jump #2 and launch over the gas station on Nelson, land on the parking lot and keep your vehicle straight. You must hit another ramp straight on so you pass through this billboard. This one may take a few tries!

4. END OF THE LINE

Shortcut between Nelson and the tracks
Grid Reference: D 10
Heading: Southeast
Description: The end of the train tracks (in this part of White Mountain at least; they can next be accessed near the Lone Stallion Ranch) pushes you east, toward a dirt ramp leading to another billboard, and a landing on Nelson Way below.

5. BANKED LEDGE

Drop west of West Lake
Grid Reference: E 10
Heading: South

Description: Drive at speed through Smash #10 from Chubb Lane, and continue keeping right, over the hump, and down the long gravel drive. Ignore the path split on your left, and stay on the ledge until you hit the billboard, and land on West Lake.

6. LAKESIDE LEDGE

Shortcut east of Chubb
Grid Reference: G 11/12
Heading: North or south (north shown)
Description: This is only accessible if you're driving south on Chubb and you exit Smash #26, or pass the gas station, and then veer left, toward and up the ledge, through the billboard, and onto the shortcut overlooking Silver Lake.

7. ALLEY OOPS!

Ramp above Chubb and West Lake
Grid Reference: F 12
Heading: South
Description: Begin a speedy dash southeast toward the intersection of Chubb and West Lake, but make sure you hit Smash #23, and enter the alley running parallel to it. Then shift to the south and over the ramp, dropping through the billboard and onto the intersection area itself. Try steering into the next shortcut, by Smash #30.

8. BACK STREET BASH

Alley west of West Lake
Grid Reference: G 12/13
Heading: South
Description: Make sure you enter the alley behind the shops at the junction of Chubb and West Lake, as the billboard requires a ramp that is north of the billboard itself. You'll pass under the billboard and then hit the ramp if you're driving north.

● BILLBOARDS: LONE PEAKS

9. DAM BUILDING ROOF

Shortcut near West Lake
Grid Reference: H/I 15
Heading: Northwest or southeast (southeast shown)
Description: This can be approached from either direction. If you're coming in from White Mountain, try hitting Smash #33 first. Whichever direction you take, steer onto a ramp and up onto the dam building. The billboard is at the southern end.

10. LONE PEAKS QUARRY: WORKINGS RAMP

Quarry north and west of South Mountain
Grid Reference: G 16
Heading: North or south (south shown)
Description: Whether you're playing in the north or south quarry areas, get a good run-up to the quarry workings towers and the large ramp leading to a gap across the water. Be at top speed as you jump the gap to the opposite tower, and crash through the billboard in the process.

11. LONE PEAKS QUARRY: OUTER ROAD

DROP 1
Quarry north and west of South Mountain
Grid Reference: H 16
Heading: North
Description: This billboard is high up above the eastern part of the quarry interior, and accessible only if you're driving counterclockwise around the quarry perimeter. When you see the ledge pointing at the billboard, accelerate off it, landing on the northern quarry interior ground.

12. LONE PEAKS QUARRY: OUTER ROAD

DROP 2
Quarry north and west of South Mountain
Grid Reference: G/H 17
Heading: Southwest
Description: This billboard is on the southern interior ground area, but isn't accessible from there. Instead, drive clockwise around the quarry perimeter, and when you see this ledge (picture 1), drive onto it and steer right ever so slightly. You'll fall through the billboard as long as you're traveling fast. This one is tricky; it takes a couple of attempts!

13. CLIFFSIDE JUMP

South Mountain
Grid Reference: E 18
Heading: North or south (north shown)
Description: This billboard is between Smashes #54 and 55, above South Mountain Drive and just north of the gas station. You must approach via the dirt cliffside road.

14. DIRT TRACK NEAR THE BARN

South Mountain
Grid Reference: C 15
Heading: Northwest or southeast (northwest shown)
Description: Instead of heading through the junction with Hans Way, ignore it and steer to the west, into this shortcut that not only cuts the corner, but allows you to split open this billboard, next to the barn that's on South Mountain Drive itself.

15. SOUTH MOUNTAIN LEAPS (SOUTH)

South Mountain
Grid Reference: B 12
Heading: South
Description: Complete the plan for smashing Billboard #16 first. When you land on the ledge beyond, keep straight and drive off the end of the ledge, flying over South Mountain, onto another ledge (picture 1). Accelerate across this ledge keeping south, and when it drops away, leap this gap (picture 2) into the billboard. Land on the next ledge if you want to attempt Super Jump #5.

16. SOUTH MOUNTAIN LEAPS (NORTH)

South Mountain
Grid Reference: B 11
Heading: South
Description: This is the beginning of some crazed leaping above the main South Mountain Road. Begin by heading south down the maintenance route shortcut from Smash #70. When you reach the junction shown, drive up the ramp, through the billboard, and land on the upper ledge beyond. You can now access Billboard #15.

● BILLBOARDS: CRYSTAL SUMMIT

17. SAILING OVER SCHEMBRI

Shortcut east of Lucas and Schembri

Grid Reference: D 12
Heading: North
Description: Crush this billboard, near the intersection of Lucas Way and Schembri Pass, after you enter the shortcut to the south, heading north through Smash #66. Drive off a concrete ramp into the billboard.

18. DOWNHILL ON UPHILL: BILLBOARD

Uphill
Grid Reference: C 8
Heading: Northeast
Description: Crash through Smash #71, complete Super Jump #7, hit Smash #76, and then continue down the last set of drops to this billboard, which overlooks the train tracks and Nelson Way. Drop off this last area.

19. UPHILL STRUGGLE

Shortcut at Uphill and Nelson
Grid Reference: C/D 8
Heading: South
Description: Unless you have a fast-accelerating car, make a very long run-up, ideally from the northern train tracks. Speed south, lining up for the dirt ramp, and sail over the tracks, through the billboard, and onto Uphill Drive.

20. BY THE WIND TURBINE

Shortcut off North Mountain
Grid Reference: B 8

Heading: North or south (north shown)
Description: Whether you're heading to or from the Wind Farm, line up the leap across the cliff near the giant wind turbine. The billboard is between the stone ramps on either side.

21. OFF THE LONG LEDGE

Train tracks north of Nelson
Grid Reference: C 6/7
Heading: South
Description: Drive at speed south from the yellow bridge on the train tracks, and steer to the right (picture 1) at the wooden shack that spans the tracks. Follow a long ledge along the right cliff wall. At the end of the wall is a gap and a billboard (picture 2). You need top speed to reach this.

22. DIRT ROAD FALL

Shortcut off North Mountain
Grid Reference: B 5
Heading: South
Description: Drive along North Mountain and pass by Smash #82. Steer left as you spot this entrance to the dirt path, and look for the billboard. Drop off the side of North Mountain Drive at a narrow angle so you pass through the billboard and land on the dirt road.

23. FOLLOW THE YELLOW BRIDGE ROAD

Train tracks west of Read
Grid Reference: C/D 5
Heading: South
Description: After negotiating the barns, keep right as you approach a yellow steel arched bridge. Steer right, through a rickety barn, and up onto a ramp. Take the ramp onto the roof of the bridge, and steer through the billboard up here. Super Jump #9 is on the left side of this bridge.

24. TRAIN BARN STORMING (NORTH)

Train tracks west of Read
Grid Reference: D 4
Heading: Southwest
Description: Drive through the tunnel from the train suspension bridge in Silver Lake, and locate the two barns. Swerve right, through Smash #84, and drive up the ramped ledge and through the billboard.

25. TRAIN BARN STORMING (SOUTH)

Train tracks west of Read
Grid Reference: D 4
Heading: Southwest
Description: Drive through the tunnel from the train suspension bridge in Silver Lake, and locate the two barns. Swerve left, through Smash #85, and drive up the ramped ledge and through the billboard.

⚠ SMASHES: SUNSET VALLEY

1. INTO SILVER LAKE MARINA
Shortcut south of East Lake and Cannon Pass
Grid Reference: F 7
Heading: East or west (east shown)
Description: On the border with Silver Lake, the marina can be reached after you cross the Marina shortcut, or if you enter (as shown) from the junction as East Lake Drive becomes West Lake Drive.

2, 3, 4. CLEARING FRANKIE'S CAMPGROUND
Shortcut east of Cannon Pass
Grid Reference: E 6
Heading: North or south (north shown)
Description: Frankie's Campground is another area that has part of its run in Silver Lake (the billboard and the fences at the northern entrance/exit). However, this southern entrance/exit is in White Mountain. Use your ramming speed! There is a second entrance/exit farther north, along Cannon Pass. This makes another good shortcut to reach Nelson Way, heading east. The third entrance/exit along Cannon Pass offers the smallest of shortcuts, and a direct route to the Silver Lake billboard. Remember that this campground also has a stone outcrop you can drop off, but only when you're heading north.

5, 6, 7. SHORTCUT ACROSS FROM THE PAINT SHOP
Shortcut at West Lake and Cannon
Grid Reference: F 7
Heading: North or south (south shown)
Description: If you're heading down Cannon Pass or along West Lake Drive, and want to cut the inside corner onto Cannon, use this small shortcut, which has two entrances (if you're heading south). The first is on Cannon itself. The second shortcut provides easier access to the crisscrossing shortcut to the ramp and Billboard #2. Approach it across from the parking lot, next to West Lake Drive.
The exit onto West Lake occurs after a short dip in the dirt path. You reach a bridge, but you can also cut across the road and enter the bridge with Super Jump #1 nearby.

8. 9. ACCESSING THE BROKEN BRIDGE
Shortcut east of West Lake
Grid Reference: E/F 7/8
Heading: Northeast or southwest (southwest shown)
Description: This shortcut allows you to gain boost as you fly over Super Jump #1, and you have a good racing line (if you're heading north) to Smash #7, and that shortcut beyond. If you're heading south, crash through this fence. Accelerate so you complete Super Jump #1, and once on the other side, drive along the concrete path and out onto West Lake Drive itself.

10, 11. CUTTING THE CORNER AT CHUBB

Shortcut at West Lake and Chubb

Grid Reference: E 9

Heading: North or south (south shown)

Description: If you're approaching the junction of Chubb Lane and West Lake Drive, you can cut the corner here, hitting Smash #10 or 11 first, depending on the direction you're traveling. Smash #10 allows you to take the longer shortcut far along West Lake to the south, and exit either into Smash #20, or Billboard #5. Smash #11 (shown here) offers a quick way to and from these roads.

12. HEADING TO VISTA POINT

Shortcut north of Nelson and Cannon

Grid Reference: D/E 5

Heading: Northeast or southwest (southwest shown)

Description: The end of the dirt road that runs alongside Nelson Way at the border with Silver Lake ends with this fence, across from Frankie's Campground.

13, 14. THE BASE OF VISTA POINT (RAMP)

Shortcut at Nelson and Chubb

Grid Reference: D 6

Heading: Northeast or southwest (southwest shown)

Description: This shortcut allows you to smash through the first billboard in White Mountain, and sets you up to climb the switchback section of Nelson Way. Enter from either direction.

Once you've driven up the ramp, smashed the billboard, and landed on the other side, you can exit onto Nelson Way. If you're heading southwest, you can head onto the natural overhang (Smash #15) almost immediately.

15. CLIMBING VISTA POINT: DIRT OVERHANG

Shortcut on Nelson

Grid Reference: D 6

Heading: Northeast or southwest (southwest shown)

Description: Just after Smash #14, you can swerve left, onto this muddy bank, and drive up and over the overhang, landing on the shortcut on the opposite side of Nelson Way. Or, you can approach the area near Smashes #16 and 17 (or the train tracks) and attempt to get enough air to land on the overhang, but this is almost Impossible.

16, 17. CLIMBING VISTA POINT: DIRT TRACK TO TRAIN TRACKS

Shortcut on Nelson

Grid Reference: C/D 7

Heading: North or south (south shown)

Description: If you're heading away from the vista drop, or toward the patch of off-road earth linking Nelson Way to the rail tracks, quicken your pace by heading through this shortcut. You might miss Smash #16 if you landed on

this area from the overhang, so double-check to make sure you didn't. Obviously, this is also a good shortcut to take in preparation for driving toward the ramp where Billboard #1 is.

18. TRAIN SHED

Shortcut on Nelson

Grid Reference: C 7

Heading: North or south (south shown)

Description: The train tracks mark the border between Sunset Valley and Crystal Summit, and this is on the cusp of both areas. Drive into the shed, either from the dirt patch near Nelson Way, or from the train tracks.

19. SUNSET VALLEY STADIUM: A CLOSER LOOK (NORTH)

Shortcut west of Chubb

Grid Reference: F 10

Heading: North or south (south shown)

Description: This is an entrance or exit, and the fence at the opposite end of the shortcut is Smash #26. This allows you to enter the path next to the stadium (the stadium can't be entered). It shaves time off the curve in Chubb Lane.

20. THE CHUBB SHORTCUT REVISITED

Shortcut near West Lake and Chubb

Grid Reference: E 10

Heading: North or south (south shown)

Description: This smash is at the southern end of the shortcut that begins on the corner of Chubb and West Lake (Smash #10). Continue along this gravel path, and elect to hit the billboard on the banked ledge exit to the right, or this small fence. This is a good shortcut if you're heading north toward Nelson, too.

21, 22, 23, 24, 25. A DASH INTO (OR OUT OF) TOWN

Shortcut between Nelson and West Lake

Grid Reference: E/F 10/11

Heading: Northwest or southeast (southeast shown)

Description: Use this cluster of shortcuts to access the main street in Sunset Valley (West Lake Drive). Or if you're heading northwest, out of town, use it to make a quick escape onto Nelson to avoid the Y-shaped intersection. Access Smash #21 near the junction with Lucas; drive onto the grassy dirt, and a second later, crash through Smash #22 (shown), onto West Lake itself. You can stop the shortcut now, or continue.

As you cross West Lake Drive, you can optionally stay on the main road as you go under the archway sign, or you can drive left, into the fenced alley. This gives you a good run-up to Billboard #7.

This smash occurs a second after Smash #23, and allows you a straight shot down the alley parallel to West Lake, avoiding the central islands and traffic.

Or, you can swerve into (or out of) this shortcut via West Lake, and join the alley just southeast of Smash #24. Accelerate to the ramp and Billboard #7. Remember to try these shortcuts in the opposite direction, too!

26. SUNSET VALLEY STADIUM: A CLOSER LOOK (SOUTH)

Shortcut west of Chubb

Grid Reference: G 11

Heading: North or south (south shown)

Description: This is an entrance or exit, and the fence at the opposite end of the shortcut is Smash #19. This allows you to enter the path next to the stadium (the stadium can't be entered). It shaves time off the curve in Chubb Lane.

27. SOUTH END OF THE STADIUM

Shortcut at West Lake and Chubb

Grid Reference: G 12

Heading: Northeast or southwest (southwest shown)

Description: The end of the alley that starts at Smash #23 (to the northwest) allows you to either take the ramp to the south (Billboard #7), or drift around to the north, and head out onto Chubb. Again, this cuts out the Chubb/West Lake intersection.

28, 29. LAKE SIDE PASSAGE (NORTHERN ENTRANCES/EXITS)

Shortcut by West Lake and Chubb

Grid Reference: G 12

Heading: North or south (north shown)

Description: The pictures show the vehicle exiting this area, onto West Lake Drive, after beginning this shortcut at Smash #32. This allows you to avoid the traffic islands and congestion of the West Lake and Chubb interchange. Smash #29 (shown) can be entered heading north only. The shortcut ends with a ledge—leap off it, gain boost, land on Chubb, and accelerate up past the stadium. This is an excellent plan if you're heading north!

30, 31. IN-TOWN ALLEYWAY

Shortcut at West Lake and Chubb

Grid Reference: F/G 12/13

Heading: Northwest or southeast (southeast shown)

Description: Take this route if you need a couple of small ramps to help your boost, and you want to avoid the congestion of the in-town road. Swerve into this fence, behind the shop fronts. After tearing down this alley, you can smash Billboard #8 (only heading southeast), and venture back onto West Lake Drive, which is now clear of the segmented traffic islands it had to the north.

32. LAKE SIDE PASSAGE (SOUTHERN ENTRANCE/EXIT)

Shortcut at West Lake

Grid Reference: G 13

Heading: North or south (north shown)

Description: Use this as an exit onto West Lake if you used the ramp to the north, crashed through Billboard #6, and used this shortcut. Or, you can head north (as shown), and take either Smash #28 or 29 (which is preferred as it has a ledge you can fly off for more boost), onto Chubb Lane.

33. EXPLORING THE DAM
Shortcut at West Lake
Grid Reference: G 13/14
Heading: Northwest or southeast (southeast shown)
Description: Head across the parking lot, passing the Hills Hotel on your left, and smash the fence to enter another section of West Lake Drive, which winds along Silver Lake to the dam in Harbor Town. There's a dam building with Billboard #9 to smash. Or, use this to exit into the parking lot.

34, 35. DIRT TRACK
Shortcut at South Mountain, Hans, and West Lake
Grid Reference: G/H 14/15
Heading: North or south (south shown)
Description: These two smashes allow you to avoid the curved section of West Lake Drive as it finishes at the junction with Hans Way and South Mountain Drive.
As you exit, you have a much better view of the intersection, and can quickly check which route you want to take next. Remember that you're close to the junkyard on Hans. Also, this a great shortcut to take northwards, heading into Sunset Valley village. Note that Smash #35 is technically in Lone Peaks.

⚠ SMASHES: LONE PEAKS

36, 37, 38, 39. TINDLE'S MINE ADVENTURE
Shortcut across Hans and Chubb
Grid Reference: E/F 13-15
Heading: Northwest to northeast or southeast to southwest (northwest to northeast shown)
Description: This entire series of shortcuts can be attempted in the opposite direction from the auto repair shop on Chubb Lane. Or, you can elect to use Smash #36 and 37 separately, and cut the corner of Hans and Chubb.
Assuming you're heading northwest, break through the previous Smash (#36), and head along the undulating dirt track to this second fence, bringing you out onto Chubb. The mine entrance/exit is just ahead.
Boost through the mine entrance, which is under the railroad area you cannot access. A moment later, you're in a tunnel, before exiting into the mine buildings area.
Keep your speed up and head into a second tunnel, and then accelerate out of the northern entrance/exit; you're close to the intersection of Chubb and West Lake, near the alleys behind the stores.

40, 41. LONE PEAKS QUARRY ENTRANCE
Off South Mountain
Grid Reference: H 16
Heading: East or west (west shown)
Description: Lone Peaks Quarry is a massive playground that doesn't appear on any in-game map. It's at the northern end of South Mountain Drive, and the entrance is wide.
So wide, in fact, that there are two sets of fences to crash through. Destroy both of them to add to your smashes total. Then take the Super Jump (#3), or drive south into the quarry complex.

42. LONE PEAKS QUARRY: SECRET EXIT
Off South Mountain
Grid Reference: H 16
Heading: East
Description: The north side of the quarry, which is separated by a river, is a vast playground with a road running around the perimeter, and three billboards (#10, 11, 12) to destroy. However, when you want to exit, don't forget this tunnel on the ground, leading into Silver Lake; it brings you out at the base of the dam.

43, 44. LONE PEAKS QUARRY: SOUTHERN ESCAPE
Off South Mountain
Grid Reference: G/H 17
Heading: North or south (south shown)
Description: If you want a quick exit from the ground interior level of the quarry, but want to stay in the White Mountain area, head up the gantry road and into the hillside.
You appear from a tunnel, at one of the lower altitude S-bends along South Mountain Drive! Alternately, head into this route from South Mountain; it's the alternate entrance into the quarry as well.

45. ALTERNATE DAM ROUTE
Off South Mountain, near Geldard
Grid Reference: H 16
Heading: Northwest or southeast (southeast shown)
Description: This short road isn't incorporated into South Mountain Drive or Geldard Drive, and it has a Rockridge Dam sign at its southern entrance/exit. Head through there, and you emerge through a smash in Harbor Town, on top of the dam itself.

46. ROCKRIDGE DAM CONSTRUCTION
South Mountain and Casey
Grid Reference: I 17
Heading: North
Description: This smash is usually destroyed as you attempt to claim the billboard at the northern end of this series of drops through a construction area. The billboard is in Harbor Town, but the entrance and this fence are at the bottom of South Mountain Drive.

47, 48, 49, 50. ON OR OFF THE TRAIN TRACKS
South Mountain
Grid Reference: H 19
Heading: East to west (both shown)
Description: These four fences, just north of the Lone Stallion Ranch area, allow you to enter or exit the railroad tracks. This smash, for example, is shown being struck while heading east. Next stop on the railroad is the suspension bridge in Harbor Town.
Or drive west from South Mountain Drive, through this smash and into this off-road four-way intersection.
A second later, you can crash into this fence, and onto the railroad tracks. However, your run on the rail lines is short-lived; the railroad line is blocked to the west, by Smash #51.
This smash is shown with the vehicle heading west, after crashing through Smash #47 and heading off the railroad. Remember this route in particular for a novel and quick route to the Lone Stallion finishing place!

51, 52. DIRT ROAD RAIL BLOCKING
Railroad and Lucas
Grid Reference: G/H 18/19
Heading: East to west (both shown)
Description: These two smashes allow you access between Lucas Way and the railroad tracks. The tracks themselves are blocked from here, all the way to the area near Billboard #4. Crash through here, and then join Lucas Way, which offers a great alternative up to Uphill Drive. It's also worth checking out as a different route to the Wind Farm, and beyond.

53. PARADISE CITY STOCK CAR RACING TRACK
South Mountain
Grid Reference: G 19
Heading: South
Description: If you wish to explore the looping figure-eight track that doesn't appear on your in-game map, the banked turns are just through here. This area is mostly used for messing about in with your online buddies.

54, 55. CLIFFSIDE PATH (NORTH AND SOUTH)
South Mountain
Grid Reference: F 19 - D 17
Heading: Northwest or southeast (northwest shown)
Description: Over in the southwestern corner of Paradise City, there's a gas station, but if you crave a shortcut instead, make a left before you reach the gas station, and head up a long, straight dirt path.
You leap the road at high speed, destroying Billboard #13, and should land on the other side. Of course, you could steer right and drop

onto the main road; a vertical takedown would be impressive if you can manage it! Rejoin the road by this smash. Remember you can choose this shortcut heading south, too.

56, 57. SHORTCUT CORNER CUT
South Mountain
Grid Reference: C/D 16/17
Heading: North or south (north shown)
Description:
Farther along South Mountain, weaving either north or south, always attempt to cut this corner and save some time during a run. Simply swerve into the inner dirt path…
…and out the other side, heading for the White Mountain Lookout sign. This shortcut has no downsides; you shouldn't even remember what the main South Mountain road looks like!

58, 59. ADAM'S WATCHTOWER: SHORTCUT CORNER CUT
South Mountain
Grid Reference: D 15/16
Heading: East or west (east shown)
Description: Choose this two-fence shortcut to quickly head east on Hans Way or south on South Mountain Drive. This first fence is just after the massive sign for Adam's Watchtower and the White Mountain Lookout.
A second later, you're careening out onto Hans Way, which becomes a severe switchback in a moment.

60, 61. HANS OFF
Shortcut off Hans
Grid Reference: E 16
Heading: North or south (north shown)
Description: White Mountain is full of two-smash shortcuts that remove seconds from your racing times. If you're traversing this section of Hans Way, be sure to look for this fence. A second later, you're out the other side, heading to the Lucas Way and Hans Way junction (or away from it, if you're traveling toward South Mountain Drive).

62, 63. AVOIDING THE BARN
Shortcut west of Hans and South Mountain
Grid Reference: C 15/16
Heading: Northwest or southeast (northwest shown)
Description: Whether you're heading down or up this long winding route, there's no need to stay on the road itself when you can steer west, into this long, narrow dirt road.
A second later, you approach a ramp next to the barn on South Mountain Drive itself. Crash through Billboard #14, and exit via the other smash.

64, 65. LONE SHORTCUT LONE PEAK
Shortcut off Lucas
Grid Reference: D 13-15
Heading: North or south (north shown)
Description: If you're traveling along Lucas Way between Hans Way and the junction with Schembri Pass (or vice versa), be sure you investigate the fence to the side of the road. It leads into an old timber building. Leap through at great speed and emerge at the dirt road and the second smash.

66. START OF THE BILLBOARD RUN
Shortcut off Schembri
Grid Reference: D 13
Heading: North
Description: Trying to figure out how to destroy Billboard #17? Head from east to west, up Schembri Pass, until you reach this fence, and smash through it.

⚠ SMASHES: CRYSTAL SUMMIT

67, 68. START OF THE SOUTH MOUNTAIN BILLBOARD JUMPS
Shortcut off Schembri and North Mountain
Grid Reference: B 11
Heading: North or south (both shown)
Description: South and North Mountain Drives stop at this junction with Schembri. If you're heading south (as shown), you can crash through this smash, or use it to reach the dirt road and go up through the maintenance route. Or, you can hit the ramp (on the left of this picture) and begin a crazed series of jumps! You can also take this smash, and head up the southern part of the maintenance route, all the way to the Wind Farm and Smashes #69 and 70.

69, 70. MAINTENANCE ROUTE TO/FROM THE WIND FARM
Shortcut near North Mountain and Uphill
Grid Reference: B 9/10
Heading: North or south (north shown)
Description: Enter the southern part of this route at Smashes #67 or 68, depending on where you're coming in from. This smash allows you access halfway through the dirt track, or lets you swerve back onto North Mountain if you're heading south.
Pass through the large concrete tube, and head through these fences to reach the Wind Farm, the western finishing place. You can also try the madness of the Uphill drop!

71. DOWNHILL ON UPHILL: 1
Shortcut at North Mountain and Uphill
Grid Reference: B 9
Heading: Northeast
Description: Time for the city's most spectacular series of drops! Begin at the Wind Farm, locate this fence, and crash through it, making sure you're driving straight ahead. Next stop is the mountain air, and Super Jump #7!

72, 73, 74, 75. DOWNHILL ON UPHILL: 2
Shortcut at Uphill
Grid Reference: B/C 8/9
Heading: North or south (north shown)
Description: If the series of spectacularly dangerous drops aren't part of your plan (if you're trying to go uphill to the Wind Farm, for example), consider the two corner-cutting shortcuts, shown here heading downhill.
The first and second fences are on the western side of the road, and cut the slight curve in the main road.
Exit Smash #73 and cross the road; it usually doesn't have much traffic to worry about. Drive onto the dirt corner that cuts out the switchback entirely.
Finally, exit heading southeast; you can swerve left and catch Smash #76, but real elite drivers drop down from the top of the hill! Remember to drive this in both directions and familiarize yourself with the shortcuts; many a race to the Wind Farms has been won using these corners!

76. DOWNHILL ON UPHILL: 3
Shortcut at Uphill
Grid Reference: C 8
Heading: Northeast
Description: Of course, you can enter this smash from Uphill Drive itself, but elite players drop down from Super Jump #7, landing on the looping route (picture 1), and dropping over the gap in the barrier to the road below (picture 2). Then accelerate through the other section of drops. Billboard #18 is just over the train tracks.

77, 78. ONTO THE TRAIN TRACKS
Shortcut on Uphill and Nelson
Grid Reference: C 8
Heading: North or south (north shown)
Description: On the border with Sunset Valley, these two fences are on the western side of the border (near Billboard #19), and can offer access to or from the tracks themselves. Hit the first smash and note the second shortcut to the right of this, allowing you to fly onto the tracks.
At the northern end of the shortcut is a second fence and the train tracks, which can be driven all the way into Silver Lake. Or, you can swerve right, and head down Nelson Way.

79, 80, 81, 82. MOUNTAIN DIRT ROAD
Shortcut off North Mountain
Grid Reference: B 5-7
Heading: North or south (north shown)
Description: You can attempt this in either direction. It's shorter than the main road, but more narrow. Begin (if you're heading north) by smashing this fence just north of Billboard #20. The second opportunity to enter this shortcut is from Smash #80, which is directly above the tunnel you can reach if you took Smash #79. Both shortcuts merge at the north exit of the tunnel, where this smash occurs. If you're traveling south, choose your exit: the shorter one to Smash #80, or the longer one to Smash #79. The northern exit occurs after you pass a lookout to the east. This is an apt description, as the lookout doesn't have a fence at its north and south ends, and you can fall down the cliff! You can also access this shortcut by falling off the road, through Billboard #22.

83. INTO ORBIT
Shortcut off North Mountain
Grid Reference: C 3
Heading: North
Description: This shortcut is a fantastic opportunity for payback against a rival. Simply drive through the smash by the diner (picture 1), and accelerate toward the northwestern finishing place: the observatory. However, the road ends with a drop just south of the finish line; what better place to try a vertical takedown?

84, 85. TRAIN TRACK DIRT ROADS
Train tracks west of Read Lane
Grid Reference: D/E 4
Heading: Southwest
Description: Leave Read Lane, enter the train tracks at the west end of the suspension bridge, and accelerate along the tracks and out of the tunnel. Then choose one of the two barns on either side of the tracks.
The left barn has Smash #85, and the right has Smash #84. You need two runs to take them both out. Combine this with the destruction of Billboards #24 and 25.

86, 87. SHORTCUTS TO SILVER LAKE
Junction of North Rouse, North Mountain, Read
Grid Reference: E/F 2/3
Heading: East or west (both shown)
Description: Take this shortcut if you miss the main road or the shortcut at Smash #87, and you're headed onto North Rouse. This immediately leads to a fallen boulder and Silver Lake. This picture shows the shortcut to the north. This, like Smash #86, is part of a two-smash shortcut either side of North Rouse; the other smash is in Silver Lake. Use this if you're coming west, and want to line up for the dirt road leading to Smashes #88–90.

88, 89, 90. INTO ORBIT
Shortcut off North Mountain
Grid Reference: E 2
Heading: East or west (west shown)
Description: From the junction with Read Lane and North Rouse Drive, head onto North Mountain, and make the left turn onto the dirt ground. This shortcut saves valuable seconds, so always take it if you're racing to the observatory. Here, the pathway splits up with the smash on your left and a path continuing under the North Mountain Drive bridge. Always take the right if you're racing because it leads to a long jump to victory!
Take the left route through Smash #89 at the fork, and you have another final fence to crash through before you're back on the main road, seconds from the finishing line!

NEIGHBORHOOD 5: SILVER LAKE

LANDMARKS AND THOROUGH-FARES: HEARTBREAK HILLS

1 CLIFFTOP DROP

A place to gain spectacular air as well as a spectacular view, this allows you access onto the railroad, which can take you quickly to the observatory, or back east to Palm Bay Heights. Note that you can also reach the train tracks via the shortcut between North Rouse and West Crawford, south of the heliport.

2 TUNNEL CONNECTIONS

West Crawford Drive, the tunnel that leads to and from Palm Bay Heights, has a pair of secret side tunnels (Smashes #1 and #2) that are easy to miss, and a billboard (#1) to destroy if you're heading west, from the train tracks that run parallel to this area.

3 HELIPORT

On the main road north (or south) through Silver Lake hills, pass the heliport, and note the smashes (#3 and 4) and billboard (#2) to the east. Use this to gauge the distance between you and the clifftop drop, or interstate junction to the south.

4 HEARTBREAK HILLS TUNNEL

This shows the southern exit, just south of the heliport. Employ this under-used shortcut to reach the northwestern area without traveling the winding North Rouse Drive.

5 END OF THE TUNNEL

This is one of the main entrances to Silver Lake; Lawrence Road disappears under the mountain range and appears in Palm Bay Heights. Remember how to return to this area for quick access to the more populated areas and the country club.

6 GABRIEL'S SHAKE SHACK

Down South Rouse Drive, this place is hardly the most convenient for a shake shop. However, it is north of the auto repair shop, and easily identified if you're dashing up or down here.

7 INTERSTATE CONSTRUCTION (NORTH)

Look to the guide map to give you the full details on the intersecting roadways here. There's an I-88 tunnel, the continuation of the interstate leading south to Harbor Town.

8 INTERSTATE CONSTRUCTION (SOUTH)

This construction also has access south toward Hubbard Street, all the way to the Harbor Town Junkyard. Two unfinished interstate sections, accessed via Super Jump #1, have billboards at their southern ends.

9 HEARTBREAK HILLS WATER TREATMENT CENTER

Overlooking the smaller of the two main lakes in this neighborhood, the water treatment center is a visible landmark along Rack Way and the southern parts of Nelson.

10 ENTERING SILVER LAKE

The junction of East Lake Drive and Nelson Way is the start of Silver Lake if you're approaching from the south. Remember that there's a gas station just south of the paint shop, but that is in Rockridge Cliffs (Harbor Town).

11 ANGUS BOAT RENTAL

The southwest corner of Silver Lake has a boat rental with a couple of smashes to run through (#14–16), and a pier you can investigate for off-road antics. It's better to approach heading north, as you can exit via Super Jump #2, back onto the road.

12 THE BOAT HIRE STORE

Next to the paint shop signage, this small boat hire store is across from the boat rental pier entrance/exit, and at the start of East Lake Drive's segmented highway. Choose the easier path if you want to avoid (or just miss) oncoming traffic!

13 SAND BANK

Here's a place you don't see much; the sand bank with the speedboat and rotting old pier, just north of the main pier entrances. A dirt road runs between the sections of East Lake Drive; drive over the rusting fishing boat en route to Super Jump #2.

14 AIRFIELD (LOOKING NORTHWEST)

A massive, hidden playground is available in the middle of this neighborhood. The southern part of the airfield offers a looping perimeter dirt track, and loads of jumping opportunities.

15 AIRFIELD (LOOKING WEST)

Here's the airfield from a different angle, showing the entrance road (bottom right of the picture) and a giant fuselage ring (middle left) which is part of Super Jump #3, a red ring on the opposite side, and more jumping areas.

16 AIRFIELD (LOOKING NORTH)

This area doesn't appear on your in-game map. The western edge is important because there's another fuselage ring to drive through (heading south), and this ramp: the key to smashing into Billboard #11.

17 PARADISE FIELD AIRFIELD ENTRANCE

This is the entrance to Paradise Field itself, which is accessible only from the southbound section of Nelson Way (either north into traffic, or south with traffic). The northbound section has a wall preventing you from crossing west, into this entrance.

18 SAWMILL YARD (NORTH ENTRANCE)

Across Nelson Way from the airfield is a large lumber yard, which has a number of interlocking dirt roads (check the guide map for them all). This is a warehouse at the north end of the yard, at the corner of Nelson Way and Ross Drive.

19 SAWMILL YARD (MAIN WAREHOUSE)

This is inside the main off-road area that can be raced in either direction. A number of smashes and a billboard (#10) are here. This is also a good way to cut the corner on Nelson and Ross (Thoroughfare #18, previously), if you want to head east into the Lawrence Tunnel and Palm Bay Heights.

20 SILVER LAKE JETTY

Take East Lake Drive northward, passing the airfield (to the east), and the gas station. You can access a lakeside road here, and exit a small tunnel (Smash #36). Hit Smash #35 to head west, out onto this jetty; the key to reaching the small island. You can also head south to this point from the East Lake/Ross junction.

Paradise

21 SILVER LAKE ISLAND

Composed of trees, a few buildings, and a ramped exit to the north, this small island is accessed via Super Jump #4 (from the jetty). Avoid the trees and the split in the middle of the dirt road, and increase your speed for the launch; this is the only way to shatter a cunningly placed billboard (#12).

22 THE EAGLE OF SILVER LAKE

A swooping eagle clutching a large salmon is a spectacular sight, and this statue is located at the intersection of Nelson and Ross. Remember that Ross leads east, all the way to the Lawrence Tunnel, so looking for this bird can be the key to making the correct turn if you're racing back into Palm Bay Heights!

23 THE LAKE HOUSE

Marking the eastern end of a fantastic shortcut across Silver Lake Marina, this structure, which shouldn't be crashed into, is next to East Lake Drive, just north of the junction with West Crawford. Look for it when searching for this shortcut.

24 SILVER LAKE MARINA (LOOKING WEST)

If you're heading west through this great short-cut, crash through Smash #53, and enter the Silver Lake Marina pier. There's a billboard (#15) you can only hit heading in this direction. As you exit (heading southwest), you can easily maneuver into White Mountain, and West Lake Drive.

25 SILVER LAKE MARINA (LOOKING EAST)

If you look on the guide map, there are two other shortcuts between Cannon Pass and the West Crawford Drive intersection with East Lake Drive. However, the marina is the quickest of the trio, and sets you up to reach either road off East Lake.

26 WATERFALL DINER

On the cusp of White Mountain, this small eatery is on the junction with Cannon Pass and East/West Lake Drive. There's a sizable parking lot in front and coach turnaround that's great to use as a shortcut. Frankie's Campground, the wilds of White Mountain, and the northern observatory finishing place are a few bends away!

27 FRANKIE'S CAMPGROUND (NORTH)

The rest of Frankie's Campground is located in White Mountain, but this entrance (or exit), contains Smash #57 and Billboard #16. The campground is excellent for cutting the corner of the Cannon Pass and Nelson Way junction. Remember that Nelson Way snakes all the way east and south back to the airfield, and down to the entrance to Rockridge Cliffs!

28 PARADISE NATIONAL PARK (WEST ENTRANCE/EXIT)

Use this as a reference when entering and exiting White Mountain via Nelson Way near the junction with Cannon Pass. Avoid two barriers, and a muddy off-road section to the north sets you up for a White Mountain billboard and ramp.

29 PARADISE NATIONAL PARK (NORTH ENTRANCE/EXIT)

At the south end of Read Lane is another park sign, and this marks the entrance to the White Mountain Crystal Summit area. Although the road to the north is looping (and away from Silver Lake), it is a reasonable road to take to reach the observatory.

30 MEADE FARM STORAGE: DEPOT 4

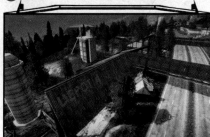

This is part of the clusters of rusting warehouses and other structures of Meade Farm Storage that line Nelson Way (which winds all the way back to the airfield). This section, however, has a number of depot buildings to race under, along the slightly quicker southern shortcut with two entrances and two exits in either direction.

31 THE JUMPING BARN

Located at the southern end of Lewis Pass (at the junction with Nelson Way), this is just east of the gas station (so remember the look of this area if you require a fill-up). It's mainly a shortcut across the junction, onto an embankment if you're heading up for Super Jump #5. Set yourself up for the depot shortcut as you continue west.

32 NICE BEAVER

The awning with the large beaver on it is located on Nelson Way, midway between the junction with Lewis Pass (northwest) and West Crawford (southeast). As the winding roads can look the same, focus on finding this landmark so you know which thoroughfare you're approaching next.

33 RICKETY BRIDGE

The junction of Nelson Way and West Crawford Drive has a number of shortcuts north and south of it, but a good one is this bridge, which allows you to zip through this intersection without any traffic problems. Also find Billboard #13 here.

34 SILVER LAKE RANGER STATION

Along Nelson Way, just southeast of the auto repair shop (and northeast of the junkyard on Ross), is a stepped visitors' center for the ranger station that provides an excellent way to gain height and boost. Plus it's a shortcut when traveling in either direction. You can position yourself for the ramp over the pond (to the south), too.

35 RAILROAD BRIDGE VALLEY (WEST)

This shows the railroad bridge, which is accessed at the eastern end of the tunnel that leads back to the northwestern corner of Palm Bay Heights. The road shown is West Crawford Drive, which stretches all the way back into Palm Bay Heights too. Use this road when navigating between the two neighborhoods.

36 RAILROAD BRIDGE VALLEY (EAST)

This shows the railroad bridge tunnel entrance (on the left), West Crawford road heading into the tunnel, and the clifftop drop (#1) above. This is also the off-road entrance that allows access to North Rouse Drive; a good plan if you need to get to the city's southeastern corner.

37 THE OLD RAILROAD BRIDGE

The railroad bridge itself looks less than sturdy, but it's fine to drive on, and can save you a load of time if you're racing to or from a nearby intersection or finishing point. Gain boost by dipping in and out of the sunken middle sections.

38 THE STONE BEAR

There's a large stone bear on the prowl at the intersection of North Rouse Drive and Lewis Pass. Lewis takes you to the railroad and winds down toward Nelson Way. North Rouse is the northern highway all the way to the observatory.

Paradise

39 HILLSIDE PASS WEATHER STATION

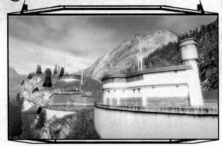

On the rocky wall north of Rouse Drive is a series of buildings making up the weather station. Don't confuse this with a finishing place; the observatory is farther west, in White Mountain. The tunnel to the southeast allows you to drop from the outer lane to the inner one.

40 THE RADIO MASTS AND COMMUNICATIONS TOWER

Lewis Pass's shortcuts are advantageous only if you're driving downhill. You can maneuver along the platform to the north, and then drop to the ramp at the communications tower to smash through Billboard #20. Enter the railroad after the next looping bend.

41 NORTH LAKE SUSPENSION BRIDGE (ENTRANCE/EXIT)

This gigantic structure dominates the North Lake area of Hillside Pass. Use it to figure out where you are, but also how to access this impressive shortcut. Check out #42 for more information.

42 RAILROAD ENTRANCE/EXIT

This shows the railroad in the opposite direction from #41, which is important because a dirt road leads off and onto the train tracks themselves. Learn this area because you can save many seconds zooming back into Palm Bay Heights and onto Crawford by using the railroad bridge.

43 NORTH LAKE SUSPENSION BRIDGE (LOOKING WEST)

The bridge itself has a couple of carriages partially narrowing the span in the middle; use the sunken middle sections to gain more boost. Remember that there are shortcut exits at either end; the one to the west is in White Mountain.

44 CLIFFTOP GAP

The highway is reasonably wide and snaking, making it a preferred way to reach (or head away from) the observatory. A gap (Super Jump #8) allows you to grab more boost, which is important on the final leg of a race.

45 THE NORTHERN ROUTE: HILLSIDE PASS

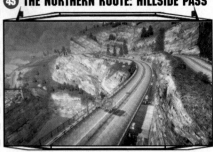

This is the "Hillside Pass" that the area is named after. There are actually three separate paths to choose from here. Enter the off-road one via the middle if you're heading west, or to the right if you're driving east.

46 THE FALLEN ROCK

You probably won't use this off-road bend during races, as the inside corner to the north is more of a shortcut, but there's still an interesting fallen rock. The junction itself allows access to Read Lane, which winds through White Mountain, and back to Landmark #29.

47 NORTH LAKE SUSPENSION BRIDGE (LOOKING EAST)

This provides a great view of the shortcut exit from the suspension bridge. If you're heading west on the bridge, choose one of two gaps between the girders and head into White Mountain, onto Read Lane. The railroad itself continues a lot farther; use it to reach the western finishing places.

DRIVETHRU AND PARKING STRUCTURE LOCATIONS

DRIVETHRU TYPE	HEARTBREAK HILLS	EASTERN SHORE	HILLSIDE PASS	TOTAL
Auto Repairs	1	1	0	2
Gas Stations	0	2	0	2
Paint Shops	1	0	0	1
Junkyards	0	1	0	1
Grand Total	2	4	0	6

AUTO REPAIR SHOPS

1. HEARTBREAK HILLS

South Rouse and Rack
Grid Reference: M 10

2. EASTERN SHORE

Nelson
Grid Reference: J 6

GAS STATIONS

3. EASTERN SHORE (SOUTH)

East Lake and Rack
Grid Reference: J 10

4. EASTERN SHORE (NORTH)

Nelson
Grid Reference: H 4

PAINT SHOPS

5. HEARTBREAK HILLS

East Lake and Nelson
Grid Reference: J/K 12/13

JUNKYARDS

6. EASTERN SHORE

Nelson and Ross
Grid Reference: K 8

NOTE

There are no parking structures in Silver Lake.

DISCOVERIES

DISCOVERY TYPE	HEARTBREAK HILLS	EASTERN SHORE	HILLSIDE PASS	GRAND TOTAL
● Super Jumps	2	2	6	10
● Billboards	7	12	1	20
△ Smashes	16	53	21	90

NOTE

Some of the super jumps, billboards, and smashes are on the border between two different areas, and may appear as one or the other (or different from this guide) on your in-game map.

● SUPER JUMPS: HEARTBREAK HILLS

☐ 1. JUMP TO THE BROKEN INTERSTATE

Shortcut east of South Rouse and Rack
Grid Reference: M 11
Barrel Roll Available: No
Heading: South
Description: Approach the concrete on-ramp that leads to this massive gap with the interstate under you. Crash through Smash #11, and then make the super jump at high speed so you land on the broken interstate section just beyond. Now choose to hit Billboard #4 or 5.

☐ 2. OUT OF ANGUS PIER

Shortcut west of East Lake
Grid Reference: J 12
Barrel Roll Available: No
Heading: North
Description: Enter the shortcut onto Angus Pier, ideally heading south, from Smash #14. Stay left, and drive over the fishing boat (as shown) just before you reach the super jump. You sail out between both lanes on East Lake. Note that you can't enter this area heading south; a low cement wall stops you.

● SUPER JUMPS: EASTERN SHORE

☐ 3. INTO THE AIRFIELD FUSELAGE

Airfield west of Nelson
Grid Reference: K 9
Barrel Roll Available: No
Heading: North
Description: The hidden airfield is a playground where you and your online friends should have a great time, but there's a discovery to be made as well! The super jump is on the inside of the fuselage that's hanging from the crane (picture 2). To enter it, approach (at top speed) the hangar with the ramp inside it (picture 1), keep straight, sail through the air, and fly through the ring itself!

☐ 4. JUMP TO SILVER LAKE ISLAND

Shortcut west of East Lake
Grid Reference: I 8
Barrel Roll Available: No
Heading: Northwest
Description: Locate Smash #35, which allows you access from the shortcut near East Lake Drive, onto the jetty, and bring your speed up as you steer right toward the ramp. Hit it at high speed, so you fly across the water and land on the island. Billboard #12 is just ahead!

● SUPER JUMPS: HILLSIDE PASS

☐ 5. INTO THE BARN

Shortcut northeast of Lewis and Nelson
Grid Reference: I 4
Barrel Roll Available: No
Heading: Southwest
Description: Crash through one of the fences (such as #70) on Lewis Pass, and head southwest toward the open barn. Make sure you're traveling at speed as you hit the ramp on the left, and fly into the top part of the barn. Continue through to reach Billboard #19.

☐ 6. THE CLIFFTOP DROP

North Rouse
Grid Reference: L 5
Barrel Roll Available: No
Heading: West
Description: This jump is as massive as it is spectacular. Charge up or down North Rouse Drive (you need to be above West Crawford to reach this place) and steer off the edge, onto the lookout area, and plunge off the ramp. Land on the railroad tracks far below.

☐ 7. WEATHER STATION SUPER JUMP

Shortcut off Lewis
Grid Reference: K 4
Barrel Roll Available: No
Heading: Southwest
Description: Advance onto the bumpy platform (via Smash #80) that parallels the northern end of Lewis Pass, but head south and continue to stay on the platform as it turns southwest, leading to a super jump that brings you close to the communications tower area and Billboard #20.

8. NORTH ROUSE ALTERNATIVE ROUTE

Shortcut off North Rouse
Grid Reference: J 3
Barrel Roll Available: No
Heading: East or west (west shown)
Description: Enter the dirt track to the south of North Rouse Drive, via either Smash #81 or 82, and accelerate toward the ramped section of dirt, ignoring the barriers. Fly across, and land on the other side.

9. HILLSIDE PASS (EAST)

Shortcut south of North Rouse
Grid Reference: H 2
Barrel Roll Available: No
Heading: East or west (west shown)
Description: Enter the dirt track that runs between the two sections of North Rouse highway, and continue to pick up speed until you reach a ramped gap. Floor it and complete the super jump. There's another one just west of you, on this stretch of shortcut.

10. HILLSIDE PASS (WEST)

Shortcut south of North Rouse
Grid Reference: G 2
Barrel Roll Available: No
Heading: East or west (west shown)
Description: Enter the dirt track that runs between the two sections of North Rouse highway, and continue to pick up speed until you reach a ramped gap. Floor it and complete the super jump. There's another one just east of you, on this stretch of shortcut.

● BILLBOARDS: HEARTBREAK HILLS

1. IN THE TUNNEL

Shortcut between the train track tunnel and West Crawford
Grid Reference: M 5
Heading: West
Description: From Palm Bay Heights, take Crawford, then enter the train tunnel that runs parallel, just north of the road tunnel itself. Look for the shortcut tunnel halfway along, on the left. Drive down this, and head through the gap in the middle, into the billboard, which is either side of Smashes #1 and 2.

2. HELIPORT DROP

Shortcut on eastern side of North Rouse
Grid Reference: M 6
Heading: South

Description: Charge down North Rouse Drive, and take the flat concrete shortcut with the cars on it. Drop off the far end, adjacent to the road, and land through the billboard, just in front of Smash #3.

3. SNAKE PASS GAP

Shortcut east of Ross and Nelson
Grid Reference: L 8
Heading: East or west (east shown)
Description: Having just slammed through Smash #18, continue through the snaking paths toward Lawrence Tunnel. At the first gap is a billboard, over the second snaking path. Next stop: Smash #10.

4. BROKEN INTERSTATE LEAP 1

Broken interstate bridge south of Rouse
Grid Reference: M/N 12
Heading: South
Description: Head south down South Rouse, hit Smash #11, complete Super Jump #1 to land on a section of broken interstate overpass, and steer left at high speed. Fly off the far drop and fall through the billboard. Keep your speed up and try to aim your car directly at the billboard.

5. BROKEN INTERSTATE LEAP 2

Broken interstate bridge south of Rouse
Grid Reference: M 12/13
Heading: South

Description: Head south down South Rouse, hit Smash #11, complete Super Jump #1 to land on a section of broken interstate overpass, and steer right at high speed. The interstate curves right slightly, and ends a second or two later with a drop onto the area just north of the toll booths. Crash through the billboard on the way down.

6. BILLBOARD TREATS AT THE TREATMENT FACILITY 1

Shortcut between lanes of Nelson
Grid Reference: K 12
Heading: North or south (north shown)
Description: At the very southern end of Nelson Way are two dirt mounds in-between the north and southbound road lanes. Drive up the muddy slope into the billboard.

7. BILLBOARD TREATS AT THE TREATMENT FACILITY 2

Shortcut between lanes of Nelson
Grid Reference: K 12
Heading: North or south (north shown)
Description: The second of the two billboards on the muddy sloping bumps southwest of the water treatment facility also allows you to gain some air and smash a billboard, before you reach Rack Way (to the north) or East Lake Drive (to the south).

● BILLBOARDS: EASTERN SHORE

8. CLIFF EDGE BILLBOARD

Shortcut east of Nelson
Grid Reference: J 6
Heading: North or south (south shown)
Description: This billboard hangs just north of the ranger station, and heading through Smash #44 to reach it is the easy way to destroy it. The hard way is approaching the ranger station steps from the south at incredible speeds, and flying through the air, into the billboard, and landing on the cliff ledge!

9. THE POND RAMP

Shortcut near Nelson and Ross
Grid Reference: K 7
Heading: North or south (north shown)
Description: Choose to crash through either Smash #40 or 41 (depending on the direction), and sail up the ramp, through the billboard without landing in the pond water, and down the other side.

10. SAWMILL PLATFORM

Shortcut east of Nelson
Grid Reference: L 9
Heading: North
Description: You can't hit this billboard heading north; you pass under it instead. Therefore, look for the entrance to the inner of the two shortcuts that run north to south (there are yellow plastic barriers to drive through), and then drive down the stepped platforms, and drop through the billboard.

11. EXITING THE AIRFIELD

Airfield west of Nelson
Grid Reference: J 9
Heading: West
Description: Enter the hidden airfield via Smashes #27 and 28, off Nelson Way, and after you've played around and completed Super Jump #3, turn and position your car heading west (picture 1). If you hit the ramp pointing out of the western perimeter of the field at high speed, you sail across and land through the billboard on East Lake, just north of the gas station.

12. SILVER LAKE ISLAND ANTICS

Island west of East Lake
Grid Reference: I 7
Heading: North
Description: Take Smash #35 onto the Silver Lake Jetty, make the super jump (#4) onto the small island, and stay in the middle dirt road, avoiding the fences or trees (picture 1). At the northern end is a ramp; speed over it and accelerate hard so you land on a grassy bank. Then steer into the billboard (picture 2) and land on East Lake Drive, at the junction with West Crawford.

13. RICKETY BRIDGE BILLBOARD

Shortcut over West Crawford and Nelson
Grid Reference: I/J 6
Heading: North or south (north shown)
Description: Whether you're heading in from Crawford, or you've just finished crashing through the Paradise Woods smashes (#47–50), line yourself up straight and hit Smash #51 (or 52), and sail through the billboard.

14. MARINA BILLBOARD (EAST)

Shortcut south of East Lake Drive
Grid Reference: G 7
Heading: East
Description: Approach this billboard at speed, heading west to east. Start by driving through the fence (in White Mountain), and accelerate across the marina, then gain air as the road slopes up slightly, allowing you to hit the billboard.

15. MARINA BILLBOARD (WEST)

Shortcut south of East Lake Drive
Grid Reference: H 7
Heading: West
Description: Approach this billboard at speed, heading east to west. Start by driving through the fence (Smash #53), and accelerate across the marina, then gain air as the road slopes up slightly, allowing you to hit the billboard.

16. FRANKIE'S CAMPGROUND

Campground east of Cannon Pass and Nelson
Grid Reference: E 5
Heading: South
Description: This is right on the edge of White Mountain. Crash through Smash #57, keep to the right so you drive onto the wooden platform, and head off the platform, into the billboard.

17. OUT FROM THE MEADE FARM STORAGE

Shortcut north of Nelson and Read
Grid Reference: E 5
Heading: Southwest
Description: Locate the junction of Nelson Way and Read Lane, head through Smash #64, then onto the raised wall section, without dropping to a lower section. Drive off the right side, through the billboard, and land near Smash #62.

18. MEADE FARM STORAGE LEAP

Shortcut south of Nelson
Grid Reference: G 4/5
Heading: West
Description: Drive into the Meade Farm Storage area and the depots, making a run through the ramped warehouse from Smash #69, and keep to the left. There's a short raised stone area; smash the barriers (as shown), then sail off the drop and through the billboard.

19. THE BARN PICNIC AREA

Shortcut by Nelson and Lewis
Grid Reference: H 4
Heading: Southwest
Description: This one takes some preparation. Speed up to the barn, head over Super Jump #5, and enter the barn's upper area. Continue to accelerate, pointing to the right slightly so you sail over Lewis Pass, to the "dirt island" just north of the Nelson/Lewis intersection. Crash through the picnic table as you point your car at the billboard, and land through it, onto Nelson.

● BILLBOARDS: HILLSIDE PASS

20. COMMUNICATIONS BREAKDOWN

Shortcut by Lewis
Grid Reference: J 4
Heading: Northwest
Description: As Lewis Pass curves north, continue to follow it downhill from the area near Super Jump #7, and steer to the right, up the gravel raised area. Head through the communications building (surrounded by masts and towers) and through the gap, into the billboard.

▲ SMASHES: HEARTBREAK HILLS

1, 2. TUNNEL SHORTCUT
Shortcut between the train track tunnel and West Crawford
Grid Reference: M 5
Heading: East or west (both shown)
Description: Whether you're heading into Crawford from Silver Lake (as shown), or coming in from the train track tunnel (in the second picture), two side tunnels split around a gap that you can hit Billboard #1 from.
You have a choice to hit the billboard or one of the smashes. You can't do all three in one straight line, so double-back to claim the other two smashes afterwards.

3, 4. HELIPORT DIRT ROAD
Shortcut east of North Rouse
Grid Reference: M 6
Heading: North or south (south shown)
Description: Drive south along North Rouse, and take the dirt track on the left side, just before you pass under the heliport bridge. Billboard #3 should be above you.

A few seconds later, the dirt track returns you back onto North Rouse Drive, and the second fence can be destroyed.

5. DIRT ROAD TO/FROM CRAWFORD
Shortcut west of North Rouse
Grid Reference: L 7
Heading: Northwest or southeast (northwest shown)
Description: If you need to reach West Crawford, down below North Rouse Drive, head along this dirt road, south of the heliport. You'll drive into a short tunnel, and emerge by Smash #17.

6, 7. OUTER EDGE OF ROUSE
Shortcut east of North Rouse
Grid Reference: L/M 7
Heading: North or south (south shown)
Description: As you roar down North Rouse, swerve into a small dirt shortcut just south of the heliport and destroy the first of two fences. The second fence is at the other end of the dirt track, before you merge back onto Rouse. Note that you can then cut across Rouse and into Smash #8.

8, 9. INNER EDGE OF ROUSE
Shortcut west of North Rouse
Grid Reference: L 7/8
Heading: North or south (south shown)
Description: You can follow this from Smashes #6 and 7 (or if heading north, continue into these smashes). Head into the short dirt path next to the white fence.

A second later you emerge back onto North Rouse, either heading for the interstate interchange (if you're moving south), or toward the heliport (if you're going north).

10. SNAKE PASS: EAST ENTRANCE/EXIT
Shortcut west of Ross and North Rouse
Grid Reference: M 8
Heading: East or west (east shown)
Description: You can either enter this snaking path from here, or (as shown) exit from it having followed one of the two winding shortcuts. You'll hit Smash #18 at the other end of this stretch, or (if heading east), find a quick route to the Lawrence Tunnel.

11. TO THE BROKEN INTERSTATE
Shortcut east of South Rouse
Grid Reference: M 11
Heading: South
Description: Tear down Rouse, and pass the auto repair shop. At the junction with Rack Way, steer left, into a worksite concrete on-ramp that leads to a spectacular super jump (#1).

12, 13. CUTTING THE CORNER
Shortcut near East Lake and Nelson
Grid Reference: K 13

Heading: East or west (east shown)
Description: To quickly reach either Nelson Way or East Lake Drive, use the shortcut to avoid the regular junction. This is a curved dirt path with one entrance/exit near the paint shop sign. The other fence is at the beginning (or end) of Nelson Way, and allows access to or from the water treatment facility area.

14, 15, 16. ANGUS PIER
Shortcut west of East Lake
Grid Reference: J/K 13
Heading: North or south (north shown)
Description: This is either the southern exit, or (as shown) the entrance onto the Angus Boat Rental pier area. This provides access to a super jump opportunity, allowing boost, but ironically, it's quicker to stay on East Lake itself. A few moments later, the pier splits into an exit (on your right), or continues on to a super jump heading north. The exit can be driven north or south, but the super jump (#2) cannot.

A second later, you can hit the exit back onto East Lake. However, traveling north out of here is dangerous; point your car to the left so you don't hit the central barrier, and watch for oncoming traffic!

⚠ SMASHES: EASTERN SHORE
17. DIRT ROAD TO/FROM CRAWFORD
Shortcut south of West Crawford
Grid Reference: K/L 6
Heading: Northwest or southeast (southeast shown)
Description: If you're planning to reach Rouse instead of remaining on Crawford, this is the place to take a shortcut. You enter a dirt road and narrow tunnel, and emerge north of the junction with Lawrence Tunnel (and hit Smash #5).

18. SNAKE PASS: WEST ENTRANCE/EXIT 1
Shortcut east of Ross and Nelson
Grid Reference: K 8
Heading: East or west (east shown)
Description: This large fence is on the opposite side of the road from the junkyard on Ross and Nelson, and the dirt track becomes two interlocking S-bends ending at Lawrence Tunnel. A second later, you'll hit Billboard #3 if you're heading east. Smash #10 is at the opposite end.

19. SNAKE PASS: WEST ENTRANCE/EXIT 2
Shortcut east of Ross and Nelson
Grid Reference: K/L 8
Heading: East or west (east shown)
Description: Study the guide map, which shows two distinct snaking paths. The western entrance/exit to this one is on Ross Drive itself, and forces you under Billboard #3, and into the other snaking path. The exit is a ramp, not Smash #10.

20, 21. SAWMILL NORTHERN ENTRANCES/EXITS
Shortcut east of Ross and Nelson
Grid Reference: K/L 8
Heading: North or south (south shown)
Description: The sawmill area has two interlocking shortcuts running north to south, and these

two smashes show the entrances (as shown) or exits in the northern part of this area. Both smashes leads you into a dirt road with scattered Meade Farm Storage. From here you are free to choose which route to take. Remember that the eastern route has a few yellow barriers to drive through.

22, 23. SAWMILL MIDDLE ENTRANCES/EXITS
Shortcut east of the lower route on Nelson
Grid Reference: L 9
Heading: North or south (south shown)
Description: The outer of the two shortcut routes offers two smashes. They are easy to spot and allow you to head back onto the main road. However, the second enables you to tear through the southern shortcut area, all the way to the next entrance/exit, and then to the junction with Rack Way. This is preferred if you're having trouble dodging the oncoming traffic when heading south.

24, 25, 26. SAWMILL SOUTH ENTRANCES/EXITS
Shortcut east of the lower route on Nelson
Grid Reference: K/L 10/11
Heading: North or south (south shown)
Description: Don't confuse the two northern fences (Smashes #24 and 25) with the middle entrance/exit smashes. Although they look very similar, these allow you back onto the road. Or, you can continue along the parallel dirt track next to Nelson Way, having cleared all of the main buildings at the sawmill.

You eventually emerge at the junction with Nelson Way and Rack Way, at the southeastern corner of the airfield. Or, use Smash #26 to start this shortcut if you're heading north.

27, 28. ENTERING PARADISE FIELD AIRFIELD
Shortcut west of Nelson
Grid Reference: K/L 9
Heading: West
Description: Travel along the western part of Nelson to reach this side fence. If you try the northbound right lane, a wall blocks your way. As soon as you spot the shed with the plane atop it, swerve left.

A second later, you're driving down the entrance road, and into the airfield itself! This area isn't seen on your in-game map, so check out the structures and roads using the guide maps. Locate a super jump (#3) and billboard (#11) here, too.

29, 30. CUTTING A CORNER ON RACK
Shortcut east of East Lake and Rack
Grid Reference: J 11
Heading: East or west (east shown)
Description: You can cut out the entire intersection with Rack Way and East Lake Drive by heading through the curved dirt road that saves you time and a more vicious drift around the corner.

A moment later, you appear (in this case) onto Rack Way, which is actually just south of the airfield that doesn't appear on your in-game map.

31. LAKE FRONT TUNNEL ENTRANCE/EXIT (SOUTH)

Shortcut west of East Lake and Rack
Grid Reference: J 10
Heading: North or south (north shown)
Description: If you are racing, are near the junction with East Lake and Rack, and don't need to use the nearby gas station, head through this fence and begin a winding shortcut by the lake. The next stop is a tunnel and Smash #36.

32, 33, 34. SHORTCUT NEAR SILVER LAKE ISLAND

Shortcut west of East Lake
Grid Reference: I/J 8/9
Heading: North or south (north shown)
Description: Drive this southern smash area east or west (west is shown). After rounding the corner after the gas station, keep left, and enter here. Or position yourself for the corner if you're heading out from this series of smashes. Round the corner, and crash through this smash, and either swerve onto East Lake Drive once again, or continue straight, into the third smash (#34). Head through this smash, which occurs a second after hitting the previous one, and then look ahead (if you're heading north); there's a final exit onto East Lake Drive (Smash #37), or a smash heading onto a jetty (#35).

35. SILVER LAKE JETTY ENTRANCE

Shortcut near East Lake
Grid Reference: I 8
Heading: West
Description: Between Smashes #34 and 37 is another fence, this one leading to a jetty over the water of Silver Lake itself. Take this only for Silver Lake Island Super Jump #4, and Billboard #12.

36. LAKE FRONT TUNNEL ENTRANCE/EXIT (NORTH)

Shortcut near East Lake
Grid Reference: I/J 9
Heading: North or south (north shown)
Description: Roar through the tunnel, having entered a lakeside shortcut via Smash #31, and head back out, onto East Lake Drive having avoided the nasty winding turn on the main road. Or, use this to enter the shortcut and appear near the junction with Rack Way.

37. SHORTCUT NEAR SILVER LAKE ISLAND (NORTHERN ENTRANCE/EXIT)

Shortcut west of East Lake
Grid Reference: I/J 8
Heading: North or south (north shown)
Description: Smash this fence either after you complete the route near Silver Lake Island, or at the beginning of the run if you're heading south. If you're heading north, you appear on East Lake, near the junction with Ross Drive.

38, 39. JUNKYARD SHORTCUT

Shortcut north of Ross

Grid Reference: J 7/8
Heading: East or west (east shown)
Description: If you're running between the junkyard and the intersection with East Lake Drive, try taking the dirt road, which has more to offer if you approach it heading east. Smash through this first fence.
The second is to the left, and it allows easy access into the intersection. Or, drive right, sail over the road, and land on the shortcut behind the junkyard. This is a quick way to head south on Nelson, near the airfield.

40, 41. RAMPED POND SKIM

Shortcut near Ross and Nelson
Grid Reference: K 7
Heading: North or south (north shown)
Description: A dirt road just west of the intersection of Ross and Nelson leads up a rickety ramped bridge, over a pond (through Billboard #9), and down the other side.
The second fence leads out onto Nelson, just south of the ranger station. Use this straight shot to keep your speed up, so you can attack Smashes #42 and onward with more aggression.

42, 43. RAMPAGE AT THE RANGER STATION

Shortcut east of Nelson
Grid Reference: J/K 6/7
Heading: North or south (north shown)
Description: Whether you completed the pond ramp into Billboard #9 or not, you can save some precious seconds and gain some boost by heading through this fence.
It leads up the steps of the ranger station, and out the other side, and the air you get increases your boost, while you shave a second off a racing time. Approach the billboard you can see (#8) from the opposite direction, unless you hit the ranger station steps at full speed and land on the cliff!

44. CLIFF LEDGE RUN

Shortcut east of Nelson
Grid Reference: J 6
Heading: North or south (south shown)
Description: The area just north of the ranger station has a billboard (#8) hanging from it. The easy way is to bust through the fence located opposite the auto repair shop, and drive off the ledge. Of course, you can land from a massive leap northward, off the ranger station steps, and drive down the cliff ledge, too!

45, 46. EAST OF THE RICKETY BRIDGE

Shortcut east of Nelson and West Crawford
Grid Reference: J 5/6
Heading: North or south (north shown)
Description: If you're heading toward the junction of Nelson and West Crawford and want to cut the corner near the rickety bridge, swing your car right before the intersection.
You emerge after a short sloping leap, into this fence, and out into Crawford. Use this shortcut if you want to quickly head south down Nelson from Crawford, or vice versa.

47, 48, 49, 50. THE WILDS OF PARADISE WOODS

Shortcut east of East Lake and Crawford
Grid Reference: I 6/7
Heading: North or south (north shown)
Description: These four smashes allow you to cut the corner on the intersection of East Lake Drive and West Crawford. If you're heading north on East Lake, you can see Smash #47 near the Paradise Woods sign on the right. As soon as you tear through Smash #47, the dirt road splits into two. The right side allows you access into this fence: Smash #48. However, if you want to reach Crawford immediately, stay left and ignore Smash #48, and hit this one instead.
Smash #50, at the northeastern end of the dirt track, offers a great racing line toward the rickety bridge and Billboard #13. Again, these are useful shortcuts for avoiding traffic.

51, 52. OVER THE RICKETY BRIDGE

Shortcut east of West Crawford and Nelson
Grid Reference: I/J 5/6
Heading: North or south (north shown)
Description: These two smashes occur at each end of a dirt track with a rickety bridge (and Billboard #13) in the middle. Make sure you've lined yourself up correctly as you reach the bridge. This is a fantastic way to avoid the traffic at the West Crawford/Nelson intersection. And afterward, you can accelerate away, especially useful in a race.

53. THE LAKE HOUSE AND MARINA SHORTCUT

Shortcut south of East Lake
Grid Reference: H 6
Heading: East or west (west shown)
Description: As East Lake Drive winds around the northern part of the lake, be on the lookout for the Lake House (Landmark #23), and drive left, onto the grass, and into the trail leading down to the beach. The billboard you drive under can't be accessed in this direction. The fence you smash as you exit is in White Mountain.

54, 55, 56. NORTH OF THE MARINA

Shortcut north of East Lake
Grid Reference: G/H 6
Heading: East or west (west shown)
Description: Think of the two smashes on the eastern entrances and exits as a choice you have to make, whether you're traveling east or west. In this case, stay right and head onto the dirt track; exit through Smash #56 if you're racing. This is the second entrance/exit (entrance in this case). It allows you to head to Smash #56 with less time on the dirt, and both routes merge before you reach Smash #56
This is the exit (or entrance if you're heading east); these three smashes mark a shortcut to avoid the East Lake traffic and the slight bend in the road.

57. WHITE MOUNTAIN CAMPGROUND

Campground east of Cannon Pass and Nelson
Grid Reference: E 5
Heading: North or south (south shown)

Description: The rest of the smashes in Frankie's Campground are located in White Mountain, but the northern entrance/exit, near the manager's office and Billboard #16, is firmly in Silver Lake. Smash it from either direction.

58. GUNNING FOR CANNON PASS

Cannon Pass and Nelson
Grid Reference: E 5
Heading: Northeast or southwest (southwest shown)

Description: There's a small fence section just northeast of the intersection with Cannon Pass and Nelson, near a White Mountain ramp and billboard. Crash through here and begin a rampage along Nelson. Next stop: Smash #59!

59, 60. NATIONAL PARK ENTRANCE (WEST)

Shortcut northwest of Nelson
Grid Reference: E 5
Heading: Northeast or southwest (northeast shown)

Description: These two fences are in the dirt track on the northern side of the Nelson, and can be approached in either direction. This shortcut is good for getting a run-up to the ramp and billboard in White Mountain to the west. However, for now, just crash through both fences as you pass along the left edge of the National Park Entrance, and then swerve back onto Nelson Way.

61, 62, 63, 64. ENTERING/EXITING THE MEADE FARM STORAGE AREA

Shortcut north of Nelson
Grid Reference: E/F 4/5
Heading: East or west (east shown)

Description: There are four fences between Nelson Way and the junction with Read Lane. Smash through the first in-between the two sections of Nelson Way.

The second fence is on the other side of the dirt stretch and leads to the second section of Nelson Way. Ignore Billboard #17 for the moment. The third fence is on the northern side of Nelson, just under the billboard. Crash through there as you drive toward the intersection with Read Lane. The final of the four fences is at the northwest part of the Read Lane/Nelson Way intersection. You can spin around to face west and go for the billboard now, if you wish.

65, 66, 67, 68. MEADE FARM STORAGE RUN

Shortcut south of Nelson
Grid Reference: F/G 5
Heading: East or west (east shown)

Description: Enter the dirt road with five entrances and exits along its path, which butts up against the southern side of Nelson Way. Find this pair of fences at the western end. Smash the first, then look for this sloped hill to the left, and drive up, through Smash #66, and back onto the road. Or, approach from the opposite direction.

The dirt path and the southern side of Nelson Way are next to each other, and this is another opportunity to enter the Meade Farm Storage

shortcut via this fence, just south of the junction with Read Lane.

This smash is a long fence that stretches across the dirt path, onto a raised stone drop that should only be approached driving east to west (when aiming at the billboard you just drove under). Otherwise, drive back onto Nelson from here, or into the eastern section of the Meade Farm Storage run.

69. MEADE FARM STORAGE RUN (EASTERN ENTRANCE/EXIT)

Shortcut south of Nelson
Grid Reference: H 4/5
Heading: East or west (west shown)

Description: Whether you've just made the spectacular launch from the barn, through Billboard #19 or not, crossing the road and entering this series of outbuildings allows you to gain boost while running parallel to Nelson Way. There's a building with a ramp through it just inside this area.

⚠ SMASHES: HILLSIDE PASS

70, 71, 72. THE BARN AREA

Shortcut near Lewis and Nelson
Grid Reference: H/I 4/5
Heading: Northeast or southwest (southwest shown)

Description: Although you can approach these fences from either direction, heading southwest allows access into the barn and the option of Super Jump #5 and Billboard #19. Zoom through the fence along Lewis.

You can now opt to take the super jump on the left, prior to reaching the barn, or enter the barn on the ground level, and take care of this fence. The final smash is at the other end of the barn, and allows quick access to the Lewis/Nelson intersection. Use this shortcut if you're heading northeast and need quick access up Lewis Pass.

73, 74, 75. OFF-ROAD TUNNEL

Shortcut on Lewis
Grid Reference: I/J 4/5
Heading: Northeast to northwest, or southeast to southwest (northeast to northwest shown)

Description: This isn't that much quicker than taking Lewis Pass itself, but you can continue from the barn area if you're heading northeast; accelerate and drift into the tunnel under the road.

A second later, you're out of the tunnel, crashing through this fence. In the distance is the large suspension bridge.

The final part of the trio of smashes occurs as you head back onto Lewis Pass, and speed under the suspension bridge rail tracks. Remember that you can swerve to face east, and head onto the tracks from here.

76, 77. ON OR OFF THE TRAIN TRACKS (EAST)

Shortcut on Lewis
Grid Reference: I/J 4
Heading: East or west (east shown)

Description: One of the best shortcuts to find,

these two sets of fences mark a narrow wooden platform that leads on or off the train tracks and is perfect for making a quick getaway to or from the train tunnel and Palm Bay Heights. Drive onto this wooden section, and gain access to the train track. If you're heading west, be sure you learn when to steer left, off the track, and onto Lewis Pass.

78, 79. ON OR OFF THE TRAIN TRACKS (WEST)

Shortcut on Lewis
Grid Reference: I 4
Heading: East or west (west shown)

Description: This allows you to enter or exit the train tracks from the opposite direction of Smashes #76 and 77. If you're following Lewis Pass Road west up the curves, find this smash to enter the wooden platform.

At the top is a second fence leading onto the tracks, and the giant suspension bridge that spans the north lake. Head onto here for a quick drive toward the north and northwestern finishing places.

80. WEATHER STATION SMASH

Shortcut south of Lewis and North Rouse
Grid Reference: K/L 3/4
Heading: South

Description: Head south from the junction with Lewis and North Rouse, and locate the fence on the right side of Lewis Pass. It leads to a bumpy platform and Super Jump #7.

81, 82. MIND THE GAP

Shortcut south North Rouse
Grid Reference: J/K 3
Heading: East or west (west shown)

Description: Take the alternate route along North Rouse Drive, and look for the dirt track to the south side. Enter it, and accelerate over the gap. Pass over this precarious drop (Super Jump #8).

Land from the super jump, and exit back onto North Rouse Drive with a refilled boost. Otherwise, this shortcut is about the same distance as the section of North Rouse itself.

83, 84. IN AND OUT OF THE CAVE

Shortcut east of North Rouse
Grid Reference: I/J 3
Heading: Northwest or southeast (northwest shown)

Description: As you can see if you study the shortcuts on the guide map, this area of rock has been carved into a curved off-road shortcut and is part of a winding track that starts/ends (to the east) with Smash #81.

It ends/starts (to the west) with Smash #86. Zoom out of this small shortcut and prepare to line yourself up with the dirt track curve that's inside the regular road (Smash #85).

85, 86. THE RURAL ROAD PROJECT

Shortcut south of North Rouse
Grid Reference: I/J 2/3

Heading: East or west (west shown)
Description: This curve south of the main thoroughfare is an excellent place to gain a second or two in a race, as long as you can precisely drive through this smash, and not hit the highway barrier. Continue accelerating and drifting through this track, appearing at the opposite end. Watch for incoming traffic if you're heading west, emerging at Smash #86.

87, 88. BETWEEN THE HILLSIDE HIGHWAY
Shortcut south of North Rouse
Grid Reference: F/G/H 2

Heading: East or west (west shown)
Description: This excellent but narrow shortcut allows you to ignore the more curved sections of North Rouse as you dash east or west. If you're heading west, position yourself in the middle of the road, and dip down between both sections.
Follow the track between the highway, and perform two super jumps (#9 and 10) along the way. The exit is a long straight area that can give you some extra air, but watch your landing! If you're

heading east, remember that this entrance/exit is on the inside of the highway.

89. INSIDE ROAD TO NORTH MOUNTAIN DRIVE
Shortcut south of North Rouse
Grid Reference: F 2
Heading: East or west (west shown)
Description: This section of dirt track wraps around the inside (or south) part of North Rouse, and exits at the junction with North Mountain Drive. The second smash is actually in White Mountain.

90. OUTSIDE ROAD TO NORTH MOUNTAIN DRIVE
Shortcut south of North Rouse
Grid Reference: F 2
Heading: Northwest or southeast (southeast shown)
Description: This can be seen as the beginning (or end) of your journey through Hillside Pass because the fence behind you, at the junction with North Mountain Drive, is in White Mountain. Don't drive too quickly through this shortcut because you can overshoot the road and fall off the cliff to the south!

05: Appendices

APPENDIX I: FREEBURN CHALLENGES

Getting online and summoning friends to lark about throughout Paradise City is the key to obtaining these online-only challenges. Press ⟳ to access the online menus, and follow the instructions from the game manual to get your Challenges started! There are 50 Challenges per number of players, from 2 to 8, making a total of 350. After completing each Challenge, check it off in the box provided. Let's ride!

TWO PLAYERS

☐ 1. GO CRASH!
Location: Anywhere
Action: Crash
Combo Actions: None
Description: Team Challenge: Crash into each other.

☐ 2. GET SOCIAL
Location: Waterfront
Action: Meet Up
Combo Actions: None
Description: Team Challenge: Meet inside the Wildcats Baseball Stadium.

☐ 3. GO JUMP!
Location: Anywhere
Action: Jump Simple
Combo Actions: None
Description: Driver Challenge: Get some air.

☐ 4. ONCOMING INTRO
Location: Anywhere
Action: Oncoming
Combo Actions: None
Description: Driver Challenge: Drive in oncoming traffic for 75 yards.

☐ 5. DRIFT INTRO
Location: Anywhere
Action: Drift
Combo Actions: None
Description: Driver Challenge: Drift your car.

☐ 6. GO CLUBBING
Location: Ocean View
Action: Meet Up
Combo Actions: None
Description: Team Challenge: Meet at the Maplemount Country Club.

☐ 7. NEAR MISS INTRO
Location: Anywhere
Action: Near Miss
Combo Actions: None
Description: Driver Challenge: Near-miss a traffic vehicle.

☐ 8. JUMP INTRO
Location: Anywhere
Action: Jump Distance
Combo Actions: None
Description: Driver Challenge: Jump 35 yards.

☐ 9. CRASH BRIDGE
Location: Paradise Avenue Bridge
Action: Crash
Combo Actions: None
Description: Team Challenge: Jump the Paradise Avenue Bridge and crash into each other in mid-air.

10. SMASH AND GRAB
Location: Anywhere
Action: Billboards
Combo Actions: None
Description: Driver Challenge: Smash through 2 Burnout billboards.

11. FOUNTAIN MISSED
Location: Twin Bridges
Action: Combo
Combo Actions: Drift / Near Miss
Description: Team Challenge: Drift a total of 1,500 yards and get 2 near misses around the Franke Avenue fountain. All drivers must contribute.

12. IN THE NAVY
Location: South Bay
Action: Meet Up
Combo Actions: None
Description: Team Challenge: Meet at the Fort Lawrence Naval Yard.

13. JUMPING EXPRESS
Location: South Bay Expressway Bridge
Action: Jump Quantity
Combo Actions: None
Description: Driver Challenge: Jump 10 times on the South Bay Expressway Bridge.

14. JUMP CASEY
Location: Rockridge Cliffs
Action: Jump Distance
Combo Actions: None
Description: Team Challenge: Jump a total of 500 yards off the ramp on Casey Pass. All drivers must contribute.

15. MINEHEADS
Location: Quarry
Action: Jump Quantity
Combo Actions: None
Description: Driver Challenge: Jump across the mine shaft in the Lone Peaks Quarry.

16. SPLASHDOWN
Location: Rockridge Cliffs
Action: Crash
Combo Actions: None
Description: Team Challenge: Crash into each other on the roof of the waterworks building behind the Rockridge Dam.

17. ROCK AND ROLLS!
Location: Quarry
Action: Barrel Roll
Combo Actions: None
Description: Team Challenge: Land a total of 10 barrel rolls in the Lone Peaks Quarry. All drivers must contribute.

18. DRIFT TRACK
Location: Stock Car Track
Action: Drift
Combo Actions: None
Description: Driver Challenge: Drift a total of 2,000 yards at the Lone Peaks Stock Car Track.

19. AIR TIME ON UPHILL
Location: Crystal Summit
Action: Jump Air Time
Combo Actions: None
Description: Team Challenge: Get a total of 12 seconds of air time from the jumps on Uphill Drive. All drivers must contribute.

20. DRIFTERS
Location: Anywhere
Action: Drift
Combo Actions: None
Description: Driver Challenge: Drift a total of 600 yards.

21. NELSON ONCOMING
Location: Nelson Way
Action: Oncoming
Combo Actions: None
Description: Driver Challenge: Drive in oncoming traffic for 500 yards on Nelson Way.

22. DARE TO JUMP!
Location: Crystal Summit
Action: Jump Quantity
Combo Actions: None
Description: Team Challenge: Land a total of 8 jumps from Dead Man's Edge. All drivers must contribute.

23. HIGH JUMP
Location: Sunset Valley
Action: Jump Distance
Combo Actions: None
Description: Driver Challenge: Jump 120 yards over the Nelson Way gas station using the railroad high jump.

24. AIR HOOP
Location: Airfield
Action: Jump Target
Combo Actions: None
Description: Driver Challenge: Jump from the hangar through the red aircraft fuselage section at the Eastern Shore Airfield.

25. BARREL HOOP
Location: Airfield
Action: Barrel Roll Target
Combo Actions: None
Description: Driver Challenge: Barrel roll from the collapsed hangar through the suspended aircraft fuselage section at the Eastern Shore Airfield.

☐ 26. FLAT SPIN INTRO
Location: Anywhere
Action: Flat Spin
Combo Actions: None
Description: Driver Challenge: Flat spin off a ramp.

☐ 27. ON THE WATERFRONT
Location: Waterfront
Action: Meet Up
Combo Actions: None
Description: Team Challenge: Meet at the Waterfront Plaza.

☐ 28. BEACHFRONT ROLLS
Location: Big Surf
Action: Barrel Roll
Combo Actions: None
Description: Driver Challenge: Land 2 barrel rolls on Big Surf beach.

☐ 29. BOOST CHAIN
Location: Anywhere
Action: Boost Time
Combo Actions: None
Description: Driver Challenge: Boost nonstop for 10 seconds.

☐ 30. MINUTE MAN!
Location: Anywhere
Action: Boost Time
Combo Actions: None
Description: Driver Challenge: Get a total of 60 seconds of boosting.

☐ 31. BOARDWALK
Location: Anywhere
Action: Billboards
Combo Actions: None
Description: Team Challenge: Get a total of 8 smashed Burnout billboards. All drivers must contribute.

☐ 32. THE I-88 FREEWAY
Location: I-88
Action: Oncoming
Combo Actions: None
Description: Driver Challenge: Get a total of 8,000 yards of oncoming on I-88.

☐ 33. NEAR MISS CHAIN
Location: Anywhere
Action: Near Miss
Combo Actions: None
Description: Driver Challenge: Near-miss 5 traffic cars without crashing.

☐ 34. DRIFT AND NEAR MISS
Location: Anywhere
Action: Combo
Combo Actions: Drift / Near Miss
Description: Team Challenge: Drift a total of 2,000 yards and 20 near misses. All drivers must contribute.

☐ 35. WAVE JUMPING
Location: Big Surf
Action: Jump Cars
Combo Actions: None
Description: Team Challenge: Jump over each other using the ramps at the Big Surf Beachfront.

☐ 36. FIND SPACE
Location: Anywhere
Action: Power Park
Combo Actions: None
Description: Driver Challenge: Power park your car.

☐ 37. INTO SPACE
Location: Waterfront
Action: Meet Up
Combo Actions: None
Description: Team Challenge: Jump from the parking garage on the EAST side of Angus Wharf to meet up on top of the parking garage on the WEST side.

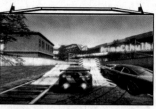

☐ 38. OFF THE RAILS
Location: Big Surf
Action: Barrel Roll
Combo Actions: None
Description: Team Challenge: Barrel roll off the ramps at the Big Surf train yard at the same time.

☐ 39. CHAIN GANG
Location: I-88
Action: Oncoming
Combo Actions: None
Description: Team Challenge: Chain 600 yards of oncoming on I-88, all at the same time.

☐ 40. READ DOUBLE
Location: Crystal Summit
Action: Barrel Roll
Combo Actions: None
Description: Driver Challenge: Jump off a ramp on Read Lane and land a double barrel roll on the railroad.

☐ 41. 720!
Location: Sunset Valley
Action: Flat Spin
Combo Actions: None
Description: Team Challenge: Get a total of 720 degrees of flat spin from the broken wooden bridge on Nelson Way. All drivers must contribute.

☐ 42. HOLE IN ONE!
Location: Lone Peaks
Action: Jump Target
Combo Actions: None
Description: Driver Challenge: Discover the jump route through the rock arch on North Mountain Drive.

☐ 43. DRIFT AND SHOUT
Location: Lone Peaks
Action: Combo
Combo Actions: Barrel Roll / Drift
Description: Driver Challenge: Land 3 barrel rolls and drift a total of 600 yards by jumping off the Rockridge cliff then driving back up.

☐ 44. 180!
Location: Anywhere
Action: Flat Spin
Combo Actions: None
Description: Driver Challenge: Flat spin your car 180 degrees.

☐ 45. LONG JUMPERS
Location: Anywhere
Action: Jump Distance
Combo Actions: None
Description: Driver Challenge: Jump 150 yards.

☐ 46. EXPRESS YOURSELF
Location: South Bay Expressway Bridge
Action: Combo
Combo Actions: Flat Spin / Oncoming
Description: Team Challenge: Get a total of 1,000 degrees of flat spin and 1,000 yards of oncoming on the South Bay Expressway Bridge. All drivers must contribute.

☐ 47. EYES BLEED
Location: I-88
Action: Boost Time
Combo Actions: None
Description: Driver Challenge: Boost nonstop for 20 seconds on I-88.

☐ 48. POWER PARKING
Location: Anywhere
Action: Power Park
Combo Actions: None
Description: Driver Challenge: Power Park and score 75% or better.

☐ 49. BILLBOARD TOP 10
Location: Anywhere
Action: Billboards
Combo Actions: None
Description: Driver Challenge: Smash 10 Burnout billboards.

☐ 50. HOOP-LA
Location: Airfield
Action: Jump Target
Combo Actions: None
Description: Driver Challenge: Jump through the suspended aircraft fuselage section at the Eastern Shore Airfield.

THREE PLAYERS

☐ 51. BOOST BABY
Location: Anywhere
Action: Boost Simple
Combo Actions: None
Description: Driver Challenge: Use boost.

☐ 52. DRIVER DESTRUCTION
Location: Anywhere
Action: Billboards
Combo Actions: None
Description: Driver Challenge: Smash a Burnout billboard.

☐ 53. GET AIR TIME
Location: Anywhere
Action: Jump Air Time
Combo Actions: None
Description: Driver Challenge: Get a total of 5 seconds of air time.

☐ 54. DRIFT INTRO
Location: Anywhere
Action: Drift
Combo Actions: None
Description: Driver Challenge: Drift a total of 100 yards.

☐ 55. COAST GUARDS
Location: Big Surf
Action: Meet Up
Combo Actions: None
Description: Team Challenge: Meet at the Coast Guard HQ.

☐ 56. JUMP CO-OP
Location: Anywhere
Action: Jump Distance
Combo Actions: None
Description: Team Challenge: Get a total of 300 yards of jump distance. All drivers must contribute.

☐ 57. ONCOMING INTRO
Location: Anywhere
Action: Oncoming
Combo Actions: None
Description: Driver Challenge: Drive in oncoming traffic for 75 yards.

☐ 58. 5 NEAR MISSES
Location: Anywhere
Action: Near Miss
Combo Actions: None
Description: Driver Challenge: Get a total of 5 near misses.

☐ 59. ALL DRIFT
Location: Anywhere
Action: Drift
Combo Actions: None
Description: Driver Challenge: Drift for 100 yards.

☐ 60. CO-OP AIR TIME
Location: Anywhere
Action: Jump Air Time
Combo Actions: None
Description: Team Challenge: Get a total of 15 seconds of air time. All drivers must contribute.

☐ 61. BARREL ROLL
Location: Big Surf
Action: Barrel Roll
Combo Actions: None
Description: Driver Challenge: Land a barrel roll at Big Surf beach.

☐ 62. 20 SECOND RUN
Location: Anywhere
Action: Boost Time
Combo Actions: None
Description: Driver Challenge: Get a total of 20 seconds of boosting.

☐ 63. FLIGHT TIME
Location: Motor City
Action: Jump Air Time
Combo Actions: None
Description: Driver Challenge: Get a total of 10 seconds of air time from the backstreet ramps off Angus Wharf.

☐ 64. GO AHEAD, JUMP!
Location: Downtown
Action: Jump Cars
Combo Actions: None
Description: Team Challenge: Each driver, jump over the other 2 drivers in the Downtown Park.

☐ 65. FLAT SPIN INTRO
Location: Anywhere
Action: Flat Spin
Combo Actions: None
Description: Driver Challenge: Flat spin off a ramp.

☐ 66. JUMP BRIDGE
Location: South Bay Expressway Bridge
Action: Jump Quantity
Combo Actions: None
Description: Driver Challenge:

Land a total of 10 jumps on the South Bay Expressway Bridge.

☐ 67. WATERWORKS
Location: Rockridge Cliffs
Action: Meet Up
Combo Actions: None
Description: Team Challenge: Meet on the roof of the waterworks building behind the Rockridge Dam.

☐ 68. EARTH MOVERS
Location: Quarry
Action: Jump Air Time
Combo Actions: None
Description: Team Challenge: Get a total of over 30 seconds of air time at the Lone Peaks Quarry. All drivers must contribute.

☐ 69. THE PARADISE JOB
Location: Crystal Summit
Action: Drive Through
Combo Actions: None
Description: Driver Challenge: Drive through the North Mountain Drive pipeline.

☐ 70. UPHILL JUMPS
Location: Crystal Summit
Action: Jump Cars
Combo Actions: None
Description: Team Challenge: Each driver, jump over the other 2 drivers at the Uphill Steps.

☐ 71. FLY ON THE EDGE
Location: Crystal Summit
Action: Jump Quantity
Combo Actions: None
Description: Driver Challenge: Jump Dead Man's Edge, once from the north side, once from the south.

☐ 72. WINDY SPINNER
Location: Crystal Summit
Action: Flat Spin
Combo Actions: None
Description: Driver Challenge: Get a total of over 360 degrees of flat spin at the Wind Farm on North Mountain Drive.

☐ 73. BARN BUSTERS
Location: Hillside Pass
Action: Meet Up
Combo Actions: None
Description: Team Challenge: Meet in the hayloft of the barn on Hillside Pass.

☐ 74. AIRFIELD MARATHON
Location: Airfield
Action: Combo
Combo Actions: Drift / Jump Quantity

Description: Team Challenge: Drift a total of 2,500 yards and land 20 jumps at the Eastern Shore Airfield. All drivers must contribute.

☐ 75. AIR PROX
Location: Airfield
Action: Near Miss
Combo Actions: None
Description: Driver Challenge: Near-miss 5 cars at the Eastern Shore Airfield.

☐ 76. HOOPS OF GLORY
Location: Airfield
Action: Jump Target
Combo Actions: None
Description: Driver Challenge: Jump from the hangar through the red aircraft fuselage section at the Eastern Shore Airfield.

☐ 77. LONG JUMP
Location: Anywhere
Action: Jump Distance
Combo Actions: None
Description: Driver Challenge: Jump a total of 500 yards.

☐ 78. TUNNEL VISION
Location: Heartbreak Hills
Action: Near Miss
Combo Actions: None
Description: Driver Challenge: Get a 5-vehicle near miss chain in the Lawrence Road Tunnel.

☐ 79. 15 SECOND BURN
Location: Anywhere
Action: Boost Time
Combo Actions: None
Description: Driver Challenge: Boost nonstop for 15 seconds.

☐ 80. OCEAN VIEW SPINS
Location: Ocean View
Action: Flat Spin
Combo Actions: None
Description: Driver Challenge: Flat spin your car 90 degrees off the Ocean View Steps.

☐ 81. BEACHFRONT DISPLAY
Location: Big Surf
Action: Jump Cars
Combo Actions: None
Description: Team Challenge: Take turns to barrel roll over the other 2 drivers using the ramps on the beach at Big Surf.

☐ 82. O2K
Location: Anywhere
Action: Oncoming
Combo Actions: None
Description: Driver Challenge: Get a total of 2,000 yards of oncoming.

☐ 83. SPLASH DRIFT
Location: Twin Bridges
Action: Drift
Combo Actions: None
Description: Team Challenge: Drift a total of 4,000 yards around the Franke Avenue fountain. All drivers must contribute.

☐ 84. DRAW JUMPING
Location: Paradise Avenue Bridge
Action: Jump Quantity
Combo Actions: None
Description: Team Challenge: Land a total of 15 jumps over the Paradise Avenue Bridge. All drivers must contribute.

☐ 85. GO WILDCATS!
Location: Waterfront
Action: Meet Up
Combo Actions: None
Description: Team Challenge: Meet inside the Wildcats Baseball Stadium.

☐ 86. NEAR MISS CHAIN
Location: Anywhere
Action: Near Miss
Combo Actions: None
Description: Driver Challenge: Get a 7-vehicle near miss chain.

☐ 87. CO-OP SMASH
Location: Anywhere
Action: Billboards
Combo Actions: None
Description: Team Challenge: Smash 10 Burnout billboards. All drivers must contribute.

☐ 88. TRAFFIC CALMING
Location: Anywhere
Action: Power Park
Combo Actions: None
Description: Driver Challenge: Power park your car.

☐ 89. COUNTDOWN
Location: Anywhere
Action: Boost Time
Combo Actions: None
Description: Driver Challenge: Get a total of 60 seconds of boost time.

☐ 90. FISH AND FLIPS
Location: Paradise Wharf
Action: Combo
Combo Actions: Flat Spin / Jump Quantity
Description: Team Challenge: Land a total of 20 jumps and get a total of 720 degrees of flat spin at the Manners Pier.

☐ 91. EXPRESS JUMPS
Location: South Bay Expressway Bridge

Action: Jump Quantity
Combo Actions: None
Description: Team Challenge: Land a total of 21 jumps on the South Bay Expressway Bridge. All drivers must contribute.

☐ 92. REVERSE CLIFF TOP
Location: Rockridge Cliffs
Action: Jump Reverse
Combo Actions: None
Description: Driver Challenge: Jump off the cliff at the Rockridge Dam in reverse.

☐ 93. ROCKFALLS
Location: Quarry
Action: Combo
Combo Actions: Drift / Flat Spin
Description: Driver Challenge: Drift a total of 3,000 yards and get 800 degrees of flat spin in the Lone Peaks Quarry.

☐ 94. JUMP FOR YOUR LIFE
Location: Crystal Summit
Action: Jump Simultaneously
Combo Actions: None
Description: Team Challenge: All drivers jump onto the railroad from the Read Lane ramps at the same time.

☐ 95. SKY DRIVER
Location: Sunset Valley
Action: Jump Distance
Combo Actions: None
Description: Driver Challenge: Jump 100 yards over the Nelson Way gas station using the railroad high jump.

☐ 96. READY TO TUMBLE
Location: River City / Paradise Wharf
Action: Barrel Roll
Combo Actions: None
Description: Team Challenge: Land a total of 10 barrel rolls off the broken bridge on 1st Street. All drivers must contribute.

☐ 97. KEEP IT GOING
Location: I-88
Action: Boost Time
Combo Actions: None
Description: Driver Challenge: Boost nonstop for 20 seconds on I-88.

☐ 98. CITY SIGHTS
Location: Waterfront
Action: Meet Up
Combo Actions: None
Description: Team Challenge: Jump from the parking garage on the EAST side of Angus Wharf to meet up on top of the parking garage on the WEST side.

☐ 99. 1ST STREET REVERSE
Location: River City / Paradise Wharf
Action: Jump Reverse
Combo Actions: None
Description: Driver Challenge: Jump over the 1st Street bridge while driving in reverse.

☐ 100. CHECK IT OUT!
Location: Downtown
Action: Meet Up
Combo Actions: None
Description: Team Challenge: Use the ramps on the Fry Avenue parking garage and meet on the roof of the DJR Sports store.

FOUR PLAYERS

☐ 101. 4 WAY PLAY
Location: Motor City
Action: Jump Quantity
Combo Actions: None
Description: Team Challenge: Land a total of 24 jumps off the backstreet ramps behind Angus Wharf. All drivers must contribute.

☐ 102. NEAR MISS INTRO
Location: Anywhere
Action: Near Miss
Combo Actions: None
Description: Driver Challenge: Near-miss a traffic vehicle.

☐ 103. DRIFT IT
Location: Anywhere
Action: Drift
Combo Actions: None
Description: Driver Challenge: Drift for 50 yards.

☐ 104. 50 YARD JUMP
Location: Anywhere
Action: Jump Distance
Combo Actions: None
Description: Driver Challenge: Jump 50 yards off a ramp.

☐ 105. AIR TIME
Location: Anywhere
Action: Jump Air Time
Combo Actions: None
Description: Driver Challenge: Get a total of 8 seconds of air time.

☐ 106. GO CLUBBING
Location: Ocean View
Action: Meet Up
Combo Actions: None
Description: Team Challenge: Meet at the Maplemount Country Club.

☐ 107. FAST OR LAST
Location: Anywhere
Action: Boost Time
Combo Actions: None
Description: Driver Challenge: Get a total of 10 seconds of boosting.

☐ 108. PAVE PARADISE
Location: Anywhere
Action: Power Park
Combo Actions: None
Description: Driver Challenge: Power park your car.

☐ 109. JUMP DISTANCE
Location: Anywhere
Action: Jump Distance
Combo Actions: None
Description: Team Challenge: Jump a total of 350 yards. All drivers must contribute.

☐ 110. DRAWING LOTS
Location: Paradise Avenue Bridge
Action: Flat Spin
Combo Actions: None
Description: Driver Challenge: Flat spin over the Paradise Avenue Bridge.

☐ 111. AIRFIELD AIR TIME
Location: Airfield
Action: Jump Quantity
Combo Actions: None
Description: Driver Challenge: Jump 4 times at the Eastern Shore Airfield.

☐ 112. 12K DRIFT
Location: Airfield
Action: Combo
Combo Actions: Drift / Near Miss
Description: Team Challenge: Drift a total of 12,000 yards and get 12 near misses at the Eastern Shore Airfield. All drivers must contribute.

☐ 113. LOOK AND LEAP
Location: Anywhere
Action: Jump Distance
Combo Actions: None
Description: Driver Challenge: Jump 100 yards.

☐ 114. BILLBOARD INTRO
Location: Anywhere
Action: Billboards
Combo Actions: None
Description: Driver Challenge: Smash through a Burnout billboard.

☐ 115. ISLAND HOPPING
Location: Eastern Shore
Action: Jump Target
Combo Actions: None
Description: Driver Challenge: Find the lakeside ramps and jump to Silver Lake Island then off again.

☐ 116. VICTORY!
Location: Nelson Way
Action: Oncoming
Combo Actions: None
Description: Team Challenge: Get a total of 2,400 yards of oncoming on Nelson way. All drivers must contribute.

☐ 117. BARREL OF LAUGHS
Location: Crystal Summit
Action: Barrel Roll
Combo Actions: None
Description: Driver Challenge: Barrel roll off the ramp on Read Lane and land on the railroad.

☐ 118. STAY ON TARGET
Location: Crystal Summit
Action: Drive Through
Combo Actions: None
Description: Driver Challenge: Drive through the pipeline on North Mountain Drive.

☐ 119. UPHILL STRUGGLE
Location: Crystal Summit
Action: Combo
Combo Actions: Drift / Oncoming
Description: Team Challenge: Drift a total of 4,000 yards and get 8,000 yards of oncoming on Uphill Drive. All drivers must contribute.

☐ 120. ALL FIRED UP
Location: Anywhere
Action: Boost Time
Combo Actions: None
Description: Driver Challenge: Boost nonstop for 10 seconds.

☐ 121. THE ROCK HOLE
Location: Lone Peaks
Action: Jump Target
Combo Actions: None
Description: Driver Challenge: Discover the jump route through the rock arch on North Mountain Drive.

☐ 122. JUMP AND MISS
Location: South Bay Expressway Bridge
Action: Combo
Combo Actions: Jump Quantity / Near Miss
Description: Team Challenge: Land a total of 30 jumps and 20 near misses on the South Bay Expressway Bridge. All drivers must contribute.

☐ 123. IN THE NAVY
Location: South Bay
Action: Meet Up
Combo Actions: None
Description: Team Challenge: Meet at the Fort Lawrence Naval Yard.

☐ 124. FOUR-SITE
Location: South Bay
Action: Meet Up
Combo Actions: None
Description: Team Challenge: Use the ramps on the roof of the Lambert Parkway parking garage and meet in the second building under construction on Hall Avenue.

☐ 125. QUICK DRAW
Location: Paradise Avenue Bridge
Action: Jump Quantity
Combo Actions: None
Description: Team Challenge: Land a total of 20 jumps on the Paradise Avenue Bridge. All drivers must contribute.

☐ 126. NEWTON DRIFT
Location: Ocean View
Action: Drift
Combo Actions: None
Description: Driver Challenge: Drift a total of 1,000 yards on Newton Drive.

☐ 127. RAILWAY ROLLER
Location: Big Surf
Action: Barrel Roll
Combo Actions: None
Description: Driver Challenge: Land a barrel roll in the Big Surf train yard.

☐ 128. FREEWAY ONCOMING
Location: I-88
Action: Oncoming Simultaneously
Combo Actions: None
Description: Team Challenge: Chain 250 yards of oncoming on I-88, all at the same time.

☐ 129. STRIKE!
Location: Waterfront
Action: Crash
Combo Actions: None
Description: Team Challenge: Crash into each other inside the baseball stadium.

☐ 130. RIGHT ANGLED ROLL
Location: Anywhere
Action: Combo
Combo Actions: Barrel Roll / Flat Spin
Description: Driver Challenge: Barrel roll off a ramp and flat spin 90 degrees.

☐ 131. DRIFT 4 FUN
Location: Anywhere
Action: Drift
Combo Actions: None
Description: Team Challenge: Drift a total of 2,000 yards. All drivers must contribute.

132. REVERSE BREAK
Location: River City / Paradise Wharf
Action: Jump Reverse
Combo Actions: None
Description: Driver Challenge: Jump over the broken bridge on 1st Street in reverse.

133. HOT TIN ROOF
Location: Motor City
Action: Meet Up
Combo Actions: None
Description: Team Challenge: Jump from the Webster Avenue parking garage and meet on the roof of the train yard.

134. STOP SPOT
Location: Anywhere
Action: Power Park
Combo Actions: None
Description: Driver Challenge: Power park and score 75% or better.

135. TUNNEL OF SHOVE
Location: Heartbreak Hills
Action: Near Miss
Combo Actions: None
Description: Team Challenge: Get a total of 16 near misses in the Lawrence Road Tunnel. All drivers must contribute.

136. CRASHWORKS
Location: Rockridge Cliffs
Action: Crash
Combo Actions: None
Description: Team Challenge: Crash into each other on the roof of the waterworks building behind the Rockridge Dam.

137. FLAT SPIN TO WIN
Location: South Bay Expressway Bridge
Action: Flat Spin
Combo Actions: None
Description: Driver Challenge: Get a total of over 720 degrees of flat spin on the South Bay Expressway Bridge.

138. WE HAVE LIFT OFF!
Location: Rockridge Cliffs
Action: Barrel Roll Boosting
Combo Actions: None
Description: Driver Challenge: Boost while barrel rolling off the cliff overlooking the Rockridge Dam.

139. DIRT BUSTER
Location: Stock Car Track
Action: Combo
Combo Actions: Drift / Near Miss

Description: Driver Challenge: Drift a total of 2,000 yards and get 4 near misses at the Lone Peaks Stock Car Track.

140. MINED THE GAP!
Location: Quarry
Action: Jump Quantity
Combo Actions: None
Description: Team Challenge: Land a total of 16 jumps over the mine shaft in the Lone Peaks Quarry.

141. QUARRY ROLLS
Location: Quarry
Action: Barrel Roll
Combo Actions: None
Description: Driver Challenge: Land a double barrel roll in the Lone Peaks Quarry.

142. ROCKRIDGE SPINS
Location: Rockridge Cliffs
Action: Flat Spin
Combo Actions: None
Description: Driver Challenge: Flat spin more than 270 degrees off the cliff overlooking the Rockridge Dam.

143. DAM BLAST!
Location: Lone Peaks
Action: Combo
Combo Actions: Drift / Jump Quantity
Description: Team Challenge: Drift a total of 4,000 yards and land 8 jumps off the cliff overlooking the Rockridge Dam. All drivers must contribute.

144. INFERNO
Location: Anywhere
Action: Boost Time
Combo Actions: None
Description: Driver Challenge: Get a total of 100 seconds of boosting.

145. STEP ON!
Location: Crystal Summit
Action: Flat Spin
Combo Actions: None
Description: Team Challenge: Get a total of over 180 degrees of flat spin off the Uphill Steps. All drivers must contribute.

146. FLATSPINNERS
Location: Sunset Valley
Action: Flat Spin
Combo Actions: None
Description: Driver Challenge: Flat spin more than 150 degrees over the Nelson Way gas station using the railroad high jump.

147. SMASH!
Location: Anywhere
Action: Billboards
Combo Actions: None
Description: Team Challenge: Get a total of 12 smashed Burnout billboards. All drivers must contribute.

148. THRU HOOP
Location: Airfield
Action: Jump Target
Combo Actions: None
Description: Driver Challenge: Jump from the collapsed hanger through the suspended aircraft fuselage section at the Eastern Shore Airfield.

149. TRAIL BLAZERS
Location: I-88
Action: Boost Time
Combo Actions: None
Description: Driver Challenge: Boost nonstop for 20 seconds on I-88.

150. BARREL HOOPLA
Location: Airfield
Action: Barrel Roll Target
Combo Actions: None
Description: Driver Challenge: Barrel roll from the collapsed hangar through the suspended aircraft fuselage section at the Eastern Shore Airfield.

FIVE PLAYERS

151. NEAR MISS INTRO
Location: Anywhere
Action: Near Miss
Combo Actions: None
Description: Driver Challenge: Get a total of 4 near misses.

152. BILLBOARD INTRO
Location: Anywhere
Action: Billboards
Combo Actions: None
Description: Driver Challenge: Smash a Burnout billboard.

153. DRIFT INTRO
Location: Anywhere
Action: Drift
Combo Actions: None
Description: Driver Challenge: Drift for 50 yards.

154. 5 JUMP
Location: Anywhere
Action: Jump Distance
Combo Actions: None
Description: Driver Challenge: Jump a total of 100 yards.

155. RUN THE TRAFFIC
Location: Anywhere

Action: Oncoming
Combo Actions: None
Description: Driver Challenge: Drive in oncoming traffic for 500 yards.

156. FREEWAY YOUR WAY
Location: I-88
Action: Near Miss
Combo Actions: None
Description: Driver Challenge: Near-miss 12 vehicles on I-88.

157. AIR TIME!
Location: Anywhere
Action: Jump Air Time
Combo Actions: None
Description: Team Challenge: Get a total of 20 seconds of air time. All drivers must contribute.

158. FLASH IN THE PAN
Location: Anywhere
Action: Boost Time
Combo Actions: None
Description: Driver Challenge: Boost nonstop for 5 seconds.

159. SINGLE ROLL
Location: Anywhere
Action: Barrel Roll
Combo Actions: None
Description: Driver Challenge: Land a barrel roll.

160. WHARF SPEED
Location: Motor City
Action: Jump Quantity
Combo Actions: None
Description: Team Challenge: Land a total of 30 jumps off the ramps in the alley behind Angus Wharf. All drivers must contribute.

161. LONE STALLION
Location: Lone Peaks
Action: Meet Up
Combo Actions: None
Description: Team Challenge: Meet at the Lone Stallion Ranch.

162. WORK IT!
Location: Rockridge Cliffs
Action: Meet Up
Combo Actions: None
Description: Team Challenge: Meet on the roof of the waterworks building behind the Rockridge Dam.

163. GOING UNDERGROUND!
Location: Crystal Summit
Action: Drive Through
Combo Actions: None
Description: Driver Challenge: Drive through the pipeline on North Mountain Drive.

164. LIVING ON THE EDGE
Location: Crystal Summit
Action: Jump Quantity

Combo Actions: None
Description: Driver Challenge: Jump over Dead Man's Edge 4 times.

165. LONG DISTANCE FALL
Location: Quarry
Action: Jump Distance
Combo Actions: None
Description: Team Challenge: Get a total of a jump distance of 1,500 yards in the Lone Peaks Quarry. All drivers must contribute.

166. DROP OFF UPHILL
Location: Crystal Summit
Action: Jump Quantity
Combo Actions: None
Description: Team Challenge: Land a total of 16 jumps off the steps on Uphill Drive. All drivers must contribute.

167. HOT STEPPER
Location: Crystal Summit
Action: Flat Spin
Combo Actions: None
Description: Driver Challenge: Get a total of 360 degrees of flat spin off the Uphill Steps.

168. HANG TOUGH
Location: Crystal Summit
Action: Jump Distance
Combo Actions: None
Description: Driver Challenge: Jump 145 yards off the double ramp on Read Lane onto the railroad.

169. HIGH FIVE
Location: Sunset Valley
Action: Jump Distance
Combo Actions: None
Description: Driver Challenge: Jump 100 yards over the Nelson Way gas station using the railroad high jump.

170. MINE'S A JUMP
Location: Quarry
Action: Jump Quantity
Combo Actions: None
Description: Driver Challenge: Jump the mine shaft in the Lone Peaks Quarry.

171. 8 TRACK!
Location: Stock Car Track
Action: Combo
Combo Actions: Drift / Near Miss
Description: Driver Challenge: Drift a total of 2,000 yards and get 4 near misses at the Stock Car Track.

172. AIRFIELD ACTION
Location: Airfield
Action: Jump Quantity

Combo Actions: None
Description: Team Challenge: Land a total of 40 jumps at the Eastern Shore Airfield. All drivers must contribute.

173. CARWRECKED!
Location: Eastern Shore
Action: Jump Target
Combo Actions: None
Description: Driver Challenge: Find the lakeside ramps and jump to Silver Lake Island then off again.

174. SMASHING!
Location: Anywhere
Action: Billboards
Combo Actions: None
Description: Driver Challenge: Jump through 2 Burnout billboards.

175. JUMP FAR
Location: Anywhere
Action: Jump Distance
Combo Actions: None
Description: Team Challenge: Jump a total of 1,500 yards. All drivers must contribute.

176. FLAME TRAIL
Location: Anywhere
Action: Boost Time
Combo Actions: None
Description: Driver Challenge: Get a total of 30 seconds of boosting.

177. COAST GUARDS
Location: Big Surf
Action: Meet Up
Combo Actions: None
Description: Team Challenge: Meet at the Coast Guard HQ.

178. BEACHFRONT POSE
Location: Big Surf
Action: Jump Quantity
Combo Actions: None
Description: Driver Challenge: Jump 4 times off the ramps on the Big Surf Beach.

179. PARK MAYHEM
Location: Big Surf
Action: Meet Up
Combo Actions: None
Description: Team Challenge: Meet on the roof of the Hudson Avenue parking garage.

180. 10K FOUNTAIN
Location: Twin Bridges
Action: Drift
Combo Actions: None
Description: Team Challenge: Drift a total of 10,000 yards at the Franke Avenue fountain. All drivers must contribute.

181. BEACHCOMBER
Location: Big Surf
Action: Flat Spin
Combo Actions: None
Description: Driver Challenge: Flat spin 70 degrees at the Big Surf beach.

182. ROOFTOP JUMPS
Location: Waterfront
Action: Meet Up
Combo Actions: None
Description: Team Challenge: Jump from the parking garage on the EAST side of Angus Wharf to meet up on top of the parking garage on the WEST side.

183. DRIFT AND NEAR MISS
Location: Anywhere
Action: Combo
Combo Actions: Drift / Near Miss
Description: Team Challenge: Drift a total of 3,000 yards and get 25 near misses. All drivers must contribute.

184. TROUBLED WATERS
Location: Paradise Avenue Bridge
Action: Jump Quantity
Combo Actions: None
Description: Team Challenge: Land a total of 15 jumps over the Paradise Avenue Bridge. All drivers must contribute.

185. SITE SEEING
Location: South Bay
Action: Meet Up
Combo Actions: None
Description: Team Challenge: Use the ramps on the roof of the Lambert Parkway parking garage and meet in the second building under construction on Hall Avenue.

186. PIER JUMP
Location: Paradise Wharf
Action: Jump Quantity
Combo Actions: None
Description: Team Challenge: Land a total of 25 jumps on the South Manners Pier. All drivers must contribute.

187. ONCOMING EXPRESS
Location: South Bay Expressway Bridge
Action: Combo
Combo Actions: Near Miss / Oncoming
Description: Team Challenge: Get a total of 4,000 yards of oncoming and 25 near misses on the South Bay Expressway Bridge. All drivers must contribute.

188. EXPRESS WHIRL
Location: South Bay Expressway Bridge
Action: Flat Spin
Combo Actions: None
Description: Driver Challenge: Get a total of 1,440 degrees of flat spin on the South Bay Expressway Bridge.

189. ROCKRIDGE RUMBLE
Location: Rockridge Cliffs
Action: Combo
Combo Actions: Barrel Roll / Drift
Description: Team Challenge: Land 25 barrel rolls off the cliff above the Rockridge Dam, and drift a total of 7,500 yards driving back up South Mountain Drive.

190. DOUBLE ROLL
Location: Rockridge Cliffs
Action: Barrel Roll
Combo Actions: None
Description: Driver Challenge: Land a double barrel roll off the cliff overlooking the Rockridge Dam.

191. LOW FLYING
Location: Airfield
Action: Jump Cars
Combo Actions: None
Description: Team Challenge: Every driver jump the other 4 at the Eastern Shore Airfield.

192. LAKEY CHALLENGE
Location: Eastern Shore / Heartbreak Hills
Action: Combo
Combo Actions: Drift / Oncoming
Description: Team Challenge: Drift a total of 5,000 yards and get a total of 1,000 yards of oncoming on East Lake Drive.

193. AFTERBURNER
Location: Crystal Summit
Action: Barrel Roll Boosting
Combo Actions: None
Description: Driver Challenge: Boost while barrel rolling off one of the Read Lane ramps to the railroad.

194. RINGO
Location: Airfield
Action: Jump Target
Combo Actions: None
Description: Driver Challenge: Jump through the suspended aircraft fuselage section at the Eastern Shore Airfield.

195. STEP OVER
Location: Ocean View
Action: Jump Cars
Combo Actions: None
Description: Team Challenge: Every driver jump the other 4 off the steps at Ocean View.

196. PARK IT
Location: Anywhere
Action: Power Park
Combo Actions: None
Description: Driver Challenge: Power park your car.

197. BEACH JUMP REVERSE
Location: Big Surf
Action: Jump Reverse
Combo Actions: None
Description: Driver Challenge: Jump off a ramp backward on Big Surf beach.

198. ARE WE THERE YET?
Location: I-88
Action: Oncoming Simultaneously
Combo Actions: None
Description: Team Challenge: Everybody chain 250 yards of oncoming on I-88 at the same time.

199. RAPID FIRE
Location: I-88
Action: Boost Time
Combo Actions: None
Description: Driver Challenge: Boost nonstop for 20 seconds on I-88.

200. ROLL THRU HOOP
Location: Airfield
Action: Barrel Roll Target
Combo Actions: None
Description: Driver Challenge: Barrel roll from the collapsed hangar through the aircraft fuselage section at the Eastern Shore Airfield.

SIX PLAYERS

201. FLOOR IT
Location: Anywhere
Action: Boost Time
Combo Actions: None
Description: Driver Challenge: Get a total of 10 seconds of boosting.

202. GO CLUBBING
Location: Ocean View
Action: Meet Up
Combo Actions: None
Description: Team Challenge: Meet at the Maplemount Country Club.

203. JUMP INTRO
Location: Anywhere

Action: Jump Distance
Combo Actions: None
Description: Driver Challenge: Jump 50 yards.

204. NEAR MISS INTRO
Location: Anywhere
Action: Near Miss
Combo Actions: None
Description: Driver Challenge: Chain 3 near misses.

205. DRIFT INTRO
Location: Anywhere
Action: Drift
Combo Actions: None
Description: Driver Challenge: Drift a total of 150 yards.

206. BILLBOARD INTRO
Location: Anywhere
Action: Billboards
Combo Actions: None
Description: Driver Challenge: Smash a Burnout billboard.

207. BARREL ROLL INTRO
Location: Big Surf
Action: Barrel Roll
Combo Actions: None
Description: Driver Challenge: Land a barrel roll on Big Surf beach.

208. ONCOMING!
Location: Anywhere
Action: Oncoming
Combo Actions: None
Description: Driver Challenge: Drive in oncoming traffic for 300 yards.

209. SKYRISE
Location: Big Surf
Action: Meet Up
Combo Actions: None
Description: Team Challenge: Meet on the roof of the Hudson Car Park.

210. BASEBALL CRASH
Location: Waterfront
Action: Crash
Combo Actions: None
Description: Team Challenge: Crash into each other inside the baseball stadium.

211. FREEWAY 500
Location: I-88
Action: Oncoming
Combo Actions: None
Description: Driver Challenge: Chain 500 yards of oncoming on I-88.

212. FOOT DOWN
Location: Anywhere

Action: Boost Time
Combo Actions: None
Description: Driver Challenge: Get a total of 45 seconds of boosting.

213. SPIN DOKTOR
Location: Anywhere
Action: Flat Spin
Combo Actions: None
Description: Driver Challenge: Flat spin off a ramp.

214. NEAR MISS TON
Location: Anywhere
Action: Near Miss
Combo Actions: None
Description: Team Challenge: Get a total of over 100 near misses. All drivers must contribute.

215. ON THE WATERFRONT
Location: Waterfront
Action: Meet Up
Combo Actions: None
Description: Team Challenge: Meet at the Waterfront Plaza.

216. CO-OP JUMPS
Location: Anywhere
Action: Jump Distance
Combo Actions: None
Description: Team Challenge: Jump a total of 400 yards. All drivers must contribute.

217. SOUTH BAY
Location: South Bay Expressway Bridge
Action: Combo
Combo Actions: Jump Quantity / Oncoming
Description: Team Challenge: Land a total of 50 jumps and 12,000 yards of oncoming on the South Bay Expressway Bridge. All drivers must contribute.

218. ROUND AND ROUND
Location: Stock Car Track
Action: Near Miss
Combo Actions: None
Description: Driver Challenge: Get a total of 10 near misses at the Lone Peaks Stock Car Track.

219. IN A TUBE
Location: Crystal Summit
Action: Drive Through
Combo Actions: None
Description: Driver Challenge: Drive through the North Mountain Drive pipeline.

220. UPHILL FLIGHT
Location: Crystal Summit
Action: Jump Air Time
Combo Actions: None
Description: Driver Challenge: Get

a total of 5 seconds of air time from the Uphill Steps.

221. READ AND ROLL
Location: Crystal Summit
Action: Barrel Roll
Combo Actions: None
Description: Driver Challenge: Jump off a ramp on Read Lane and land a barrel roll on the railroad.

222. HOLE LOTTA JUMPS
Location: Quarry
Action: Jump Quantity
Combo Actions: None
Description: Team Challenge: Land a total of 18 jumps over the mine shaft in the Lone Peaks Quarry. All drivers must contribute.

223. OPEN FACE-OFF
Location: Quarry
Action: Combo
Combo Actions: Barrel Roll / Drift
Description: Driver Challenge: Land 2 barrel rolls and drift a total of 2,000 yards in the Lone Peaks Quarry.

224. BLAST OFF!
Location: Quarry
Action: Jump Air Time
Combo Actions: None
Description: Driver Challenge: Get a total of 15 seconds of air time in the Lone Peaks Quarry.

225. ALL JUMP
Location: Rockridge Cliffs
Action: Jump Distance
Combo Actions: None
Description: Team Challenge: Jump a total of 3,000 yards from the cliff overlooking the Rockridge Dam. All drivers must contribute.

226. AIRFIELD ROLLERS
Location: Airfield
Action: Barrel Roll
Combo Actions: None
Description: Driver Challenge: Land 4 barrel rolls at the Eastern Shore Airfield.

227. AIRFIELD SPINS
Location: Airfield
Action: Flat Spin
Combo Actions: None
Description: Team Challenge: Get a total of 2,500 flat spin degrees at the Eastern Shore Airfield. All drivers must contribute.

228. PASS YOU BY
Location: Hillside Pass
Action: Combo
Combo Actions: Drift / Oncoming

Description: Team Challenge: Drift a total of 6,000 yards and get a total of 1,200 yards of oncoming on Baer Pass. All drivers must contribute.

229. ROUSE LONG JUMP
Location: Hillside Pass
Action: Jump Target
Combo Actions: None
Description: Driver Challenge: Jump from the ramp at the scenic view on Rouse onto the railroad track below.

230. BURN THE BARN
Location: Hillside Pass
Action: Meet Up
Combo Actions: None
Description: Team Challenge: Meet in the hayloft of the barn in Hillside Pass.

231. CO-OP DRIFT
Location: Anywhere
Action: Drift
Combo Actions: None
Description: Team Challenge: Drift a total of 6,000 yards. All drivers must contribute.

232. ALL TOGETHER NOW
Location: Nelson Way
Action: Oncoming Simultaneously
Combo Actions: None
Description: Team Challenge: Everybody get 200 yards of oncoming on Nelson Way at the same time.

233. ROCK AND ROLL
Location: Quarry
Action: Barrel Roll
Combo Actions: None
Description: Driver Challenge: Land a double barrel roll in the Lone Peaks Quarry.

234. 6 CARS-A-LEAPING
Location: Rockridge Cliffs
Action: Jump Quantity
Combo Actions: None
Description: Team Challenge: Land a total of 24 jumps from the cliff overlooking the Rockridge Dam. All drivers must contribute.

235. DIRT TRACK MARATHON
Location: Stock Car Track
Action: Drift
Combo Actions: None
Description: Team Challenge: Drift a total of 18,000 yards at the Lone Peaks Stock Car Track. All drivers must contribute.

236. IN THE NAVY
Location: South Bay

Action: Meet Up
Combo Actions: None
Description: Team Challenge: Meet at the Fort Lawrence Naval Yard.

237. MISSING LINK
Location: I-88
Action: Near Miss
Combo Actions: None
Description: Driver Challenge: Chain 5 near misses on I-88.

238. IN YOUR FACE
Location: I-88
Action: Oncoming Simultaneously
Combo Actions: None
Description: Team Challenge: All drivers chain 250 yards of oncoming on I-88 at the same time.

239. SPRAY AND DISPLAY
Location: Downtown
Action: Combo
Combo Actions: Drift / Near Miss
Description: Team Challenge: Drift a total of 15,000 yards and get 20 near misses at the Downtown fountain. All drivers must contribute.

240. CAN YOU MAKE IT?
Location: Big Surf
Action: Jump Cars
Combo Actions: None
Description: Team Challenge: One driver jumps the other 5 on Big Surf beach.

241. SANDY DISPLAY
Location: Big Surf
Action: Combo
Combo Actions: Barrel Roll / Flat Spin
Description: Driver Challenge: Land 4 barrel rolls and flat spin a total of 270 degrees on Big Surf beach.

242. MEET AND GREET
Location: Waterfront
Action: Meet Up
Combo Actions: None
Description: Team Challenge: Jump from the parking garage on the EAST side of Angus Wharf to meet up on top of the parking garage on the WEST side.

243. EXPRESSO
Location: South Bay Expressway Bridge
Action: Combo
Combo Actions: Flat Spin / Near Miss
Description: Driver Challenge: Accumulate 5 near misses and 360 flat spin degrees on the South Bay Expressway Bridge.

244. STONE POSES
Location: Lone Peaks
Action: Jump Target
Combo Actions: None
Description: Driver Challenge: Discover the jump route through the rock arch on North Mountain Drive.

245. SPIN CITY
Location: Crystal Summit
Action: Flat Spin
Combo Actions: None
Description: Driver Challenge: Get a 270-degree flat spin off Dead Man's Edge.

246. OFF TRACK
Location: Sunset Valley
Action: Jump Distance
Combo Actions: None
Description: Team Challenge: Jump a total of 700 yards over the Nelson Way gas station using the railroad high jump. All drivers must contribute.

247. BILLBOARD HUNT
Location: Anywhere
Action: Billboards
Combo Actions: None
Description: Driver Challenge: Smash 5 Burnout billboards.

248. AIRFIELD REVERSAL
Location: Airfield
Action: Jump Reverse
Combo Actions: None
Description: Driver Challenge: Land a reverse jump at the Eastern Shore Airfield.

249. FLYING THRU
Location: Airfield
Action: Jump Target
Combo Actions: None
Description: Driver Challenge: Jump from the hangar through the red aircraft fuselage section at the Eastern Shore Airfield.

250. ROLLING HOOP
Location: Airfield
Action: Barrel Roll Target
Combo Actions: None
Description: Driver Challenge: Barrel roll from the collapsed hangar through the aircraft fuselage section at the Eastern Shore Airfield.

SEVEN PLAYERS

251. FAST START
Location: Anywhere
Action: Boost Simple
Combo Actions: None
Description: Driver Challenge: Use boost.

252. AIR TIME
Location: Anywhere
Action: Jump Air Time
Combo Actions: None
Description: Driver Challenge: Get a total of 5 seconds of air time.

253. BOOST INTRO
Location: Anywhere
Action: Boost Time
Combo Actions: None
Description: Driver Challenge: Get a total of 10 seconds of boosting.

254. BILLBOARD INTRO
Location: Anywhere
Action: Billboards
Combo Actions: None
Description: Driver Challenge: Smash a Burnout billboard.

255. BEACHFRONT AERIALS
Location: Big Surf
Action: Jump Air Time
Combo Actions: None
Description: Team Challenge: Get a total of 35 seconds of air time on Big Surf beach. All drivers must contribute.

256. NEAR MISS INTRO
Location: Anywhere
Action: Near Miss
Combo Actions: None
Description: Driver Challenge: Get a total of 4 near misses.

257. DRIFT INTRO
Location: Anywhere
Action: Drift
Combo Actions: None
Description: Driver Challenge: Drift for 50 yards.

258. MY LOVELY JUMPS
Location: Anywhere
Action: Jump Distance
Combo Actions: None
Description: Driver Challenge: Jump 60 yards.

259. 7TH HEAVEN
Location: Anywhere
Action: Jump Quantity
Combo Actions: None
Description: Team Challenge: Land a total of 21 jumps. All drivers must contribute.

260. GO WILDCATS!
Location: Waterfront
Action: Meet Up
Combo Actions: None
Description: Team Challenge: Meet inside the Wildcats Baseball Stadium.

261. LONE STALLION
Location: Lone Peaks
Action: Meet Up
Combo Actions: None
Description: Team Challenge: Meet at the Lone Stallion Ranch.

262. TUBE RIDE
Location: Crystal Summit
Action: Meet Up
Combo Actions: None
Description: Driver Challenge: Drive through the North Mountain Drive pipeline.

263. TIME TO BOOST
Location: Anywhere
Action: Boost Time
Combo Actions: None
Description: Driver Challenge: Get a total of 45 seconds of boosting.

264. WATER METER
Location: Rockridge Cliffs
Action: Meet Up
Combo Actions: None
Description: Team Challenge: Meet on the roof of the waterworks building behind the Rockridge Dam.

265. CO-OP JUMP
Location: Anywhere
Action: Jump Distance
Combo Actions: None
Description: Team Challenge: Jump a total of 1,800 yards. All drivers must contribute.

266. AIR TODAY...
Location: Crystal Summit
Action: Jump Air Time
Combo Actions: None
Description: Team Challenge: Get a total of 30 seconds of air time, jumping from Dead Man's Edge. All drivers must contribute.

267. READ ROLLER
Location: Crystal Summit
Action: Barrel Roll
Combo Actions: None
Description: Driver Challenge: Jump off a ramp on Read Lane and land a barrel roll on the railroad.

268. HIGH JUMP
Location: Sunset Valley
Action: Jump Distance
Combo Actions: None
Description: Team Challenge: Jump a total of 1,000 yards over the Nelson Way gas station using the railroad high jump. All drivers must contribute.

269. DON'T QUARRY
Location: Quarry
Action: Combo
Combo Actions: Barrel Roll / Drift
Description: Driver Challenge: Drift 1,000 yards and land 2 barrel rolls in the Lone Peaks Quarry.

270. EXPRESS RACE
Location: South Bay Expressway Bridge
Action: Oncoming
Combo Actions: None
Description: Driver Challenge: Get a total of 4,000 yards of oncoming on the South Bay Expressway Bridge.

271. LOST
Location: Eastern Shore
Action: Crash
Combo Actions: None
Description: Team Challenge: Jump to Silver Lake Island and crash into each other.

272. AIRFIELD DRIFT
Location: Airfield
Action: Drift
Combo Actions: None
Description: Team Challenge: Drift a total of 4,000 yards at the Eastern Shore Airfield. All drivers must contribute.

273. AIRFIELD DISPLAY
Location: Airfield
Action: Jump Cars
Combo Actions: None
Description: Team Challenge: One driver jumps over the other 6 at the Eastern Shore Airfield.

274. AIRFIELD ANGLE
Location: Airfield
Action: Flat Spin
Combo Actions: None
Description: Driver Challenge: Land a 90 degree flat spin from the ramps at the Eastern Shore Airfield.

275. WRONG WAY A LONG WAY
Location: I-88
Action: Oncoming
Combo Actions: None
Description: Team Challenge: Get a total of 10,000 yards of oncoming on I-88. All drivers must contribute.

276. NEAR MISS I-88
Location: I-88
Action: Near Miss
Combo Actions: None
Description: Team Challenge: Get

a total of 140 near misses on I-88. All drivers must contribute.

277. SIM FREEWAY
Location: I-88
Action: Oncoming Simultaneously
Combo Actions: None
Description: Team Challenge: All drivers chain 250 yards of oncoming on I-88 at the same time.

278. ROLLING STOCK
Location: Big Surf
Action: Barrel Roll
Combo Actions: None
Description: Driver Challenge: Land a barrel roll off the train yard ramp in Big Surf.

279. NEWTON SLIDE
Location: Ocean View
Action: Drift
Combo Actions: None
Description: Driver Challenge: Drift 120 yards on Newton Drive.

280. QUICK PARK
Location: Anywhere
Action: Power Park
Combo Actions: None
Description: Driver Challenge: Power park and score 75% or better.

281. QUICK DRAW
Location: Paradise Avenue Bridge
Action: Combo
Combo Actions: Jump Quantity / Near Miss
Description: Team Challenge: Get a total of 7 near misses and 14 jumps on the Paradise Avenue Bridge. All drivers must contribute.

282. STEP TO IT
Location: Ocean View
Action: Jump Cars
Combo Actions: None
Description: Team Challenge: Six drivers park on the Ocean View steps while the other jumps over them all.

283. PIER
Location: Paradise Wharf
Action: Flat Spin
Combo Actions: None
Description: Driver Challenge: Flat spin a total of 360 degrees on the Manners Pier.

284. COAST GUARDS
Location: Big Surf
Action: Meet Up
Combo Actions: None
Description: Team Challenge: Meet at the Coast Guard HQ.

285. HEAD SPINS
Location: Anywhere
Action: Combo
Combo Actions: Barrel Roll / Flat Spin
Description: Team Challenge: Land 35 barrel rolls and flat spin a total of 1,300 degrees. All drivers must contribute.

286. VALLEY HUNT
Location: Anywhere
Action: Billboards
Combo Actions: None
Description: Driver Challenge: Smash 3 Burnout billboards.

287. BARNSTORMING
Location: Hillside Pass
Action: Meet Up
Combo Actions: None
Description: Team Challenge: Meet in the hayloft of the barn in Hillside Pass.

288. WIDE BODY
Location: Airfield
Action: Jump Target
Combo Actions: None
Description: Driver Challenge: Jump from the collapsed hanger through the suspended aircraft fuselage section at the Eastern Shore Airfield.

289. BURNOUT WAY
Location: Nelson Way
Action: Combo
Combo Actions: Drift / Oncoming
Description: Team Challenge: Drift a total of 7,000 yards and get a total of 1,400 yards of oncoming on Nelson Way. All drivers must contribute.

290. QUARRY BARRELS
Location: Quarry
Action: Barrel Roll
Combo Actions: None
Description: Driver Challenge: Land a double barrel roll in the Lone Peaks Quarry.

291. 3K LEAP
Location: Rockridge Cliffs
Action: Jump Distance
Combo Actions: None
Description: Team Challenge: Jump a total of 3,000 yards from the cliff overlooking the Rockridge Dam.

292. QUARRY TAKEOFFS
Location: Quarry
Action: Jump Quantity
Combo Actions: None
Description: Team Challenge: Land

a total of 50 jumps at the Lone Peaks Quarry. All drivers must contribute.

293. DRIFT AND DIRT
Location: Stock Car Track
Action: Drift
Combo Actions: None
Description: Driver Challenge: Drift 3,000 yards at the Lone Peaks Stock Car Track.

294. HALF CENTURY
Location: Rockridge Cliffs
Action: Barrel Roll
Combo Actions: None
Description: Team Challenge: Land 50 barrel rolls from the cliff overlooking the Rockridge Dam. All drivers must contribute.

295. SHOOTING HOOPS
Location: Airfield
Action: Jump Target
Combo Actions: None
Description: Driver Challenge: Jump from the hangar through the red aircraft fuselage section at the Eastern Shore Airfield.

296. SOUTH BAY EXPRESS
Location: South Bay Expressway Bridge
Action: Combo
Combo Actions: Flat Spin / Jump Quantity
Description: Team Challenge: Flat spin a total of 8,000 degrees and jump 50 times on the South Bay Expressway Bridge. All drivers must contribute.

297. DAM
Location: Rockridge Cliffs
Action: Jump Distance
Combo Actions: None
Description: Driver Challenge: Jump 75 yards on Casey Pass.

298. BURNOUTS
Location: I-88
Action: Boost Time
Combo Actions: None
Description: Driver Challenge: Boost nonstop for 20 seconds on I-88.

299. FLY FOR WEBSTER!
Location: Motor City
Action: Meet Up
Combo Actions: None
Description: Team Challenge: Jump from the Webster Avenue parking garage and meet on the roof of the train yard.

300. 4 BILLBOARDS
Location: Anywhere
Action: Billboards
Combo Actions: None
Description: Driver Challenge: Smash 4 Burnout billboards.

EIGHT PLAYERS

301. QUICK FIRE
Location: Anywhere
Action: Boost Simple
Combo Actions: None
Description: Driver Challenge: Use boost.

302. BATTER UP
Location: Waterfront
Action: Meet Up
Combo Actions: None
Description: Team Challenge: Meet in the Wildcats Baseball Stadium.

303. CO-OP JUMP DISTANCE
Location: Anywhere
Action: Jump Distance
Combo Actions: None
Description: Team Challenge: Jump a total of 800 yards. All drivers must contribute.

304. LEARN TO DRIFT
Location: Anywhere
Action: Drift
Combo Actions: None
Description: Driver Challenge: Get a 100-yard drift.

305. NEAR MISS INTRO
Location: Anywhere
Action: Near Miss
Combo Actions: None
Description: Driver Challenge: Get a total of 4 near misses.

306. BILLBOARD INTRO
Location: Anywhere
Action: Billboards
Combo Actions: None
Description: Driver Challenge: Smash a Burnout billboard.

307. 50 YARD JUMP
Location: Anywhere
Action: Jump Distance
Combo Actions: None
Description: Driver Challenge: Jump 50 yards.

308. BARREL ROLL INTRO
Location: Big Surf
Action: Barrel Roll
Combo Actions: None
Description: Driver Challenge: Land a barrel roll on Big Surf beach.

309. STUNTMAN!
Location: Big Surf
Action: Jump Cars
Combo Actions: None
Description: Team Challenge: One driver jumps the other 7 on Big Surf Beach.

310. OVER A MILE
Location: Anywhere
Action: Oncoming
Combo Actions: None
Description: Team Challenge: Get a total of 16,000 yards of oncoming. All drivers must contribute.

311. PARADISE JUMP
Location: Paradise Avenue Bridge
Action: Jump Quantity
Combo Actions: None
Description: Driver Challenge: Jump over the Paradise Avenue Bridge.

312. WHARF LEAPS
Location: Motor City
Action: Jump Quantity
Combo Actions: None
Description: Team Challenge: Land a total of 50 jumps off the ramps in the alley behind Angus Wharf. All drivers must contribute.

313. IN THE NAVY
Location: South Bay
Action: Meet Up
Combo Actions: None
Description: Team Challenge: Meet up at the Fort Lawrence Naval Yard.

314. MR. BRIDGER
Location: South Bay Expressway Bridge
Action: Jump Quantity
Combo Actions: None
Description: Team Challenge: Land a total of 160 jumps on the South Bay Expressway Bridge. All drivers must contribute.

315. PARKING PROBLEM
Location: Anywhere
Action: Power Park
Combo Actions: None
Description: Driver Challenge: Power park your car.

316. QUICK BURST
Location: Anywhere
Action: Boost Time
Combo Actions: None
Description: Driver Challenge: Boost for a total of 10 seconds.

317. RUSH HOUR
Location: I-88
Action: Oncoming Simultaneously
Combo Actions: None
Description: Team Challenge: All drivers chain 200 yards of oncoming on I-88 at the same time.

318. SIMPLE...
Location: I-88
Action: Near Miss
Combo Actions: None
Description: Driver Challenge: Chain 5 near misses on I-88.

319. FLOOR FILLER
Location: South Bay
Action: Meet Up
Combo Actions: None
Description: Team Challenge: Use the ramps on the roof of the Lambert Parkway parking garage and meet in the second building under construction on Hall Avenue.

320. PIER PRESSURE
Location: Paradise Wharf
Action: Jump Quantity
Combo Actions: None
Description: Driver Challenge: Jump the pier on Manners Avenue 6 times.

321. DAM CO-OP
Location: Rockridge Cliffs
Action: Jump Distance
Combo Actions: None
Description: Team Challenge: Jump a total of 1,000 yards on Casey Pass. All drivers must contribute.

322. WATERWORKS
Location: Rockridge Cliffs
Action: Meet Up
Combo Actions: None
Description: Team Challenge: Meet on the roof of the waterworks building behind the Rockridge Dam.

323. DIRT TRACK FUN
Location: Stock Car Track
Action: Combo
Combo Actions: Drift / Near Miss
Description: Driver Challenge: Drift a total of 2,000 yards and get a total of 5 near misses at the Lone Peaks Stock Car Track.

324. DON'T LOOK DOWN
Location: Quarry
Action: Jump Quantity
Combo Actions: None
Description: Driver Challenge: Jump the Lone Peaks Quarry mine shaft 4 times.

325. TUBE TRAIN
Location: Crystal Summit
Action: Drive Through
Combo Actions: None
Description: Driver Challenge: Drive through the North Mountain Drive pipeline.

☐ 326. MOUNTAIN MISS
Location: Lone Peaks
Action: Near Miss
Combo Actions: None
Description: Team Challenge: Get a total of 45 near misses on South Mountain Drive. All drivers must contribute.

☐ 327. WIND FARM MEET
Location: Crystal Summit
Action: Meet Up
Combo Actions: None
Description: Team Challenge: Meet at the Wind Farm.

☐ 328. JUMP HIGH
Location: Sunset Valley
Action: Jump Distance
Combo Actions: None
Description: Driver Challenge: Jump 100 yards over the Nelson Way gas station using the railroad high jump.

☐ 329. BOOST CHASE
Location: Anywhere
Action: Boost Time
Combo Actions: None
Description: Driver Challenge: Boost for a total of 45 seconds.

☐ 330. LONG CO-OP JUMPS
Location: Anywhere
Action: Jump Distance
Combo Actions: None
Description: Team Challenge: Jump a total of 2,000 yards. All drivers must contribute.

☐ 331. CO-OP DRIFT
Location: Anywhere
Action: Drift
Combo Actions: None
Description: Team Challenge: Drift a total of 8,000 yards. All drivers must contribute.

☐ 332. BILLBOARDS... GO!
Location: Anywhere
Action: Billboards
Combo Actions: None
Description: Driver Challenge: Smash 5 Burnout billboards.

☐ 333. FILL THE BARN!
Location: Hillside Pass
Action: Meet Up
Combo Actions: None
Description: Team Challenge: Meet in the hayloft in the barn on Hillside Pass.

☐ 334. WHAT A BLAST!
Location: Quarry
Action: Combo
Combo Actions: Drift / Jump Quantity
Description: Driver Challenge: Drift 2,000 yards and land 10 jumps in the Lone Peaks Quarry.

☐ 335. DIRT TRACK SMASH
Location: Stock Car Track
Action: Crash
Combo Actions: None
Description: Team Challenge: Crash into each other at the Lone Peaks Stock Car Track.

☐ 336. MIRACLE MILE
Location: South Bay Expressway Bridge
Action: Combo
Combo Actions: Flat Spin / Near Miss
Description: Driver Challenge: Get a total of 10 near misses and 720 degrees of flat spin on the South Bay Expressway Bridge.

☐ 337. LIFT-OFF
Location: Airfield
Action: Combo
Combo Actions: Jump Air Time / Near Miss
Description: Team Challenge: Get 40 near misses and 120 seconds of air time at the Eastern Shore Airfield. All drivers must contribute.

☐ 338. ROLLING
Location: Airfield
Action: Barrel Roll
Combo Actions: None
Description: Team Challenge: Land 40 barrel rolls at the Eastern Shore Airfield.

☐ 339. GO AROUND
Location: Airfield
Action: Near Miss
Combo Actions: None
Description: Driver Challenge: Get a total of 40 near misses at the Eastern Shore Airfield.

☐ 340. HOLD THE BUTTON
Location: Anywhere
Action: Boost Time
Combo Actions: None
Description: Driver Challenge: Boost for a total of 90 seconds.

☐ 341. ON THE WATERFRONT
Location: Waterfront
Action: Meet Up
Combo Actions: None
Description: Team Challenge: Meet at the Waterfront Plaza.

☐ 342. FIND A SPACE
Location: Anywhere
Action: Power Park
Combo Actions: None
Description: Driver Challenge: Power park and score 75% or better.

☐ 343. STEP OVER
Location: Ocean View
Action: Jump Cars
Combo Actions: None
Description: Team Challenge: Seven drivers park on the Ocean View steps while the other jumps over them all.

☐ 344. HOOP DREAMS
Location: Airfield
Action: Jump Target
Combo Actions: None
Description: Driver Challenge: Jump from the collapsed hangar through the suspended aircraft fuselage section at the Eastern Shore Airfield.

☐ 345. DEAD MAN'S REVERSE
Location: Crystal Summit
Action: Jump Reverse
Combo Actions: None
Description: Driver Challenge: Land a reverse jump over Dead Man's Edge.

☐ 346. FAST FUEL
Location: I-88
Action: Boost Time
Combo Actions: None
Description: Driver Challenge: Boost nonstop for 20 seconds on I-88.

☐ 347. THE ISLAND
Location: Eastern Shore
Action: Jump Target
Combo Actions: None
Description: Driver Challenge: Find the lakeside ramps and jump to Silver Lake Island then off again.

☐ 348. EDGY
Location: Crystal Summit
Action: Jump Quantity
Combo Actions: None
Description: Driver Challenge: Land a total of 4 jumps over Dead Man's Edge.

☐ 349. ANGUS LEAP
Location: Waterfront
Action: Meet Up
Combo Actions: None
Description: Team Challenge: Jump from the parking garage on the EAST side of Angus Wharf to meet up on top of the parking garage on the WEST side.

☐ 350. ROLLER HOOP
Location: Airfield
Action: Barrel Roll Target
Combo Actions: None
Description: Driver Challenge: Barrel roll from the collapsed hangar through the aircraft fuselage section at the Eastern Shore Airfield.

APPENDIX II: PS3 PARADISE AWARDS

If you're playing the PlayStation 3 version of this game, you have 60 Paradise Awards to complete. They are automatically unlocked once you complete them. Check the game menu for a running total of the awards you've earned.

☐ 1. LOOKIN' GOOD
Details: Repair your first wrecked car
Description: Easily completed early on. Just listen to DJ Atomika telling you about the auto repair on Angus Wharf and head over there to get this award.

☐ 2. WATT?
Details: Set a Time Road Rule on Watt Street
Description: Wait until you can turn Road Rules on after the fourth event and set a Time Road Rule on Watt Street. You can get the Time Road Rule in the Hunter Cavalry, but if you want to make this easy, just wait till you get a faster car.

3. IT'S SHOWTIME

Details: Set a Showtime Road Rule on East Crawford Drive

Description: Again, wait until Road Rules are active, press ✛ L1 ↙ and R1 ↙ to trigger Showtime, and go crashing in to every bit of traffic you see. See the separate Showtime section for more info.

4. GREAT START

Details: Win a race

Description: Just win any race in any car at any time. Easy right?

5. MISDEMEANOR

Details: Collect 5 billboards

Description: See the separate Billboard section for more info. This one is pretty easy because you should be able to smash 5 billboards within the first hour or so.

6. OFF THE BEATEN PATH

Details: Collect 25 smashes

Description: See the separate Smash section for more info. You'll come across your first 25 smashes pretty early on, maybe even within your first race!

7. GETTING AWAY WITH IT

Details: Win a race without crashing

Description: Not as hard as it sounds. Choose a short race if you're scared of crashing. See the separate Race section for more info.

8. BOTTOM OF THE CLASS

Details: Get your Class D License

Description: Get 2 event wins, and the Class D License is yours. See the Progression section for more info on number of wins for each license.

9. YATTA!

Details: Shut down the SI-7

Description: The SI-7 is the first car that will be roaming around Paradise City after 3 wins. Keep an eye out for it and take it down to get this award.

10. SHOWBOATING

Details: Get a x5 multiplier in Showtime

Description: Once Road Rules are active, nail 5 buses to get a x5 multiplier. See the separate Showtime section for more info.

11. PERFECT RAGE

Details: Get 10 Takedowns in Road Rage without wrecking

Description: Pick yourself a huge muscley aggression car for this one. The Carson Inferno Van or the Hunter Takedown 4x4 are good choices here. You are allowed to crash for this one, just not wreck. If your car is looking beat up, find an auto repair and keep on going.

12. RISING FROM THE ASHES

Details: Repair your car at critical damage in a Road Rage event

Description: Play any Road Rage event and repair your car when you're at Damage Critical. See the separate Drivethru section for more info on where the drivethrus are.

13. SPINNIN' AROUND

Details: Perform a 360 flat spin in any car

Description: You have to perform a full 360-degree flat spin to get this award. Try this one from the jump on South Mountain Drive, in the quarry, or the super jump on Read Lane. These huge jumps give you the maximum amount of air time to get a full spin out of your car.

14. FRENZY!

Details: Get a Takedown Frenzy

Description: Best completed in a Road Rage where all the cars are battling like crazy. Just take down 5 of them in quick succession to score this award.

15. UNDERACHIEVER

Details: Get your Class C License

Description: Win 9 events and the Class C License is yours. See the Progression section for more info on number of wins for each license.

16. LEARNING TO FLY

Details: Successfully land 5 super jumps

Description: Find 5 super jumps and land them.

17. GETTING IN THE GROOVE

Details: Get a x2 Boost Chain

Description: You can get this award as soon as the Nakamura SI-7 enters the world. Shut it down, go the junkyard, and get a x2 Boost Chain.

18. TAKING DOWN YOUR ELDERS

Details: Shut down the Rossolini LM Classic

Description: The LM Classic enters Paradise City after 19 wins. Shut it down for this award.

19. DUCKIN' AND WEAVIN'
Details: Win a Marked Man without being taken down
Description: The sooner you do this the better, because the farther you get through the game, the more aggressive the black cars get. If you're struggling with this, try the Marked Man from Angus and Watt Street. There are plenty of off-roads along the way to the finish at the naval yard. See the separate Marked Man section for more tips on Marked Man.

20. 7 STUNT WONDERS
Details: Win 7 unique Stunt Runs
Description: Just find at least 7 of the Stunt Run junctions and win them. When you find a Stunt Run and see how much fun it is, chances are you'll just go and find all 14 of them. See the separate Stunt Run section to find all the locations.

21. CURB JOB
Details: Power park with at least 80% rating
Description: Find some parked traffic with a gap large enough to fit your car in to (easiest to find in Downtown). Drive up to the space at a fair speed and handbrake your car into the space without hitting either vehicle. Your rating depends on how you lined up. Practice makes perfect!

22. THE SHOW MUST GO ON
Details: Get a x10 multiplier in Showtime
Description: For this one you have to hit 10 buses within a single Showtime attempt. The best places to try this are Hamilton Avenue, Evans Boulevard, Southbay Expressway, East Crawford Drive, Young Avenue, Angus Wharf, and the top section of Webster. See the separate Showtime section for more tips on Showtime.

23. GATE CRASHER
Details: Collect 200 smashes
Description: Just smash through 200 gates. See the separate Discovery Smash section for more info.

24. ROAD BLOCK
Details: Set a Showtime Road Rule on 30 roads
Description: Smash the offline Showtime Road Rule par scores on 30 roads. See the separate Showtime section for more info.

25. SPEED FREAK
Details: Set a Time Road Rule on 30 roads

Description: Set the offline time record for 30 of the roads in Paradise City. You can set a Time Road Rule on any 30 roads, not just the same ones as Showtime. See the separate Road Rules section for more info.

26. FEELING THE BURN
Details: Win 10 Burning Routes
Description: Once you've shut down 10 cars, you can attempt the Burning Routes for these cars. You can attempt this award when you're at License C. See the separate Burning Route section for more info

27. RAMPAGE!
Details: Get a Takedown Rampage
Description: A Takedown Rampage is 10 Takedowns in quick succession without crashing. Your best bet for this award is to start a Road Rage and take it up to White Mountain and Silver Lake; the roads are narrower, making Takedowns easier.

28. THE MEAN MILE
Details: Set a record of 1 mile driving in oncoming
Description: This one can be very easy. Just head to the interstate and stay on oncoming for a mile.

29. MUST TRY HARDER
Details: Get your Class B License
Description: Earn your Class B License. See the separate License progression section for more info.

30. MANHATTAN PROJECT
Details: Shut down the Hunter Manhattan
Description: The Hunter Manhattan enters Paradise City just before you get your Class B License. See the separate Unlock section for more info.

31. UN-CHAINED FELONY
Details: Get a x10 Boost Chain
Description: You've hopefully already have "Getting in the Groove" before you attempt this one, so you know how boost chaining works. Attain this one easily by heading to the interstate again and sticking to oncoming. A x10 boost chain is near enough a whole lap around the interstate.

32. PARALLEL PARK
Details: Power park with a 100% rating
Description: Once you've got the "Curb Job" award you can try your luck at "Parallel Park." Practice makes perfect and remember not

to touch the parked cars. If you do, the car alarms go off and you have to find another location.

33. YOU'VE JUST HIRED THE B-TEAM

Details: Shut down the Carson Inferno Van

Description: Ahhh, an old Burnout favorite. Once you've got your Class A License, take down the Inferno Van and use it to make Road Rages easier.

34. MILLIONAIRES' CLUB

Details: Score over 1,000,000 in Stunt Run

Description: Can you get in the Millionaire's Club? See the separate Stunt Run section for more info on how to score insane combos.

35. HANGTIME

Details: Successfully land 25 super jumps

Description: Land half of the super jumps in the world. See the separate Super Jump section for details on where to find them.

36. CHAIRMAN OF THE BOARDS

Details: Collect 60 billboards
Description: Find and smash through half of the billboards scat-

tered throughout Paradise City. Billboards are great multipliers for Stunt Run, so go find them all! See the separate Discovery section for details on the billboard locations.

37. DAREDEVIL

Details: Land a 2 barrel roll jump
Description: Barrel roll jumps are another great multiplier earner in Stunt Run! Head for the dam or the quarry, pick a stunt class like the P12, and nail those rolls.

38. BOOSTING AROUND THE WORLD

Details: Get a x20 Boost Chain
Description: Just like the x10 Boost Chain Award, this one can be easily gained by heading on the interstate. Do you have nerves of steel? Prove it by getting a x20 Boost Chain without going on the interstate.

39. FLYING COLORS

Details: Get your Class A License
Description: Earn your Class A License. See the separate License progression section for more info.

40. THE FULL MONTY

Details: Shut down the Montgom-

ery GT 2400
Description: Get the opportunity to shut down this car after 42 event wins. See the separate Progression section to see exactly where this car enters Paradise City.

41. STUNT SUPERSTAR

Details: Score a x40 multiplier in Stunt Run

Description: Get this award and you are truly on your way to being Stunt Superstar. See the separate Stunt Run section for more info on how to score insane combos. How far can you go above 40?

42. SUPERCHARGED

Details: Win 25 Burning Routes
Description: Once you've shut down 25 cars, you can attempt the Burning Routes for these cars. You can attempt this award when you've got your Class A License. See the separate Burning Route section for more info

43. KING OF THE ROAD

Details: Shut down the Jansen X12 Supercar

Description: Shut down this pocket rocket and you'll have yourself a great stunt car. See the separate Progression section to see exactly where this car enters Paradise City.

44. CAR IN A CHINA SHOP

Details: Get 500 Takedowns (including online and offline)
Description: You can get this award when working toward your Burnout License. Check on your progress by looking at your Records in Driver Details.

45. FALL GUY

Details: Shut down the Hunter 4x4
Description: If you've been shutting down every car up until now, when you shut down the Hunter 4x4 you'll get this award and can go for the Supercharged Award.

46. PARADISE WON

Details: Win your Burnout Driving License

Description: Get 90 wins under your belt and you'll get your Burnout Driving License. Now go for that Elite License for even more kudos.

47. ELEMENTARY

Details: Win a race in the Watson 25 V16 Revenge

Description: This is the souped up version of another old favorite. See the separate Progression sec-

tion to see exactly where this car enters Paradise City.

☐ 48. ALL PIMPED OUT

Details: Win all Burning Routes
Description: You can get this achievement only when you've shut down the Krieger Racing WTR on the way to your Elite License. See the separate Progression section to see exactly where this car enters Paradise City.

☐ 49. EXPLORER

Details: Find all events
Description: Travel around the world and find all event junctions. If you've toured the world for the discoverables you should have discovered these events. See the separate Event section to see where they all are. You can check your progress from the License screen in Driver Details.

☐ 50. PAID AND DISPLAYED

Details: Visit www.burnout.ea.com to find out more
Description: You may have guessed already. For this one you have to find and smash into all the car parks throughout Paradise City. See the separate Discovery sections for more info.

☐ 51. LONG HAUL

Details: Drive 750 miles
Description: This may seem like a long haul, but you'll have so much fun in Paradise City that this award can be attained way before you've got your Burnout License.

☐ 52. BUSTIN' OUT

Details: Collect all billboards
Description: Check your progress toward billboards from the Discovery screen in Driver Details. See the separate Discovery section for more info on where to find all the billboards.

☐ 53. TOTALLY SMASHED

Details: Collect all smashes
Description: Check your progress toward smashes from the Discovery screen in Driver Details. See the separate Discovery section for more info on where to find all the smashes.

☐ 54. RUNNING SCARED

Details: Win a Marked Man with the Krieger Racing WTR
Description: The Krieger Racing WTR has only 2 lives, so this award can be quite hard. Try the

Marked Man from Angus Wharf and Watt Street because there are plenty of shortcuts for this route. See the separate Marked Man section for more tips.

☐ 55. FLYING HIGH

Details: Successfully land all super jumps
Description: You can check your progress toward super jumps from the Discovery screen in Driver Details. See the separate Discovery section for more info on where to find all the super jumps.

☐ 56. SPEED KING

Details: Set a Time Road Rule on every road
Description: You can check your progress toward Time Road Rules from the License screen in Driver Details. See the separate Road Rules section for each road's par times.

☐ 57. CRASHIN' ALL OVER THE WORLD

Details: Set a Showtime Road Rule on every road
Description: You can check your progress toward Showtime Road Rules from the License screen in Driver Details. See the separate Road Rules section for each road's par scores.

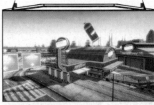

☐ 58. SHOPAHOLIC

Details: Find all drivethrus
Description: Find drivethru numbers on the Discovery screen of Driver Details. See the separate Discovery section for their locations.

☐ 59. ELITE

Details: Win your Burnout Elite License
Description: This is the penultimate award. Win every event in Paradise City and get your Elite License. See the Progression section for more details.

☐ 60. CRITERION ELITE

Details: Get your Elite License, win every event, find all discoverables, and beat every Road Rule
Description: You truly are Criterion Elite! Go take your Platinum cars online and gloat that you own Paradise City.

APPENDIX III: XBOX 360 ACHIEVEMENTS

If you're playing the Xbox 360 version of this game, you have 50 Achievements to complete. They are automatically unlocked once you complete them, and each is worth a specific number of points, adding to 1,000. Check the game menu for a running total of the Achievements you have completed.

1. LOOKIN' GOOD

Details: Repair your first wrecked car

Description: This is easily completed early on. Just listen to DJ Atomika telling you about the auto repair on Angus Wharf and head over there to get this award.

Points: 5

2. WATT?

Details: Set a Time Road Rule on Watt Street

Description: Wait until you can turn Road Rules on after the fourth event and set a Time Road Rule on Watt Street. You can get the Time Road Rule in the Hunter Cavalry, but if you want to make this easy, just wait till you get a faster car.

Points: 10

3. IT'S SHOWTIME

Details: Set a Showtime Road Rule on East Crawford Drive

Description: Again, wait until Road Rules are active, press ↗Ⓐ and ↙Ⓐ to trigger Showtime, and go crashing in to every bit of traffic you see. See the separate Showtime section for more info.

Points: 10

4. GREAT START

Details: Win a race

Description: Just win any race in any car at any time. Easy right?

Points: 10

5. MISDEMEANOR

Details: Collect 5 billboards

Description: See the separate Billboard section for more info. This one is pretty easy because you should be able to smash 5 billboards within the first hour or so.

Points: 10

6. OFF THE BEATEN PATH

Details: Collect 25 smashes

Description: See the separate Smash section for more info. You'll come across your first 25 smashes pretty early on, maybe even within your first race!

Points: 10

7. BOTTOM OF THE CLASS

Details: Get your Class D License

Description: Win 2 events and the Class D License is yours. See the Progression section for more info on number of wins for each license.

Points: 20

8. PERFECT RAGE

Details: Get 10 Takedowns in Road Rage without wrecking

Description: Pick yourself a huge muscley aggression car for this one. The Carson Inferno Van or the Hunter Takedown 4x4 are good choices here. You are allowed to crash for this one, just not wreck. If your car is looking beat up, find an auto repair and keep on going.

Points: 5

9. RISING FROM THE ASHES

Details: Repair your car at critical damage in a Road Rage event

Description: Play any Road Rage event and repair your car when you're at Damage Critical. See the separate Drivethru section for more info on where the drivethrus are.

Points: 10

10. SPINNIN' AROUND

Details: Perform a 360 flat spin in any car

Description: You have to perform a full 360-degree flat spin to get this award. Try this one from the jump on South Mountain Drive, in the Quarry, or the super jump on Read Lane. These huge jumps give you the maximum amount of air time to get a full spin out of your car.

Points: 10

11. UNDERACHIEVER

Details: Get your Class C License

Description: Win 9 events and the Class C License is yours. See the Progression section for more info on number of wins for each License.

Points: 30

12. LEARNING TO FLY

Details: Successfully land 5 jumps

Description: Find 5 super jumps and land them.

Points: 10

13. DUCKIN' AND WEAVIN'

Details: Win a Marked Man without being taken down

Description: The sooner you do this the better, because the farther you get through the game, the more aggressive the black cars get. If you're struggling with this, try the Marked Man from Angus and Watt Street. There are plenty of off-roads along the way to the finish at the naval yard. See the separate Marked Man section for more tips on Marked Man.

Points: 10

Burnout License. Burnout License Check on your progress by looking at your Records in Driver Details.
Points: 20

☐ 14. THE SHOW MUST GO ON

Details: Get a x10 multiplier in Showtime

Description: For this one you have to hit 10 buses within a single Showtime attempt. The best places to try this are Hamilton Avenue, Evans Boulevard, Southbay Expressway, East Crawford Drive, Young Avenue, Angus Wharf, and the top section of Webster. See the separate Showtime section for more tips on Showtime.
Points: 20

☐ 15. RAMPAGE!

Details: Get a Takedown Rampage
Description: A Takedown Rampage is 10 Takedowns in quick succession without crashing. Your best bet for this award is to start a Road Rage and take it up to White Mountain and Silver Lake. The roads are narrower, making Takedowns easier.
Points: 20

☐ 16. MUST TRY HARDER

Details: Get your Class B License
Description: Earn your Class B License. See the separate License progression section for more info.
Points: 40

☐ 17. PARALLEL PARK

Details: Power park with a 100% rating

Description: Once you've got the "Curb Job" award you can try your luck at "Parallel Park." Practice makes perfect and just remember not to touch the parked cars. If you do, the car alarms will go off and you'll have to find another location.
Points: 20

☐ 18. DAREDEVIL

Details: Land a 2 barrel roll jump
Description: Barrel roll jumps are another great multiplier earner in Stunt Run! Head for the dam or the quarry, pick a stunt class like the P12, and nail those rolls.
Points: 25

☐ 19. BOOSTING AROUND THE WORLD

Details: Get a x20 Boost Chain
Description: Just like the x10 Boost Chain award, this one can be easily gained by heading on the interstate. Do you have nerves of steel? Prove it by getting a x20 Boost Chain without going on the interstate.
Points: 25

☐ 20. FLYING COLORS

Details: Get your Class A License
Description: Earn your Class A License. See the separate License progression section for more info.
Points: 50

☐ 21. MILLIONAIRES' CLUB

Details: Score over 1,000,000 in Stunt Run

Description: Can you get in the Millionaire's Club? See the separate Stunt Run section for more info on how to score insane combos.
Points: 25

☐ 22. SUPERCHARGED

Details: Win 25 Burning Routes
Description: Once you've shut down 25 cars, you can attempt the Burning Routes for these cars. You can attempt this award when you've got your Class A License. See the separate Burning Route section for more info.
Points: 20

☐ 23. CAR IN A CHINA SHOP

Details: Get 500 Takedowns (including online and offline)
Description: You can get this award when working toward your

☐ 24. PARADISE WON

Details: Win your Burnout License
Description: Get 90 wins under your belt and you'll get your Burnout License. Now go for that Elite License for even more kudos.
Points: 60

☐ 25. ALL PIMPED OUT

Details: Win all Burning Routes
Description: You can get this achievement only once you've shut down the Krieger Racing WTR on the way to your Elite License. See the separate Progression section to see exactly where this car enters Paradise City.
Points: 10

☐ 26. EXPLORER

Details: Find all events
Description: Travel around the world and find all event junctions. If you've toured the world for the discoverables, you should have discovered these events. See the separate Event section to see where they all are. You can check your progress from the License screen in Driver Details.
Points: 10

☐ 27. PAID AND DISPLAYED
Details: Visit www.burnout.ea.com to find out more
Description: You may have guessed already. For this one you have to find and smash in to all the car parks throughout Paradise City. See the separate Discovery sections for more info.
Points: 20

☐ 28. BUSTIN' OUT
Details: Collect all billboards
Description: You can check your progress toward billboards from the Discovery screen in Driver Details. See the separate Discovery section for more info on where to find all the billboards.
Points: 20

☐ 29. TOTALLY SMASHED
Details: Collect all smashes
Description: You can check your progress toward smashes from the Discovery screen in Driver Details. See the separate Discovery section for more info on where to find all the Smashes.
Points: 20

☐ 30. FLYING HIGH
Details: Successfully land all super jumps

Description: You can check your progress toward super jumps from the Discovery screen in Driver Details. See the separate Discovery section for more info on where to find all the super jumps.
Points: 20

☐ 31. SPEED KING
Details: Set a Time Road Rule on every road
Description: You can check your progress toward Time Road Rules from the License screen in Driver Details. See the separate Road Rules section for each road's par times.
Points: 20

☐ 32. CRASHIN' ALL OVER THE WORLD
Details: Set a Showtime Road Rule on every road
Description: You can check your progress toward Showtime Road Rules from the License screen in Driver Details. See the separate Road Rules section for each road's par scores.
Points: 20

☐ 33. SHOPAHOLIC
Details: Find all drivethrus
Description: Find drivethru numbers on the Discovery screen of Driver Details. See the separate Discovery section for their locations.
Points: 10

☐ 34. ELITE
Details: Win your Burnout Elite License
Description: This is the penultimate award. Win every event in Paradise City and get your Elite License. See the progression section for more details.
Points: 70

☐ 35. CRITERION ELITE
Details: Get your Elite License, win every event, find all discoverables, and beat every Road Rule
Description: You truly are Criterion Elite! Go take your Platinum cars online and gloat that you own Paradise City.
Points: 20

☐ 36. ONLINE RACER
Details: Complete an online race
Description: Just get online and take part in an online race. Try the new Easy Drive menu by pressing ➲This is the simplest way to get online in Paradise City.
Points: 10

☐ 37. FIRST WIN
Details: Win your first 8-player online race
Description: You'll need a lobby of

8 players and you have to win the race. You can get this Achievement in either a ranked or unranked race.
Points: 10

☐ 38. ONLINE CHAMPION
Details: Win 10 online races
Description: Win 10 races online. This can be with 2–8 players. This Achievement is easier with fewer drivers and in an unranked race.
Points: 20

☐ 39. ONLINE AND KICKING
Details: Complete 20 online events
Description: Win 20 races online. This can be with 2–8 players. This Achievement is easier with fewer drivers and in an unranked race.
Points: 30

☐ 40. FIRESTARTER
Details: Make 50 online rivals
Description: Take down 50 different people online. Not only do you get this Achievement, but you'll have also collected 50 mugshots.
Points: 20

☐ 41. JUST FOR PICS
Details: Make your first online rival

Description: Take down your first victim online. Once you start you'll be addicted!
Points: 10

42. HAPPY SNAPPER

Details: Send 5 camera shots
Description: Send your mugshot out 5 times. You need an Xbox Live Vision camera for this one.
Points: 10

43. NOTORIOUS

Details: Send 50 camera shots
Description: Send your mugshot out 50 times. You need an Xbox Live Vision camera for this one.
Points: 20

44. HOTSHOTS

Details: Get 50 snapshots in your lineup
Description: Collect 50 snapshots. You can get these from Freeburn Mugshots, Race Mugshots, Rulebreaker Smugshots, and Photo Finishes. With this many opportunities, getting 50 snapshots shouldn't be a problem.
Points: 20

45. JOIN THE PARTY

Details: Complete 1 online challenge
Description: There are more than 300 Freeburn Challenges, each tailored to the number of players in your lobby. Pull up the Easy Drive menu by pressing ◇ and complete a challenge for this one.
Points: 10

46. PARTY CRASHER

Details: Complete 25 online challenges
Description: There are more than 300 Freeburn Challenges, each tailored to the number of players in your lobby. Pull up the Easy Drive menu by pressing ◇ and complete 25 challenges for this one.
Points: 15

47. PARTY ANIMAL

Details: Complete 250 online challenges
Description: There are more than 300 Freeburn Challenges, each tailored to the number of players in your lobby. You'll have had lots of practice for these by now. Complete 250 of them and earn another 20 points.
Points: 20

48. BLOCK PARTY

Details: Complete a whole section of online challenges (excluding PDLC)
Description: There are 50 challenges in each section of Freeburn

Challenges. The easiest way to get this Achievement is to complete the 2-player or 3-player Freeburn Challenges.
Points: 40

49. BURNOUT SKILLS

Details: In 8-player online Freeburn, lead 6 of the Today's Best Scores
Description: Get 8 of your friends in a Freeburn Lobby and own 6 of the Today's Best Scores. Play nicely and this one can be easy for all 8 of you.
Points: 30

50. CRITERION FEVER

Details: Catch Criterion Fever. Visit www.burnout.ea.com to find out more.
Description: A great viral Achievement. Take down one of the developers to get this. This one would be really difficult if you could only take down the developers, because we hear they're some of the best Burnout players around. Luckily this Achievement passes on from players who have taken down the team. Play online frequently, and you'll get this Achievement.
Points: 20

TOTAL POINTS: 1,000

APPENDIX IV: GOLD ELITE AND PLATINUM ELITE MEMBERS

One of the main reasons you are completing all the different aspects available in this game is to ensure envy and demand respect! The highest accolade is to become a

true "Elite" member, and receive a special "gold" or "platinum" coat of paint for your vehicles. Show this off to your online friends! Here's how to reach this level of Elite status:

GOLD ELITE MEMBER

Details: Choose "Gold" as a car color option after achieving the following: Gain the Burnout Elite License (Complete all 120 events listed below after upgrading to your Burnout License):

- [ ] Complete Race Events (40).
- [ ] Complete Road Rage Events (16).
- [ ] Complete Marked Man Events (8-35 depending on those already completed).
- [ ] Complete Burning Route Events (35).
- [ ] Complete Stunt Run Events (14).

PLATINUM ELITE MEMBER

Details: Choose "Platinum" as a car color option after achieving the following:
Complete the game 100 percent:

- [ ] Gain the Burnout Elite License (183-210 events from start).
- [ ] Complete Road Rules: Time Events (64).
- [ ] Complete Road Rules: Show-time Events (64).
- [ ] Locate all 11 parking structures and drive to the roof of each.
- [ ] Complete all 50 super jumps.
- [ ] Locate and crash into all 120 billboards.
- [ ] Locate and crash into all 400 smashes.
- [ ] Complete two sets of online Freeburn Challenges (100).